the BLUE DUCKS

plum. Pan Macmillan Australia

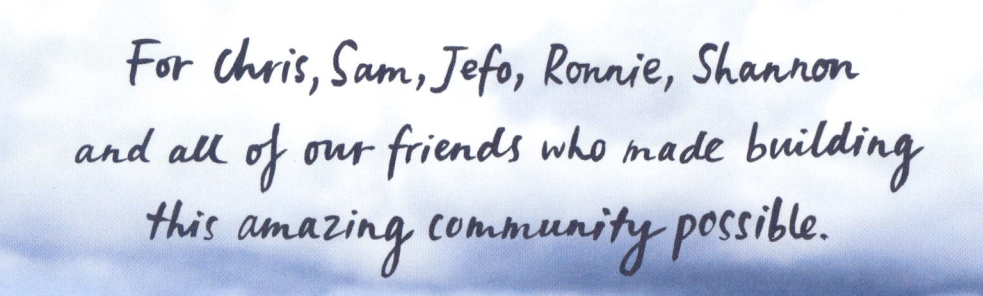

For Chris, Sam, Jefo, Ronnie, Shannon and all of our friends who made building this amazing community possible.

G'day A+A, thank you for 'car sitting' with love J&M xx 2014.

MARK LABROOY
DARREN ROBERTSON
with Hannah Reid

the BLUE DUCKS

DELICIOUS FOOD, THE IMPORTANCE OF COMMUNITY AND THE JOY OF SURFING

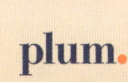

plum. Pan Macmillan Australia

CONTENTS

Introduction 1

THE WATER
Seafood 8

THE LAND
Meat & Poultry 40
Savoury Grains 82
Sweet Grains 91

THE GARDEN
Vegetables 108
Honey 148
Savoury preserves 156
Sweet preserves 160
Eggs 172
Desserts 185

Big thanks! 195
Index 197

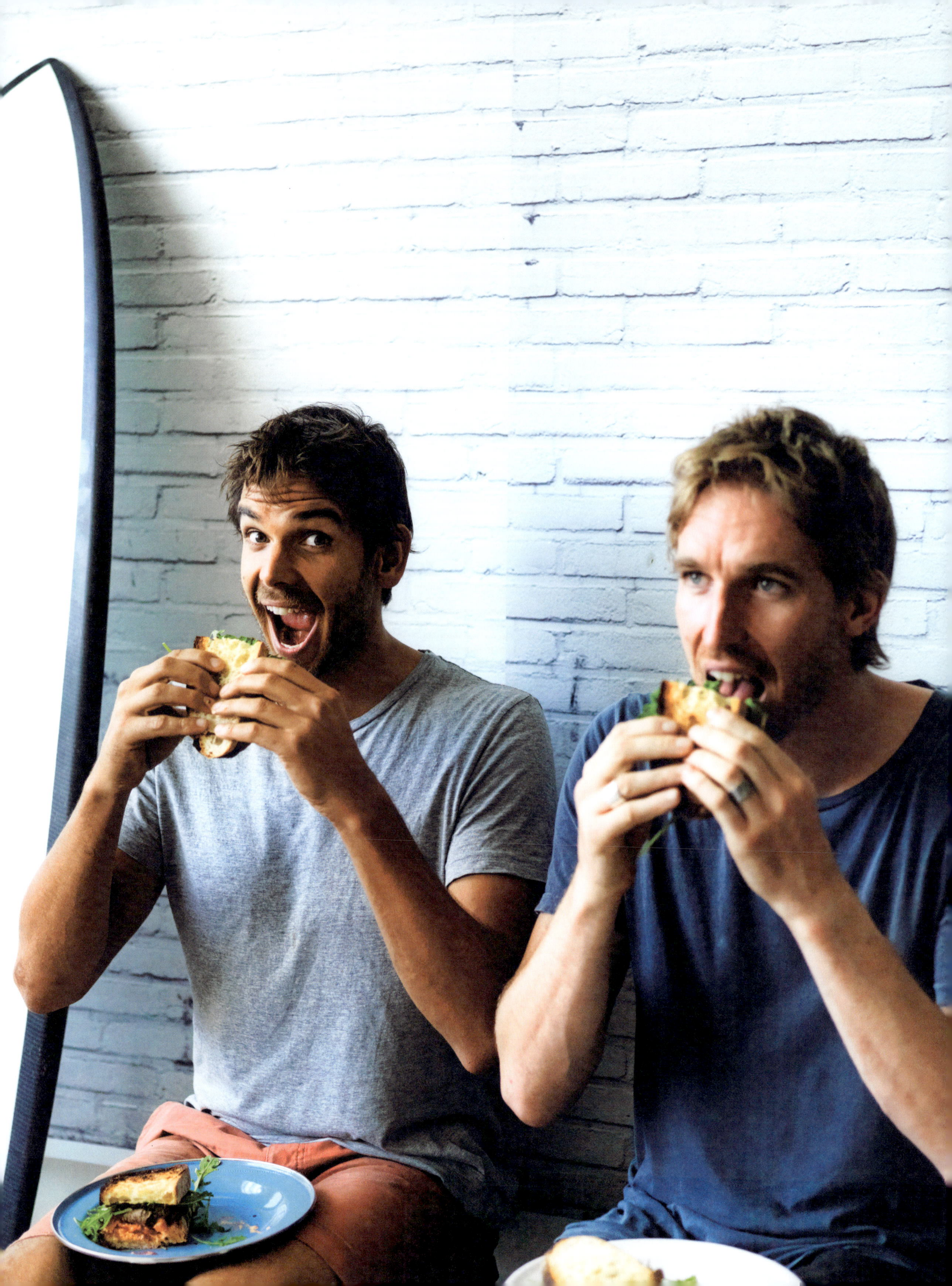

INTRODUCTION

The story of the Blue Ducks is a story of food. It was born in the surf, but it picked up in Morocco. In 2007, Mark LaBrooy followed the scent of fried sardines stuffed with chermoula, and salty, 6-foot-plus right-hander point breaks, to the southwest coast of Morocco where his friend Chris Sorrell was running a surf camp. Mark had finished an apprenticeship at Tetsuya's, and then spent five years cooking in a restaurant in Zurich in the winter before travelling throughout the summer. Another visitor to the camp in Tamraght was Chris's good friend Sam Reid-Boquist, on leave from his job – managing a surf shop in Bondi – to carry out an intercontinental search for the perfect wave. A few months later, Chris and Sam travelled to Switzerland to visit Mark for a few weeks snowboarding metre-deep dumps of Swiss pow pow in the resort of Flims Laax. Throughout the trip, the boys spent time talking about what they were going to do with themselves, and it became apparent they were all on the same page, looking for a better, more sustainable approach to living, and believing in good, ethical food.

Mark takes up the story...

We reunited back in Australia, and began talking about the idea of opening something. We discussed the idea of a café with everything made from scratch, run like a restaurant. Sam had a space in mind; an old roast chicken shop in Bronte. We had a look through the greasy window, then went up the road, drained our bank accounts and leased it on the spot. The build wasn't pretty. It's at 143 Macpherson Street, and there were 143 problems with it, including dead pigeons in the ventilation and cockroach nests behind the wallpaper. Because the budget was so small, we were limited with the fit-out of the restaurant. We'd go to auctions and lie in wait for rare deals on fridges and ovens. We've probably done a million bacon and egg rolls on the old stovetop we bought.

It was during this time that we met Jeff Bennett. He had just opened a pizza shop next door. Our relationship with Jeff went to the next level when he offered up his backyard to be used as our rubbish dump. It was an intense man-courtship; he understood our needs and we made him breakfast in the morning.

The first day we opened was a circus. We did a trial run the night before for friends and family; everyone had a drink and something to eat. There was such a sense of excitement. We got back at 5 am to do the baking, and when the doors were pulled open a little while later, there were five people outside the shop waiting. From the start, it was a monster. Originally we had thought we would cruise through the day with just the three of us. Sam planned on putting a couch out the back with a TV and a guitar, so during quiet times in the service, we could watch surf movies and play tunes for sweet ladies who got lost on the way to the bathrooms. That idea never materialised. I did 75 meals alone on day one. Sam's Aunt Pix came in for breakfast at 9 am and we begged her to help. She set to work on the dishes and stayed for five hours.

Two days after opening, I decided to rustle the branches of my own family tree and call in my brother Grant to start in the kitchen. Grant remains an integral part of the Ducks, reigning el supremo over the garden. That first month we were doing 100-hour weeks, but we couldn't maintain it, so we decided to close Mondays. The time we really felt it was when the surf was pumping. Then we'd close early and rush the clean up to run down and chase fat slabs at Bronte Point. The ocean is an integral part of the Ducks. We needed a café that was close to the ocean so we could carry out regular surf checks throughout the day, and get down there as soon as we could after signing off. Even now, the phrase 'I haven't been for a surf in a week' indicates an absolutely unreasonable workweek.

Jeff left the pizza shop next door and joined the Ducks partnership about a year after we opened. He had experience with craft beer, having been an owner of the Local Taphouse in Darlinghurst and St Kilda. He once told us something a brewer had said to him: that the difference between beer and craft beer is that craft beer is made by the brewer and not the accountant. There's something so honest about that, and it's definitely our own philosophy. Some of our most popular dishes – comprised of many and expensive elements – yield a minute profit, but they are signature dishes and people order them again and again.

During this time, Darren Robertson held a pop-up dinner at the Ducks. I had worked with Darren at Tetsuya's, where he spent three years as head chef. When he left, he travelled the world, going to food festivals and cooking demonstrations, talking to other chefs, and eating and eating. Then he came back and launched The Table Sessions, hosting pop-up dinners around Sydney. The night The Table Sessions took over the Ducks, we served an eight-course dégustation to a packed restaurant. Darren always says it was the most enjoyable event he had done to date. A couple of weeks later, we were out the back in the garden and I asked Darren if he wanted to hang around here. And that was it. One more Duck.

When we were boys, we ate what our mothers cooked. We learnt what 'salty' meant from Saturday nights stripping the fat off a leg of roast lamb. We learnt what 'sweet' meant because our grandmothers would cook our birthday cakes with cream cheese icing, and we knew 'burnt' from the smell of toast in the mornings. But it wasn't until we travelled that we learnt about spice – cardamom, coriander, coconut, curry leaf, chilli, garlic and cinnamon. We travelled and we ate and the world was suddenly full of flavour and we could access all of it – from salty, dry and bitter, to smoky, tender, and spicy.

Alongside the impulsivity and emotion involved with creating dishes, is a need to practise common sense cooking. One of the most accessible and important points of sustainability is how you treat food. We need to think more to avoid being wasteful. For example, instead of peeling prawns and discarding the shells, we eat the prawns and use the shells to make shellfish oil, which can be mixed into pasta. Even with garden produce, you can make food go further. With the fennel from the Ducks garden, for example, we braise the fennel bulbs for fennel jam, use the stalks for fennel ice cream and the fennel pollen to garnish a meat dish.

'Sustainability' is a fashionable word. It is used unreservedly, and has become feel-good jargon for doing the right thing. To us, however, it is not just about the produce that you use and the meat that you buy, but also about how sustainable your workweek is, and how you relate to the people around you. Do you have love? Do you have interests? Do you have balance? Sustainability is not exclusively about purchasing and eating ethically sourced food. It's multidimensional – sustainability is a lifestyle. We're trying to create sustainability at the Ducks both in the food we make and the work we oversee. We are trying to break some of the moulds that are associated with restaurants. We have a four-day workweek, we're compassionate about time off, we want our staff to take holidays and be rested, and we provide good, nutritious staff meals.

At this stage we cannot claim to be 100 per cent sustainable. You can't operate sustainably in an ecological sense if you can't operate sustainably as a business. We're a young business and still growing, and our backyard garden is young too. Having an exclusive approach to using only organic or locally sourced food is good, but if it sends your food costs through the roof, then it's not going to be sustainable. Organic produce is going to be more expensive and that's just the reality. And it is not just the vegetables, the fish and meat that must be sustainable, but loads of other things like the salt and pepper, the rice and oil. It's no longer a matter of whether a business does or doesn't adopt environmentally and socially sustainable strategies — but how.

Keeping dish costs down is an important consideration. The pressure on suppliers to provide affordable organic food is increasing as informed businesses and communities make choices about what they will and won't eat, buy and consume. So, while we haven't called ourselves sustainable, it's a conversation that we're having, and this is the first step. We hope that by reading this book you will start having that conversation as well, that you will ask questions about the source of the food you buy and eat.

WE ENCOURAGE YOU TO:
- Grow what you can
- Buy food mindfully
- Buy it locally
- Cook it thoughtfully
- Waste nothing

So the story of the Three Blue Ducks really is the story of a few guys who were taught a few things and then learnt a few more things, and travelled a few roads, surfed a few breaks and came to the realisation that they wanted to live lives of hard work, eat real food from good, ethical sources, cooked well and served without pretension to people with the sun on their backs and salt in the air, by people who care about the world they have inherited, and the one to come.

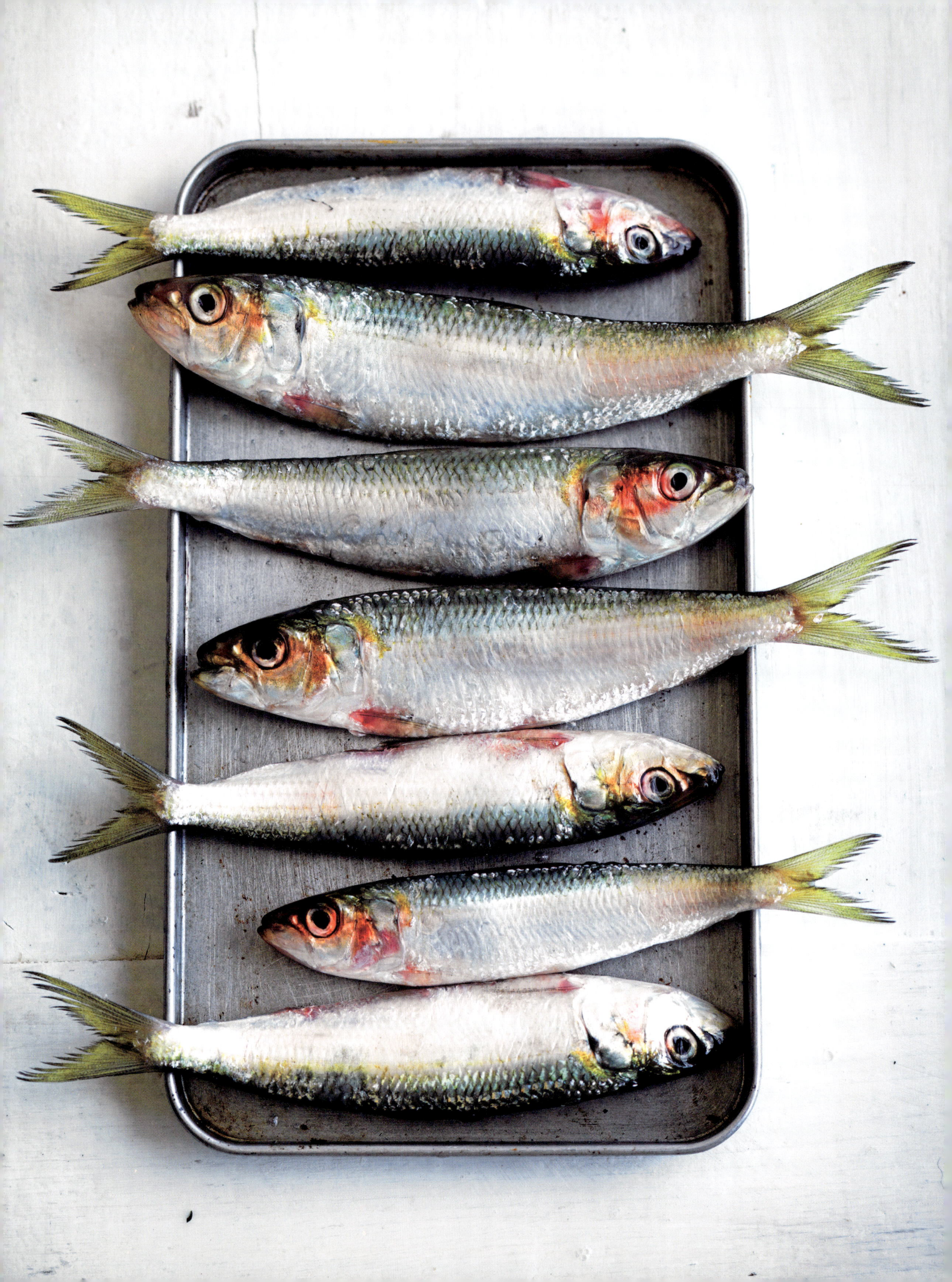

THE WATER

Seafood

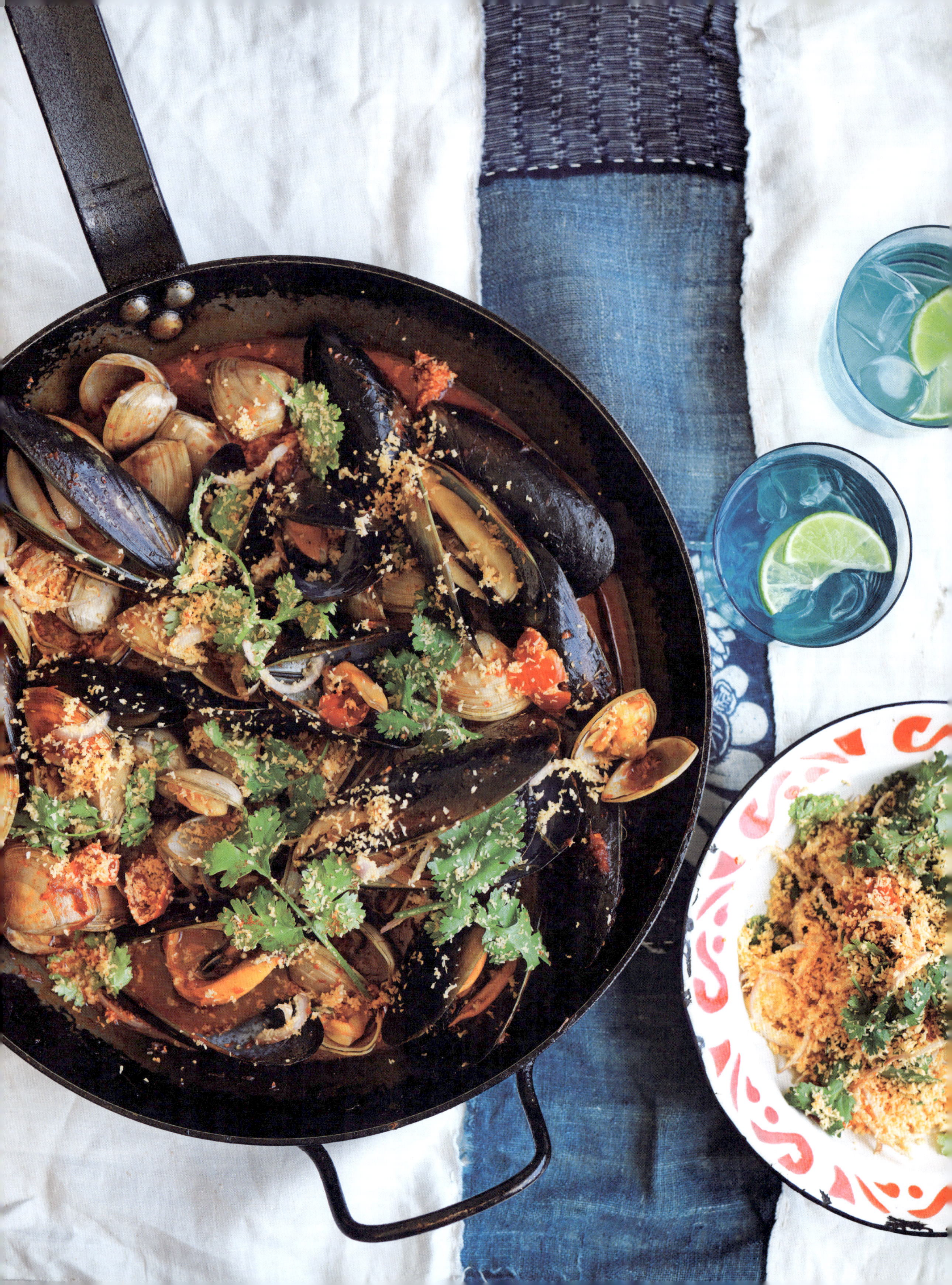

MUSSELS and PIPIS with CHILLI and COCONUT

This is a dish to make for your mother-in-law – if she doesn't love you after this, you have got no hope!

Make the chilli paste first. Separate the leaves from the coriander and set aside for the seafood. Put the coriander stalks and other ingredients into a medium-sized saucepan, cook over high heat until soft in texture and the chillies are translucent. Add a splash of water if the mixture becomes too dry and starts to stick to the pan.

When the mixture looks as though it will blend easily, tip it into a food processor and blend for about 45 seconds until it is a smooth paste.

For the seafood, pour the oil into a large saucepan and heat to almost smoking point. Add the cleaned mussels, pipis and the chilli paste, give it a quick stir and cover with a lid for 2 minutes. Add the coconut milk and put the lid back on. After 2 minutes, open the lid to check. As soon as the mussels and pipis start to open up, add the reserved coriander leaves, pour into a serving bowl.

For the sambal, mix all the sambal ingredients together and scatter over the dish before serving.

SERVES 6

3 tablespoons vegetable oil
2 kg mussels, cleaned, beard off
1 kg pipis, cleaned, beard off
1 x 330 ml can coconut milk

CHILLI PASTE
1 bunch of coriander
5 garlic cloves, chopped
10 long red chillies, seeded and chopped
1 knob of ginger, roughly chopped
50 g palm sugar, grated
2 tablespoons sweet soy sauce

COCONUT SAMBAL
1 cup desiccated coconut
½ bunch of coriander, leaves picked
pinch of chilli powder
½ teaspoon salt
2 cherry tomatoes, finely diced
juice of 1 lemon

BARBECUED CALAMARI
with TOMATO *and* OLIVE SALSA

6 medium-sized whole calamari, cleaned and scored
salt and pepper

TOMATO AND OLIVE SALSA
4 vine-ripened tomatoes, chopped
½ red onion, finely chopped
1 handful of Kalamata olives, chopped
1 long red chilli, seeded and finely diced
½ bunch of flat-leaf parsley, roughly chopped
50 ml extra virgin olive oil
zest and juice of 1 lemon

Soaking the calamari in milk with a pinch of bicarb soda in it the night before will help keep it really tender. Your barbecue or grill should be really hot, because you want to cook the calamari fairly quickly but get a good strong charred flavour. And make sure the tomatoes are vine-ripened and have plenty of flavour (with luck you might have even grown them in your own garden).

To make the salsa, mix all the ingredients in a bowl, season with salt and pepper and let it sit for 15 minutes for the flavours to develop.

Heat the barbecue or put the char-grill on a very high heat.

Season the calamari well with salt and pepper and place on the grill side of the barbecue. Once the calamari begin to shrink and become charred, turn them over to cook the other side. It depends how hot your barbecue is but you want a good strong charred flavour – don't let the calamari start to 'stew'.

To serve, put the barbecued calamari on plates and top with two or three healthy spoons of salsa with plenty of the juice.

SERVES 6

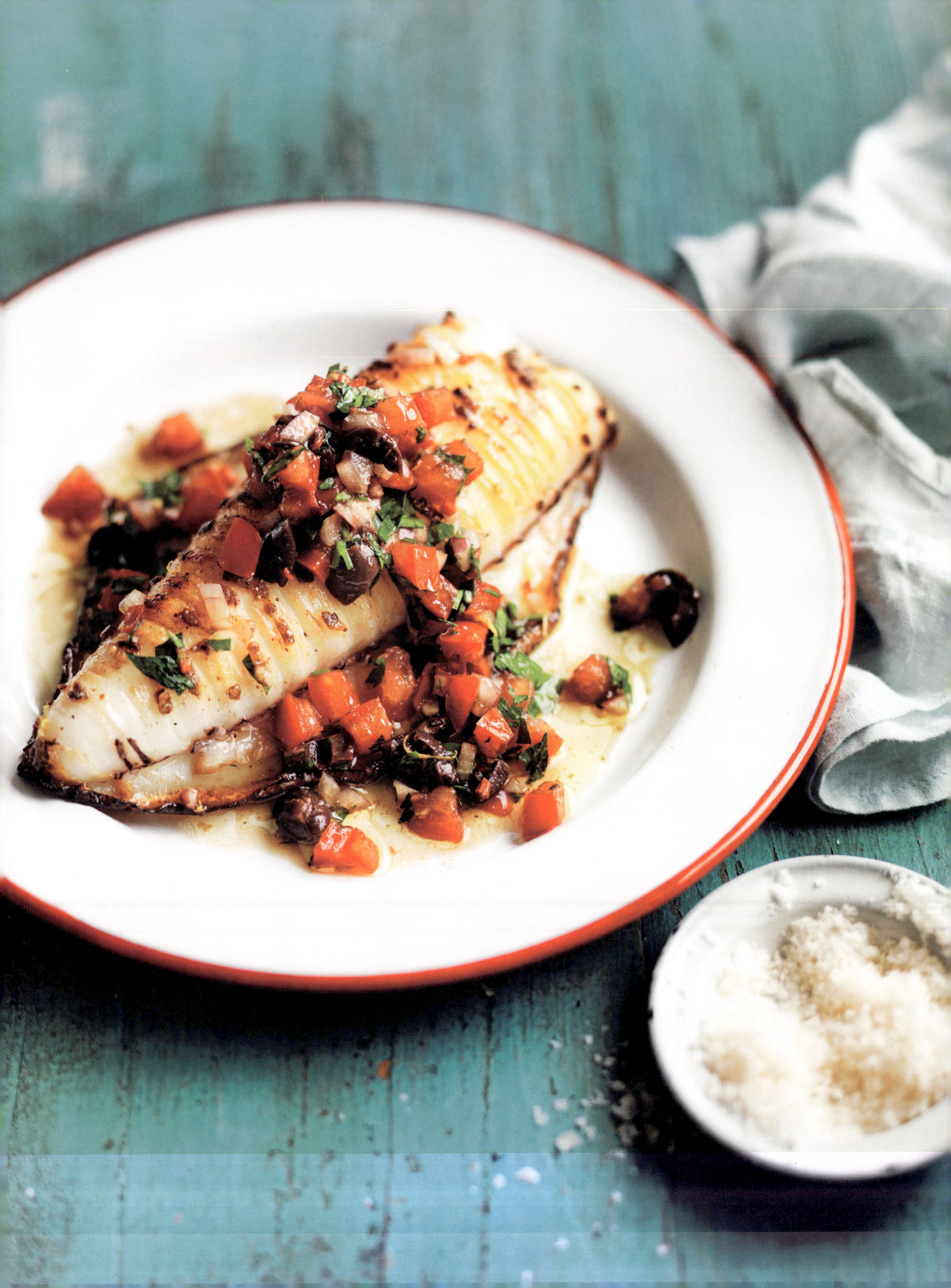

SALMON and POACHED EGG on TOAST for 6 HUNGRY PEOPLE

1 x 1.2 kg side of salmon, skin on, pin-boned
2 tablespoons Dijon mustard
1 bunch of dill, chopped
zest and juice of 1 lemon
1 tablespoon capers, chopped
½ red onion, finely diced
salt and pepper
6 fresh eggs (fresh eggs are better for poaching)
6 slices of good sourdough bread
butter, for toast

This method of cooking salmon was first shown to me when I was an apprentice. It has served me well over the years as it is easy, no fuss and always a great result – a cracker of a breakfast.

Preheat the oven to 190°C. Line a baking tray with baking paper.

Place the salmon skin-side down on the prepared tray, smear with the Dijon mustard, scatter on the dill, lemon zest, capers and onion, pour over the lemon juice and season with salt and pepper.

Place in the oven and bake for 16 minutes, until the salmon is opaque in colour. Remove from the oven and allow it to rest for 5 minutes.

Soft-poach the eggs (the yolk should be still runny). Toast the bread and lightly butter.

Break the salmon into pieces by hand, pile it on the toast, place a poached egg on top and serve immediately.

SERVES 6

PRAWN, CORN and AVOCADO SALAD

This salad is a serious mix of textures, inspired by a cooking demo by chef Matt Wilkinson and our passion for chilli and seafood – fresh prawns, crunchy corn, creamy avocado and buttermilk. If you can't get buttermilk you could use sour cream. For a little variation try blow-torching the avocado puree to introduce a smoky flavour.

Put the oil in a pan over low heat, add the garlic and stir-fry for 3 minutes, then add the prawns and cook for 2 minutes. Using tongs, remove the prawns and set aside.

In a food processor, blend the avocado and buttermilk, and season with salt and pepper. Pour this into a serving bowl, arrange the cooked prawns, corn, basil, onion, tomatoes, jalapenos on top. Pour over the fresh lime juice and serve.

SERVES 4

4 tablespoons grapeseed oil
1 garlic clove, thinly sliced
12 prawns, peeled and deveined
1 avocado, halved
200 ml buttermilk
salt and pepper
2 corn cobs, kernels cut away from the cob
1 handful of basil leaves, torn
1 small red onion, thinly sliced
12 cherry tomatoes, halved
3 jalapeno peppers, sliced
juice of 1 lime

Instead of throwing out the shells from the prawns or scampi, try making this simple oil. It is packed with flavour!

SHELLFISH OIL

Prawn shells contain loads of flavour and that beautiful orange colour, so instead of putting them in the rubbish, why not turn them into a delicious shellfish oil? You can use scampi or prawn shells – this recipe works well with either. There is not much difference – the scampi have claws and are generally sweeter but are touch more expensive.

To roast the scampi or prawn shells, preheat the oven to 180°C. Put the shells on the tray and roast for 5–10 minutes, or until golden brown.

In a large pot heat a little of the oil, add carrot, onion and tomato paste and fry for 5 minutes, stirring occasionally. Add the roasted shells and all the other ingredients, including remaining oil, and cook for about 2 hours, or until most of the water has evaporated. Leave it to cool for a while.

Line a strainer with muslin, place over a bowl and tip in the scampi mixture. When the oil has drained into the bowl, skim off any extra water, pour the shellfish oil into a jar, seal and and refrigerate.

The oil should keep in a sealed jar in the fridge for around 1 month.

MAKES ABOUT 500 ML

300 g scampi or prawn shells
500 ml grapeseed oil
1 carrot, chopped and minced
1 small brown onion, chopped and minced
100 g tomato paste
1 garlic clove, chopped
1 bay leaf
2 litres water

SHELLFISH, CHILLI and LEMON PASTA

50 ml shellfish oil (see page 15)
100 g prawns or scampi, peeled, tails removed and deveined
1 teaspoon chopped long red chilli
1 teaspoon soy sauce
juice of 1 lemon
salt and pepper
100 g tagliatelle
1 handful of pea tendrils

An elegant-but-easy dish that you'll never tire of eating. Making the shellfish oil takes time but it adds a whole other level of flavour. Serve plenty of crusty bread with this to soak up the juices.

In a non-stick frying pan over medium heat, warm the oil, add the prawns or scampi and heat for about 30 seconds, or until just cooked (they'll look a little more pink). Add the chilli, soy sauce and lemon juice, and season with salt and pepper.

Cook the pasta until al dente, drain, add to the prawns, and serve immediately in warmed bowls with a few pea tendrils on top.

SERVES 4

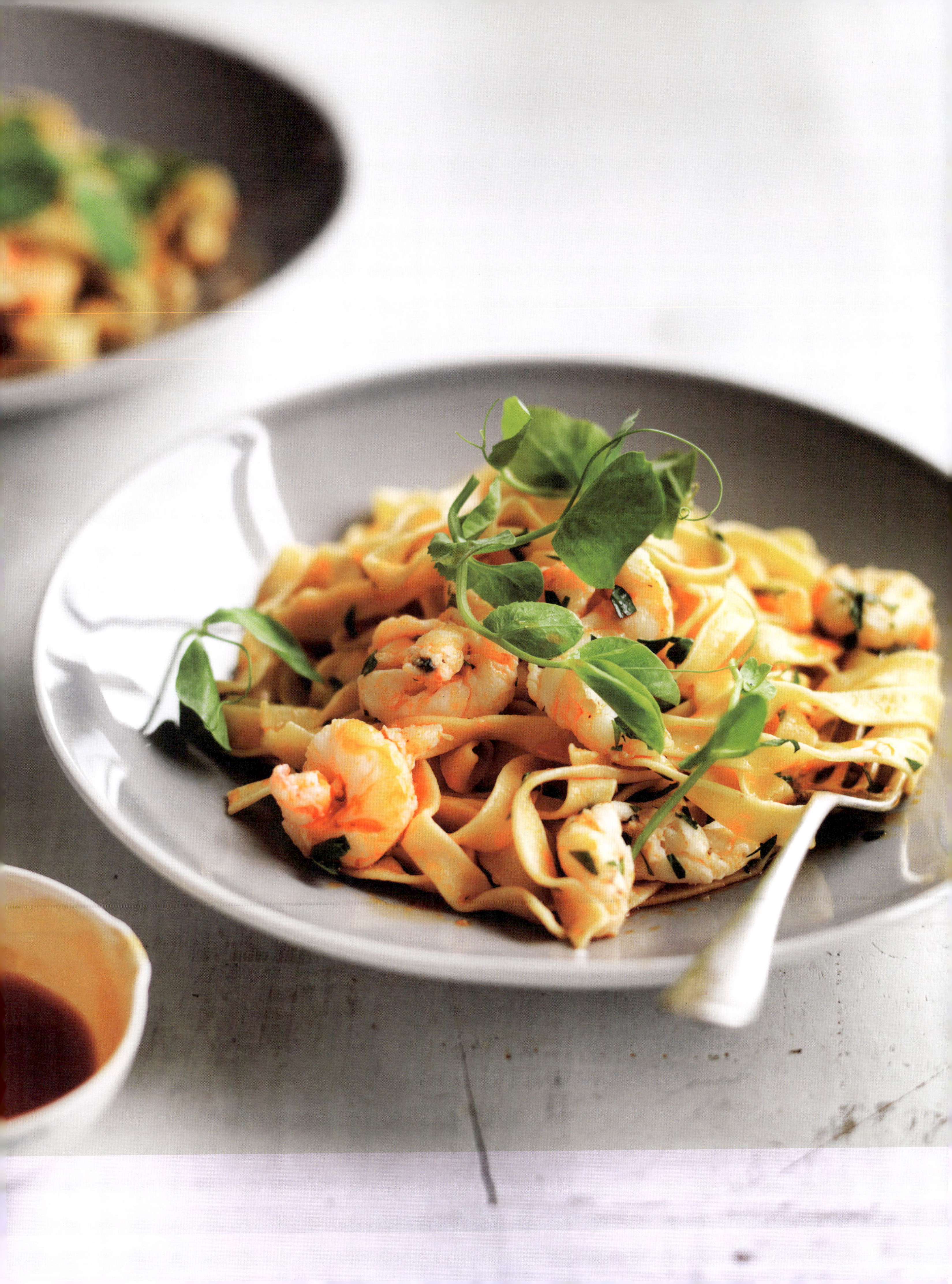

OYSTERS

Awesome oyster toppings

Wasabi and cucumber granita

juice of 1 lime
1 small cucumber, roughly chopped
1 teaspoon wasabi paste

Place lime juice and cucumber in a food processor and blitz until smooth, strain into a bowl, stir in the wasabi. Freeze for 4 hours.

To serve, scratch the green ice with a fork to produce a snow-like consistency and spoon on top of an oyster.

Chilli and lime

1 long red chilli
1 pinch of caster sugar
juice of 1 lime

Chop the chilli or better still, smash using a pestle and mortar. Add the sugar and lime juice and serve.

Rice wine and shallot vinegar

1 small spring onion, finely chopped
50 ml rice wine vinegar

Mix ingredients together and serve. You can add a pinch of sugar if it's a little harsh.

Fried chorizo

1 chorizo sausage, cut into 5mm slices
olive oil

Fry slices of the chorizo in a little olive oil for a few minutes until browned.

Oysters are the bad boys of seafood. Denuded of their shells and washed down in a swill of their own sultry brine, there is nothing sweet about them. They are sexy and delicious. French poet Léon-Paul Fargue said 'eating oysters is like kissing the sea on the lips' and Casanova is said to have feasted on 50 oysters every morning, to increase his faculties of seduction. At the Ducks, we soak them in nahm jim dressing, or sweet vinegar and shallots, sometimes wasabi granita, or just a squeeze of lemon.

Coastal communities have eaten oysters for thousands of years, but with an increasingly arresting price tag, they've unfortunately become the mollusc of the wealthy. Traditionally oysters were handpicked in shallow coastal waters, but today almost all oysters consumed have been farmed. Oyster farming in Australia is an important aquaculture industry, with oysters cultivated and available throughout the year. Historically, the farming process involved growing the oysters on tarred hardwood frames. Some farmers still move partially grown oysters into tarred, mesh-bottomed trays for their final growth stage, giving a more uniform shape to the shell. These days farming is more commonly undertaken using baskets suspended from ropes in the lake, estuary or waterway.

There are many species of oysters, though not all are edible. In Australia the most popular eating oysters are Sydney Rock and Pacific, but there are other varieties, including the native Australian Angasi (sometimes called a Flat oyster) and the Pearl oyster. The Pacific oyster is native to Japan, and the Sydney Rock to Australia. The Rock oyster is smaller and softer than the Pacific oyster, with a stronger flavour and a smoother-textured, triangular-shaped shell. The Pacific has a shell that is spiky and oval shaped.

Oysters are filter feeders, so how they taste is unique to the environment in which they are grown. The more nutrient-rich the water, the stronger the flavour. The colder the water, the slower the oysters grow and the smaller they are when harvested. Because of these variations they are often sold by location rather than species. For example, the pristine waters of Wallis Lake on the mid-north coast of New South Wales are said to produce creamy, full-bodied oysters, free of biological defects.

When buying oysters give some thought to food miles and how far your oysters have to be transported. Most of our commercial oysters are farmed in growing regions on the northern and southern coasts of New South Wales, including Merimbula, Clyde River, Shoalhaven, Hawkesbury River, Port Stephens, Wallis Lake and the Macleay River. Moreton Bay in Queensland is a huge growing region, and Coffin Bay and Streaky Bay in South Australia are two well-known areas for oyster farming. The Angasi oyster grows wild in South Australia and throughout the sandy seafloors of the Tasmanian coastline.

The Pacific oyster takes 12–18 months to reach maturity, while the Rock oyster takes about three years. Growing time accounts for the recent rise in production of Pacific oysters, as they are ready for sale more quickly than the Sydney Rock.

THAT SALTY TASTE

Oysters are an entirely natural food, reared beneath a constant wash of seawater. They should smell like saltwater, and be plump and slippery not shrivelled and dry. The Sydney Rock should have a clean, consistent colour, which may vary from white to light straw or even pale lime, and a creamy, firm texture, with a slight saltiness on the palate. Pacific oysters should be plump with a creamy white colour and a clean, fresh aftertaste.

Rock oysters are available year-round with oysters from the north coast of New South Wales being in peak condition in summer and those from the south coast in the winter. They also have the longest shelf life of any oyster – they can be kept alive for up to 21 days, at a temperature of 10–15°Celsius. In comparison, the Pacific oyster can be kept alive for 7–10 days, preferably at a temperature of 1–10°Celsius. Pacific oysters are more commonly found in good condition from early autumn to early summer, but are best in the cool of winter and spring. For natives such as the Angasi, May to August are the prime months.

Both varieties are highly nutritious, brimming with calcium, protein and iron, as well as other vitamins and minerals and Omega 3 fatty acids. It's best to eat them raw to benefit from their full nourishing effect.

CHOOSING, STORING, SHUCKING

Oysters are best bought live, and shucked just before serving. It is essential that your oysters are fresh, particularly if you intend to eat them raw. Choose oysters that are closed and have a fresh ocean smell. If you buy them opened, they should be unwashed, in brine and appear wet.

Store oysters unopened in the warmest part of the fridge, covered with a damp cloth. You can keep them for a few days; however, they are highly perishable so are best consumed as soon as possible, or within a day or two of buying them. Avoid oysters where the shell is cracked or has opened.

There are various ways to open oysters, but we tend to crack them from the hinge of the shell as opposed to the lip. Either way, use an oyster knife, which has a special blunt blade, to pry the shell open. Make sure to wash the oyster shell well before opening the oysters. Oyster purists would deny any other method of eating them besides slurping them from their shell. However, they can also be poached in broth or deep-fried and served with a spicy dressing. If you're steaming, sautéing, grilling, frying or baking them, discard any that fail to open during cooking.

While oysters aren't endangered, they are very sensitive to water pollution and coastal contamination, drawing toxins into their flesh. Always buy from a reliable seafood outlet or fishmonger.

BARRAMUNDI, PEAS and BACON

6 x 180–200 g barramundi steaks (ask your fishmonger to cut them for you)
salt and pepper
1 tablespoon vegetable oil
4 bacon rashers, diced
1 garlic clove, chopped
2 red onions, diced
500 g frozen peas
1 small bunch of mint leaves, torn
zest and juice of 1 lemon

Barramundi is a fantastic-tasting white fish, low in fat and very nutritious. It's much more readily available these days (farmed and even wild barramundi). The skin is quite thick, but frying it before baking gives it a crispy, crackly finish.

Preheat the oven to 200°C.

Season the steaks well with salt and pepper. Heat half the oil in a heavy-based, ovenproof frying pan, add the barramundi, skin-side down, and fry over high heat until you get some good colour on the skin. Turn the steaks over and fry the other side for 2 minutes. Turn them skin-side down again, put the frying pan in the oven and cook for 8 minutes.

Remove the steaks from the oven and let them rest for 5 minutes.

Meanwhile, heat the remaining vegetable oil in a medium-sized frying pan over medium heat. Add the bacon, garlic and onion and fry until the bacon is the way you like it and onion is soft. Add the peas and cook, stirring occasionally, for 3–4 minutes, or until soft, then stir through the mint, lemon zest and juice, and season with salt and pepper.

To serve, put a generous scoop of bacon, peas and mint on each plate, then place the barra steaks, crispy skin side up, on top.

SERVES 6

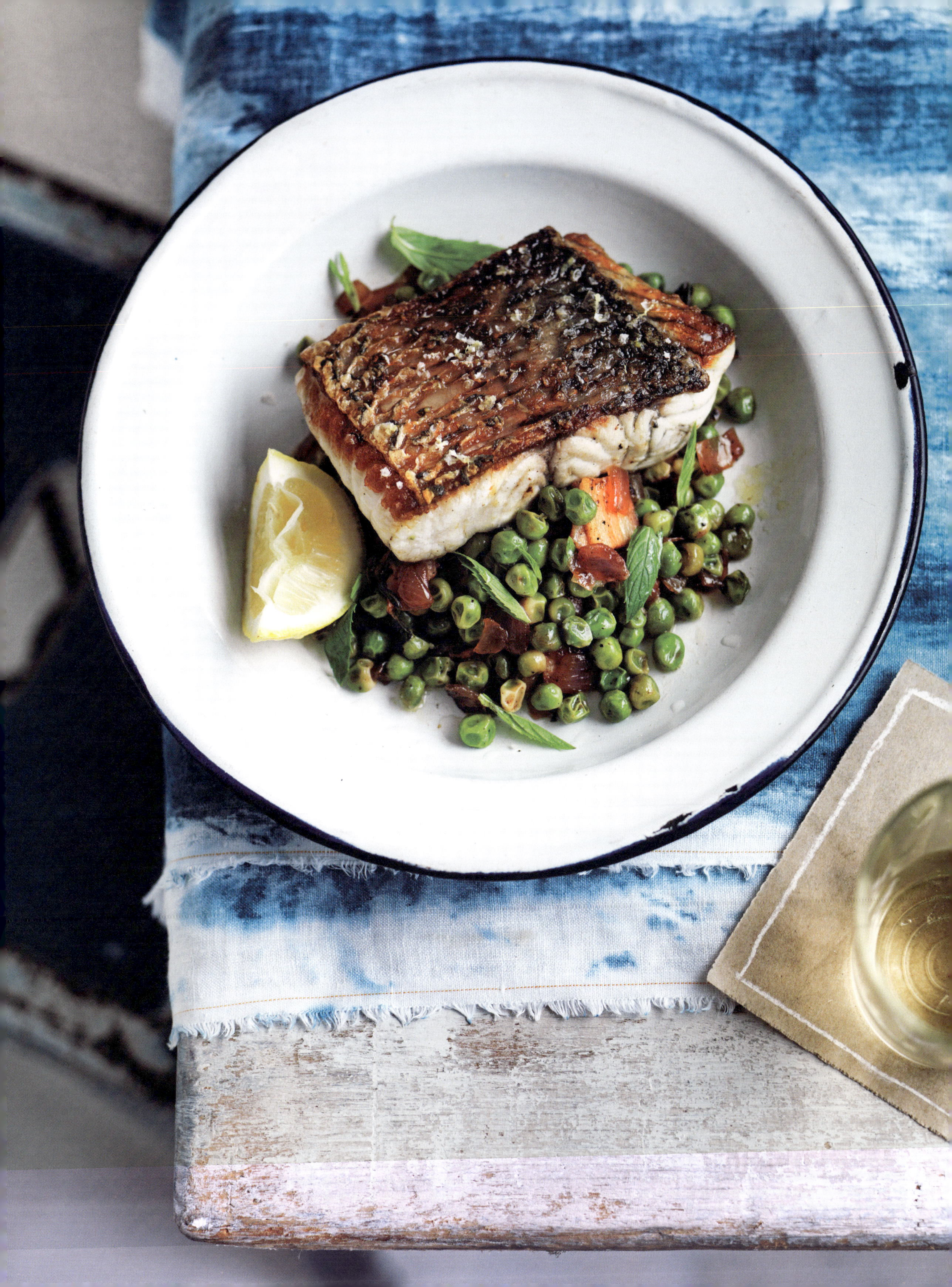

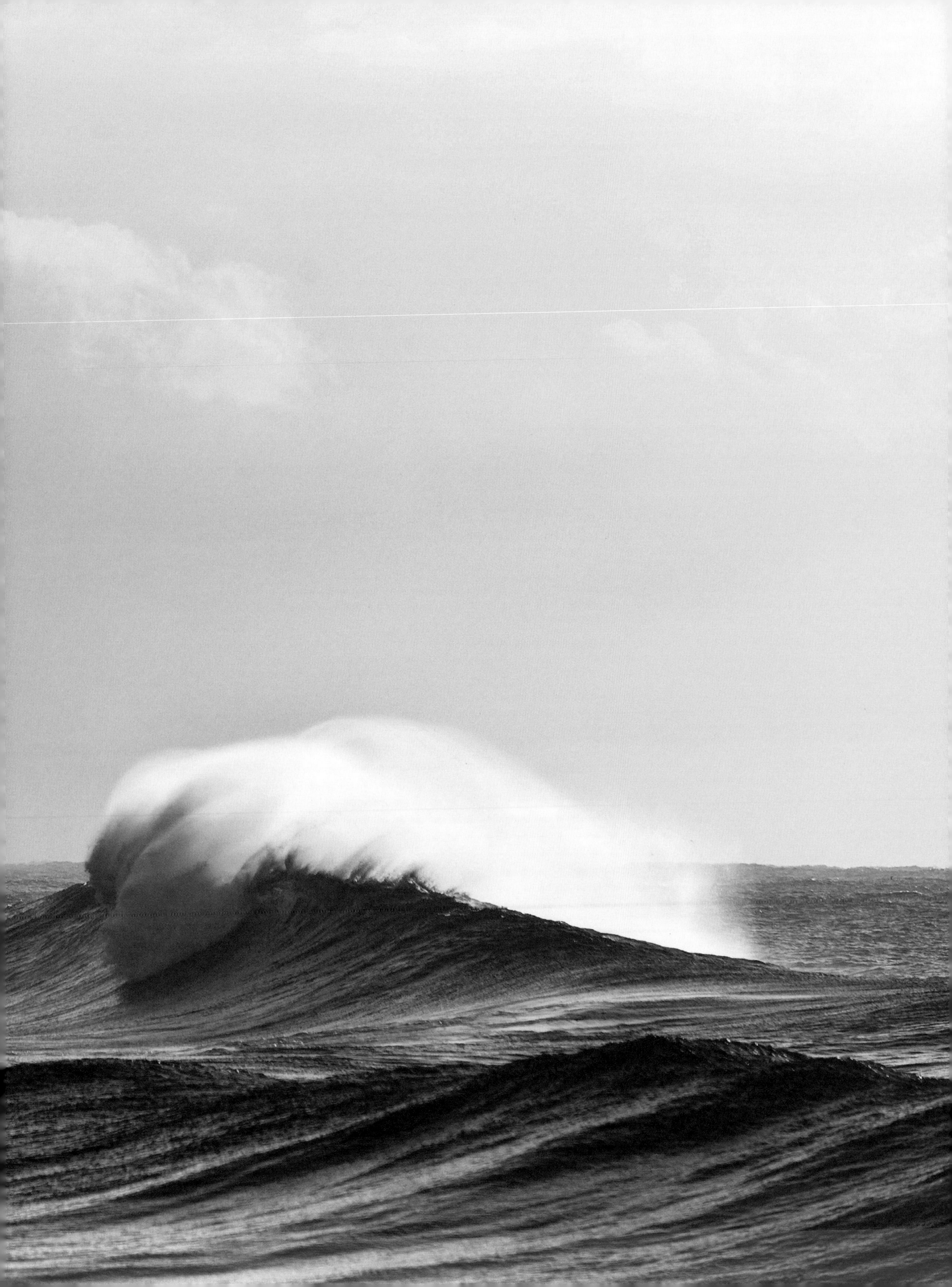

Sustainable
SEAFOOD

Cooking seafood is a pirate's game; filleting soft fish bodies, making stock out of the heads, frying the skin until it's crispy, shucking oysters, and crushing bright orange sea urchin into a soft whipped butter. We love cooking with seafood. There are so many variables of tastes and textures from the ocean.

When surfing, you often look down into the water to see schools of fish roaming in scaly packs around your feet. It's a great feeling, like you're a part of the ocean. In a way, when we eat fish we're just another part of the intricate food web of the ocean's ecosystem. As humans, though, we also have a responsibility towards maintaining the balance of that ecosystem and ensuring the sustainability of the seafood we consume. The environmental impact of fishing, the killing power of new fishing technology, and consumers' apathy to the future of fish species, has led to a worldwide decline in fish stocks. The world's current fishing practices are unsustainable. Modern fishing equipment is stealthy and powerful, with super trawler nets potentially collecting all species that lie in their path. Along with the catch comes an excessive amount of bycatch, that is, unwanted, usually juvenile species that are discarded overboard, dead. For example, 89 per cent of hammerhead sharks have disappeared from the north-east Atlantic Ocean in the last 20 years, due to bycatch. Each year, shrimp trawlers haul in over 35 million juvenile red snappers in the Gulf of Mexico, only to toss them back, dead. The oceans are resilient, however, and fish species can bounce back if we give them a chance.

As fish stocks rise and fall in different areas, affected by seasonal and environmental change as well as the effects of commercial fishing, it's difficult to set clear guidelines on what 'sustainable fish' is. At present, the best approach appears to be encouraging the eating of a wide variety of fish that are caught sustainably.

According to the Australian Marine Conservation Society, 'sustainable seafood' is 'fish or shellfish that reaches our plates with minimal impact upon fish populations or the wider marine environment'. The AMCS stress that 'it's not just the numbers of fish left in the ocean that matters, it's the way in which the fish are caught, the impact on the seafloor, other marine wildlife and how fishing affects the healthy and natural functioning of marine ecosystems'.

Different fishing practices have varying levels of impact on the oceans, so knowing how your seafood was raised and caught will help you make a good choice. The two main fishing methods are wild catch and aquaculture farming. Wild-caught fish have firm, clean tasting meat and have lived a natural life hunting and gathering. Although, there is a problem with bycatch, as well as 'bottom trawling,' which involves dragging weighted nets across the seafloor, disturbing seafloor ecosystems. Moreover, overfishing removes large numbers of fish species from the ecosystem, affecting the marine food chain. In comparison, aquaculture farming has become popular because theoretically it allows the demand for seafood to be met despite the depletion of wild fish stocks. In reality, some farms actually increase the pressure on wild fish stocks, through the use of wild fish to feed farmed fish, and the waste footprint created by farms on marine and coastal environments. In an ideal scenario, farms would be clean, ethically managed, with a low impact on the environment. In fact many farms are considered to produce an excess of waste, and the fish are kept in overcrowded cages that can provide refuge for diseases. If farmed fish escape, they can spread the disease to wild fish.

If you do eat seafood, it's worth taking the time to make an informed choice. Websites such as GoodFishBadFish present information to help consumers make sustainable choices. Some of the species recommended by GoodFishBadFish at present include Australian salmon, bream, bonito, crabs, mussels, oysters, octopus, squid, calamari, trevally and whiting.

SO, HOW SHOULD YOU SELECT YOUR SEAFOOD?

- Ask questions – of fishmongers, supermarket assistants and waiters, before you buy. How and where was the fish caught or farmed? Is it a species that's overfished?
- Eat locally sourced seafood – this ensures traceability and means you will have more information on the origin of your fish.
- Purchase species that are lower on the food chain – smaller fish are usually fast breeding, making their species capable of surviving pressure from fishing. In the same way, avoid larger, longer aging species such as tuna and shark (flake), as they breed infrequently and are in the frontline of overfishing.
- Eat more sustainable varieties – there is a sustainable alternative readily available for every species. Download the Australia's Sustainable Seafood Guide app on your phone and take it with you to the supermarket or fishmonger as a reference to check if the fish is sustainable before you buy.

There isn't a high enough level of demand for sustainable seafood in the restaurant supply chain yet, to ensure regular, reasonably priced supplies. Sustainable seafood is to the Ducks, what satisfaction is to the Rolling Stones. We try, but we can't get enough. We see it as the responsibility of chefs and restaurants to influence the supply chain by their choices, and influence consumers by what they supply. Chefs have the potential to be instigators of change, and their menus tools for education. For the dinner menu at the Ducks, all the seafood is line-caught, so fully sustainable. The menu changes naturally, but we have served mussels and pipis, as well as snapper, blue mackerel and bonito. The fish we choose now, at home and in restaurants, will affect the content of our seas in the future.

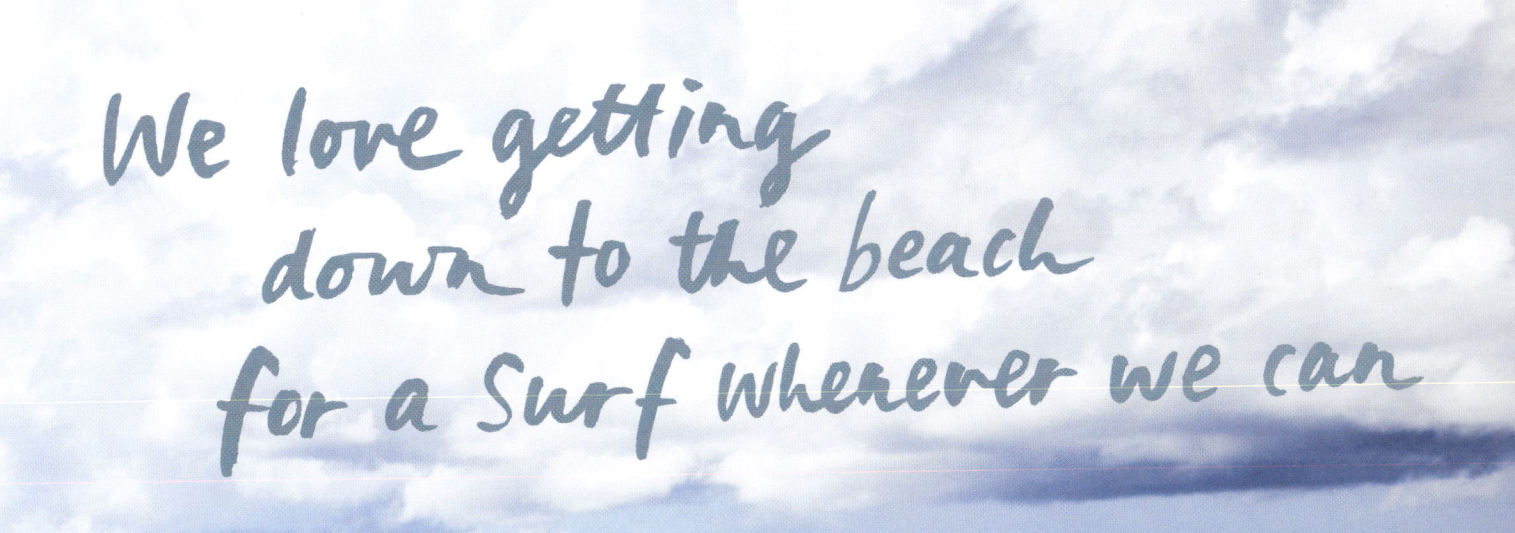

We love getting down to the beach for a surf whenever we can

DEAD SIMPLE CHAR-GRILLED SARDINES

8 x 80 g fresh sardines, gutted and scaled
1 teaspoon grapeseed oil
salt and pepper
30 g butter, diced
1 small garlic clove, thinly sliced
1 teaspoon soy sauce
juice of 1 lemon
3 tablespoons coarsely chopped flat-leaf parsley

One of the best ways to enjoy seafood is as fresh from the ocean as possible, then straight off the barbecue, finished with plenty of lemon juice and a dash of sea salt. With a little butter, garlic and fresh herbs this might be simple but it really takes some beating.

Preheat the char-grill to medium.

Brush the sardines with oil and season with salt and pepper. Cook them on the grill for 1 minute on each side, turning them carefully. Take them off the grill and arrange on a large, warmed plate.

Heat a frying pan over high heat, then add the butter. When the butter begins to turn nut brown, add the garlic and soy sauce. Remove the pan from the heat, stir through the lemon juice and parsley. Pour over the sardines and serve.

SERVES 4

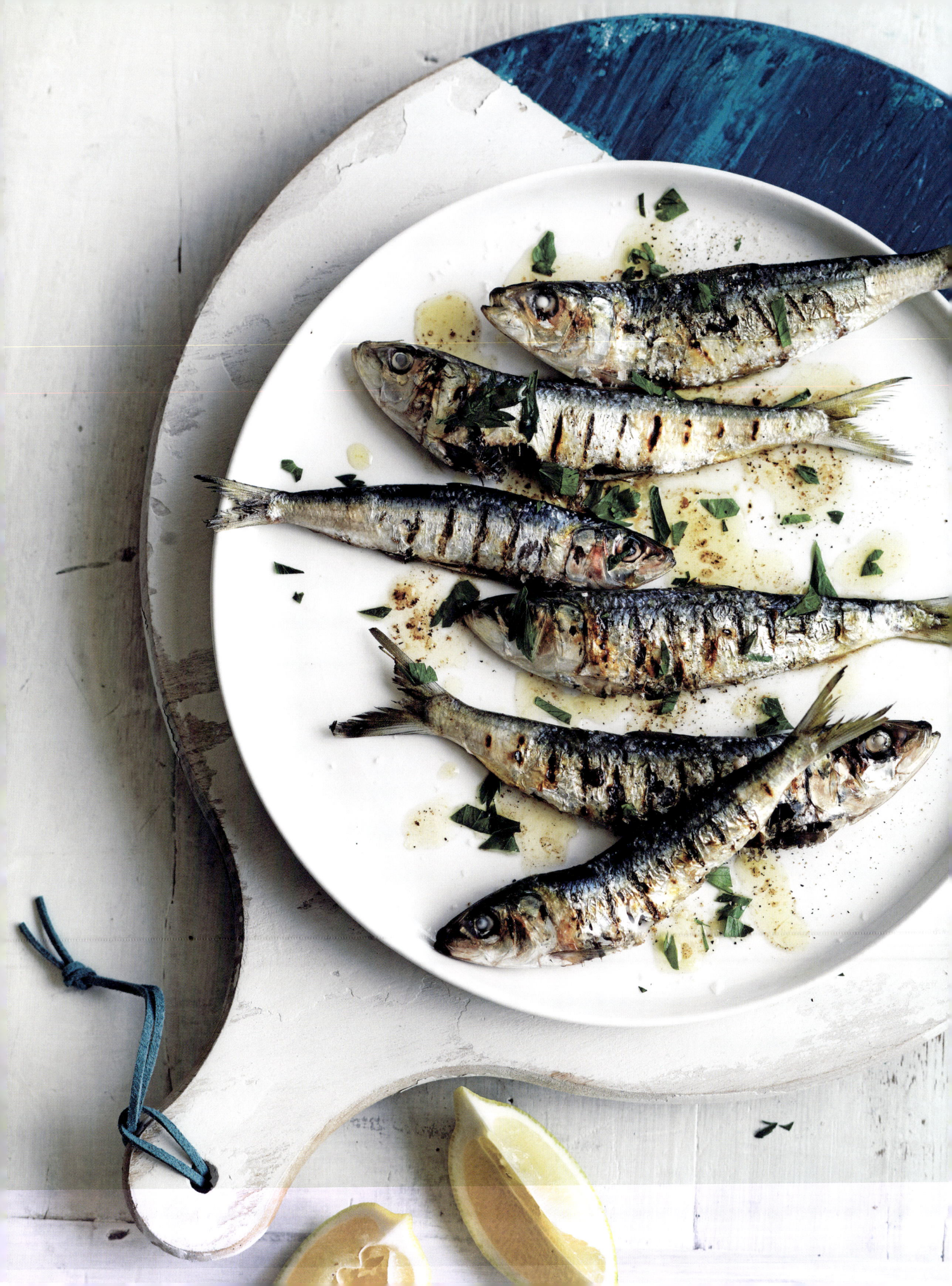

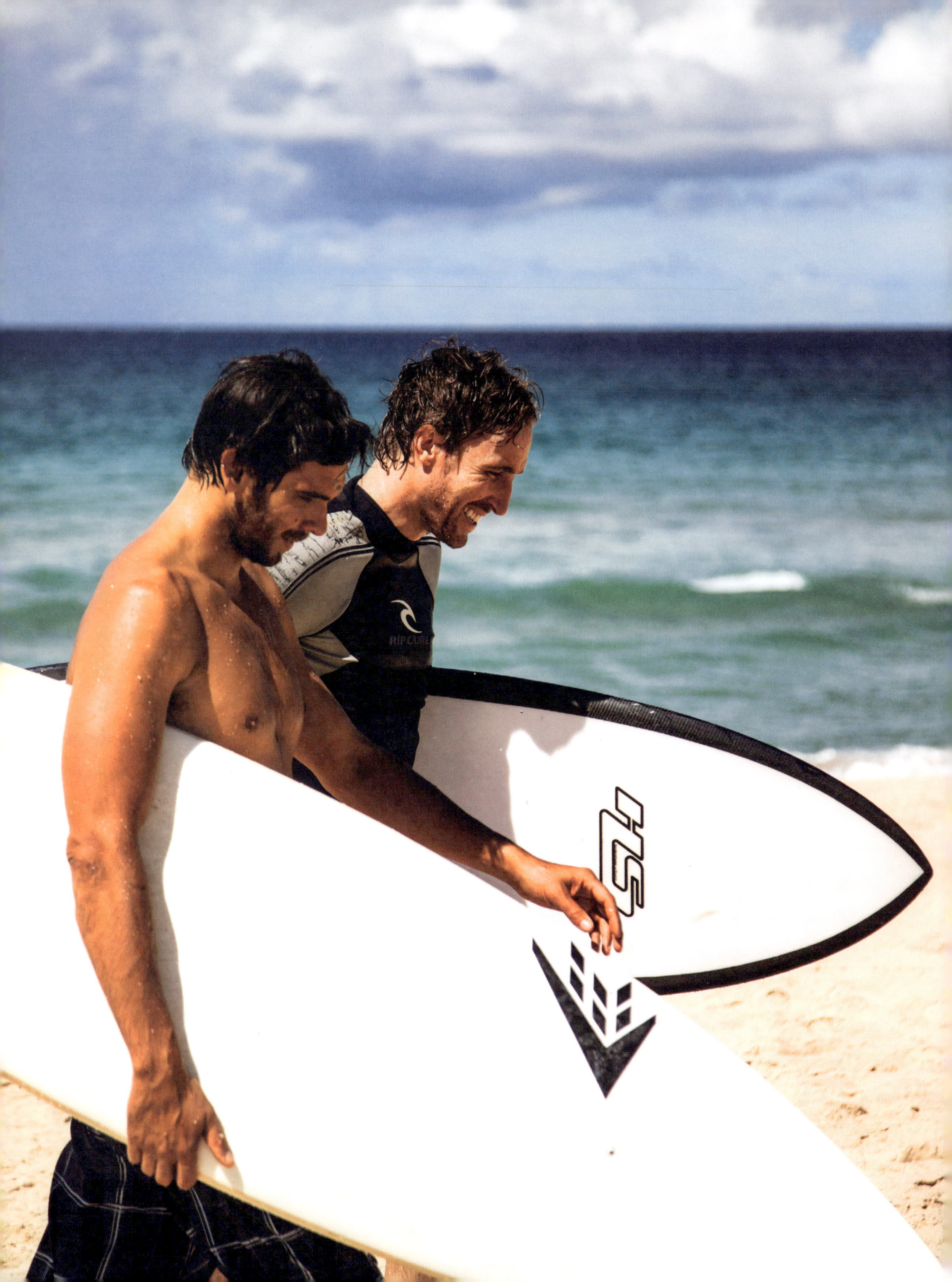
RIP CURL

BRONTE FISH CAKES

The humble fish cake has been around for donkey's years but we often have them at the Ducks either for lunch or for staff meals. Fish cakes are a really practical way of using fish offcuts. This recipe suggests barramundi and flathead, but we also use salmon, trout, snapper, mulloway, john dory, yellowtail, swordfish, smoked cod or mackerel too. You can boil your potatoes if you're short of time but baking them removes more moisture from the spuds, concentrating the flavour and giving you a tastier cake.

Preheat the oven to 180°C.

Roast the potatoes in their skins for 50 minutes. Remove from the oven, cut in half and scoop the potato flesh into a large bowl.

Heat water to boiling in a saucepan and place a bamboo steamer on top. Put the fish in and steam for 5–10 minutes until just cooked (it will depend on the type of fish and how thick the fillets are).

Flake the fish, removing any skin and bones, and add to the potato. Mix well, breaking up the potato and fish. Add the egg yolks, capers, parsley, mustard, lemon zest and juice, and season with salt and pepper. Leave the mixture to cool for 5 minutes.

Shape the mixture into cakes – this should make around 10 fish cakes.

Put the cakes in the refrigerator for 30 minutes to help firm them, then dust both sides in cornflour.

Heat the oil in a large, non-stick frying pan over medium heat and shallow fry the cakes for 3 minutes on each side until golden brown.

Serve with lemon cheeks, mayonnaise or a fresh slaw.

MAKES 10 FISH CAKES

1 kg desiree potatoes
250 g flathead fillets
250 g barramundi fillets
2 egg yolks
1 tablespoon capers, chopped
2 tablespoons chopped flat-leaf parsley
1 tablespoon grain mustard
zest and juice of 1 lemon
salt and pepper
50 g cornflour
200 ml vegetable oil
lemon cheeks, mayonnaise or slaw, to serve

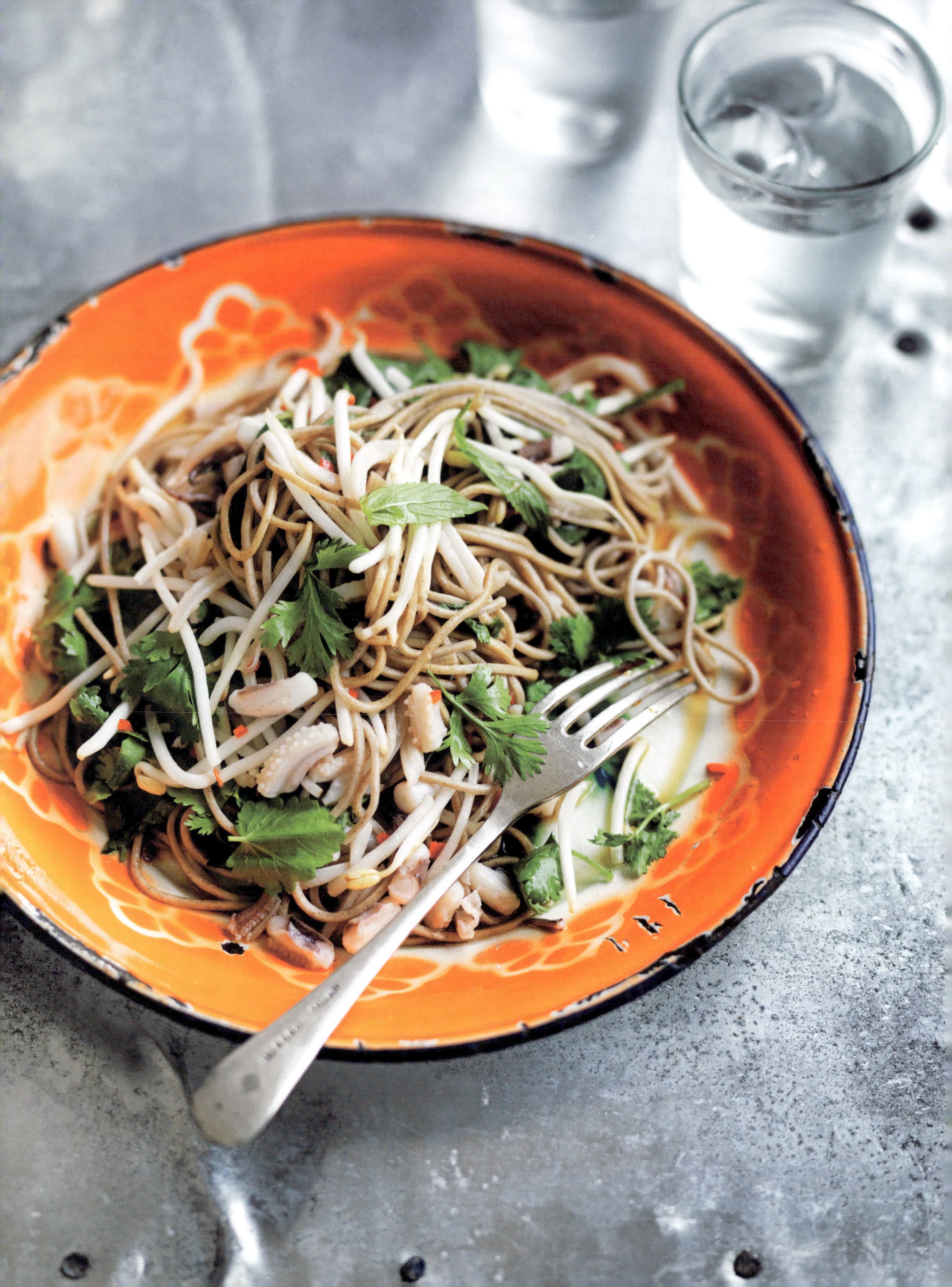

CUTTLEFISH and SUMMER HERB SOBA NOODLE SALAD

A tasty and easy little dish this one, which literally takes minutes to prepare. The Asian flavours – fish sauce, chilli, lime and coriander – give it quite a kick. If you can't get your hands on fresh cuttlefish, then shredded duck, pork or prawns will do the job.

Heat a non-stick pan over low heat, add the oil and garlic and cook for 2 minutes, without letting it colour. Add the cuttlefish and gently cook for about 1 minute, until it just begins to lose its translucency, then tip into a large serving bowl.

Place the pan back on the heat, add the soy sauce, fish sauce, palm sugar and the water (you can use water left from cooking the noodles). Warm the liquid to dissolve the sugar. Remove from the heat, add the lime juice and pour the liquid over the cuttlefish.

Add the noodles, bean sprouts, chilli, coriander and mint to the bowl and mix, saving a few of the fresh herbs to sprinkle on top. Season with salt and pepper and serve.

SERVES 4

30 ml grapeseed oil
1 garlic clove, sliced
400 g cuttlefish, cleaned and cut into thin strips
1½ tablespoons soy sauce
2 tablespoons fish sauce
1 tablespoon grated palm sugar
40 ml water
juice of 2 limes
300 g soba noodles, cooked and refreshed
100 g bean sprouts
1 long red chilli, seeded and finely chopped
1 bunch of coriander, leaves picked
1 bunch of mint, leaves picked
salt and pepper

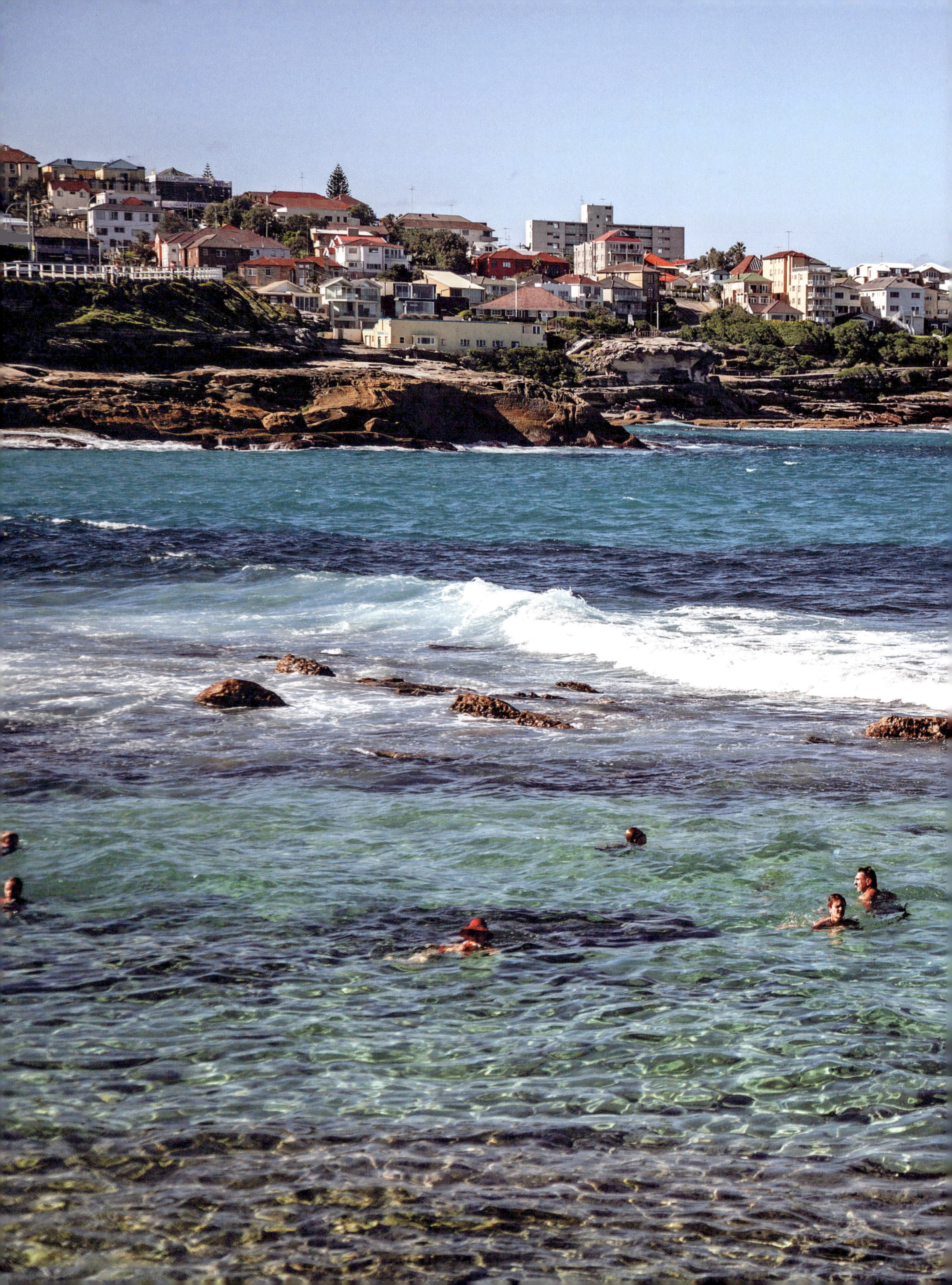

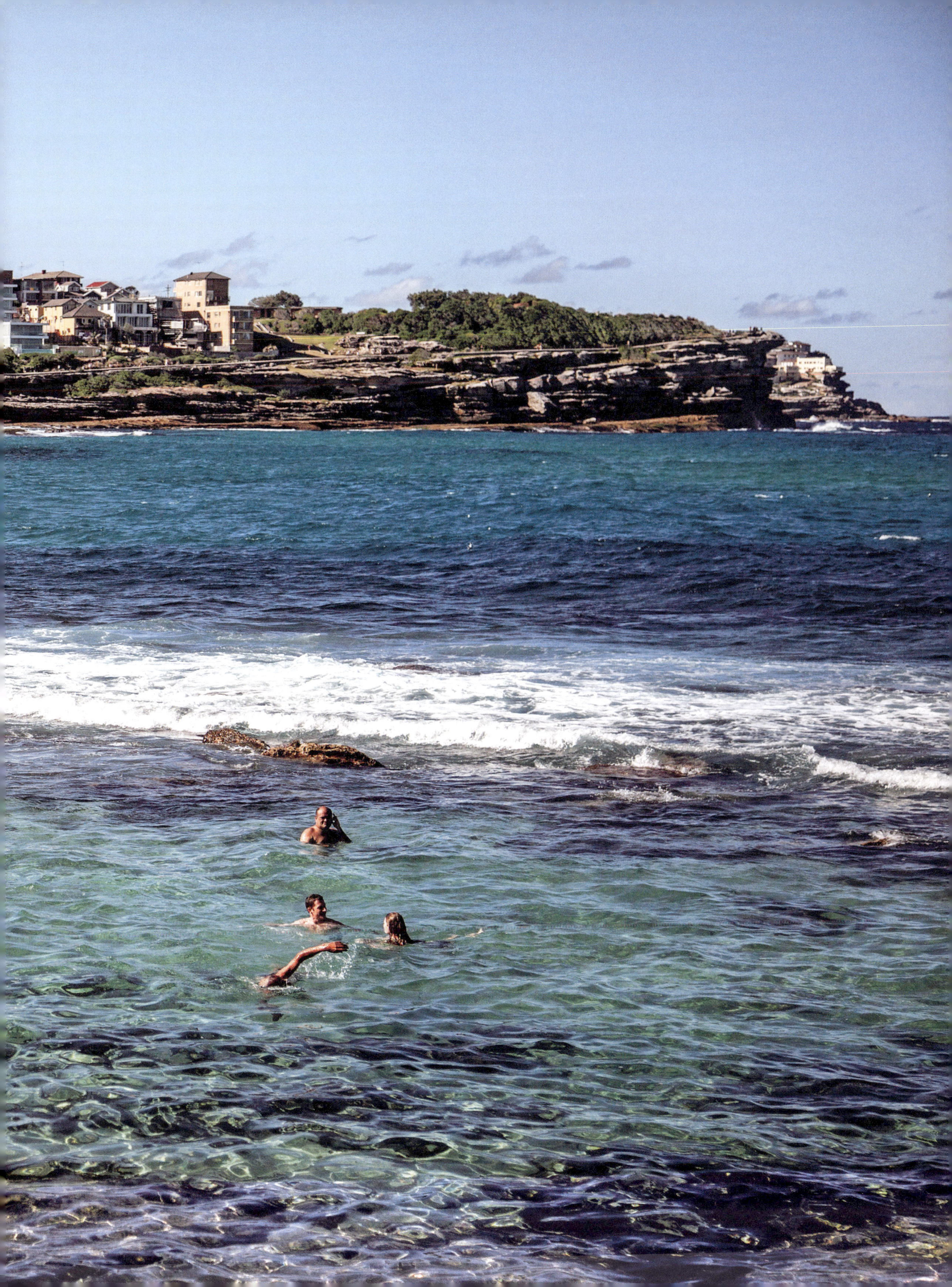

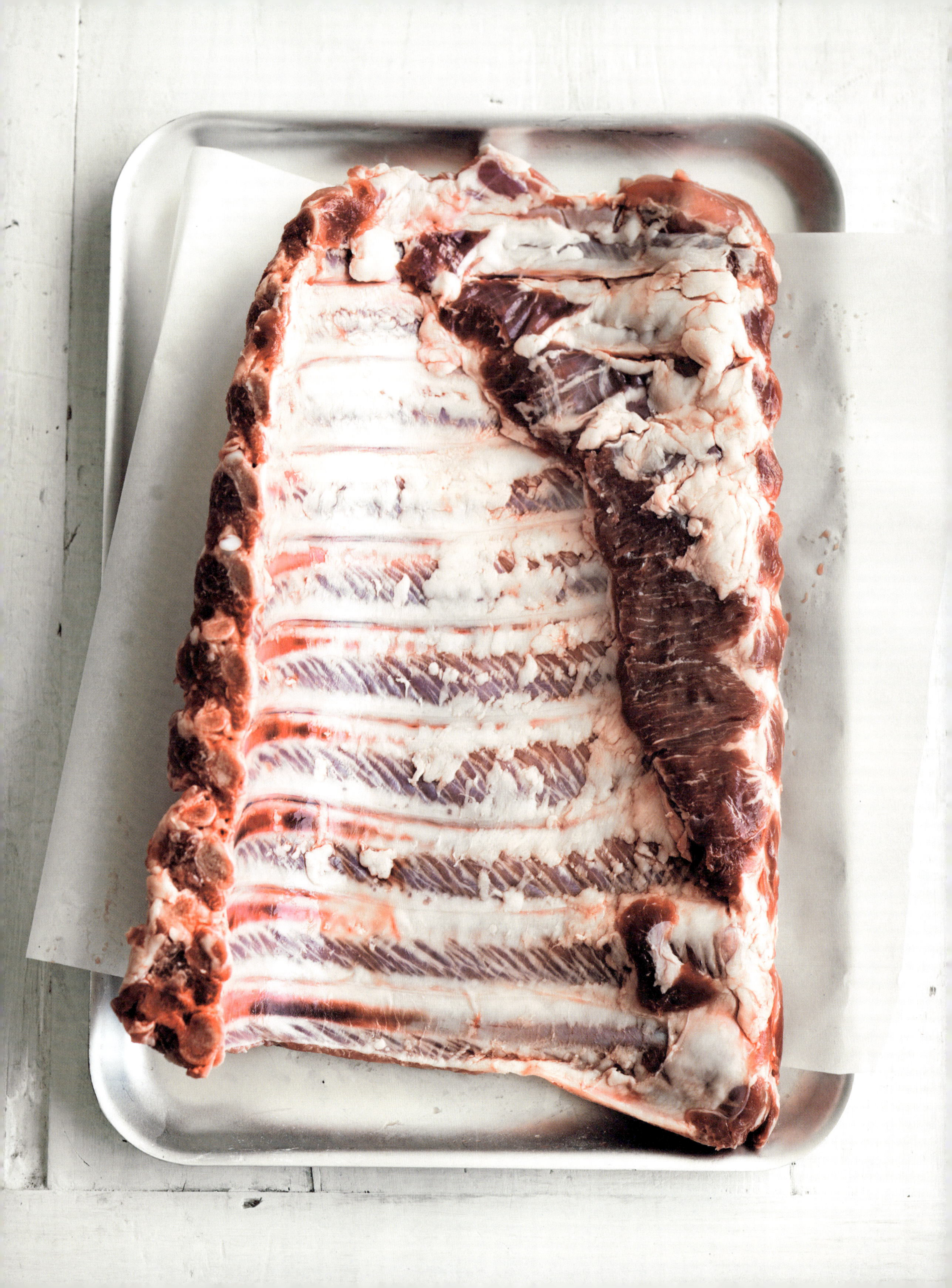

THE LAND

Meat & Poultry
Savoury Grains
Sweet Grains

Bloody delicious!

KICK-ARSE STEAK SANDWICH

This isn't just any old steak sandwich – we've spent a lot of time getting all the elements just right, so we can highly recommend it. It's a sandwich with heart and soul and a lot of good fresh ingredients. If you can, fire up the barbecue to cook the steak, but if not, a really hot pan will do.

To make the marinade, place the chilli, rosemary, thyme, garlic and olive oil in a food processor and blitz until smooth.

Pour the marinade over the sliced rump steak, put it in the fridge and let it sit for a couple of hours.

Put a heavy-based frying pan on high heat, add the vegetable oil, onion, and 2 pinches of salt (this will help the onion break down faster) and cook until soft and translucent. Add the sugar and stir, and a caramel will start to form. Add the vinegar and red wine, cook and reduce until most of the wine has evaporated and the onion marmalade is dark and sticky. Season to taste.

Take the whole capsicums, cover with olive oil and season heavily. Char-grill them on a naked flame on your burner, or turn your oven as high as it will go and put them in for 10 minutes, until the skin goes black. Take them out of the oven, place in a bowl and cover with cling film, so the capsicums will steam a little. When they cool down enough to handle, peel off the black skin and discard, put the capsicum flesh into the blender and blend to a puree.

Add the capsicum puree to the mayo and stir well.

Toss the rocket into a bowl with the balsamic vinegar and olive oil, and season with salt (don't use pepper as the rocket is peppery enough).

Season the sliced tomatoes with cracked pepper and salt, and set them aside.

CONSTRUCTING THE STEAK SAMBO
The meat is best cooked on a barbecue, but if you can't do that, just cook it in a frying pan on high heat. Season the meat and cook for 1 minute on either side.

Toast the sourdough and have it ready when the meat's cooked.

Spread the red capsicum mayo and onion marmalade on the sourdough, then the meat, the tomato, the rocket and then the sourdough lid. Eat. Enjoy.

SERVES 4

1 long red chilli, whole
¼ bunch of rosemary, leaves picked
¼ bunch of thyme, leaves picked
5 garlic cloves, peeled
75 ml good olive oil
800 g beef rump, cut into 1-cm thick slices

ONION MARMALADE
2 tablespoons vegetable oil
2 red onions, thinly sliced
salt
2 tablespoons caster sugar
1 tablespoon apple cider vinegar
1½ cups red wine

RED CAPSICUM MAYO
2 red capsicums
good olive oil
salt and pepper
1 quantity Mayonnaise (page 113)

SALAD
4 handfuls of rocket
splash of balsamic vinegar
splash of extra virgin olive oil
salt and cracked pepper
3 tomatoes, sliced
1 loaf sourdough bread

THE LAND

Meat & Poultry

CHILLI DUCK SALAD with GREEN MANGO and MINT

2 large duck breasts, skin on and scored
1 tablespoon vegetable oil
1 green mango
250 g snow pea sprouts
1 red onion, thinly sliced
1 punnet cherry tomatoes, halved
1 bunch of coriander, leaves picked
½ bunch of mint leaves, torn
nahm jim dressing (page 111)
75 g unsalted peanuts, crushed
75 g deep-fried shallots (from Asian supermarkets)
1 lime quartered, to serve

CHILLI JAM
1 bunch of coriander, chopped
5 garlic cloves, chopped
10 long red chillies, seeded and chopped
1 knob of ginger, peeled and chopped
100 g palm sugar, grated
2 tablespoons sweet soy sauce (kecap manis)

This is one of our signature dishes and when we bring it out at festivals like Big Day Out, it is a real crowd-pleaser. Save the duck fat and use it the next time you bake potatoes to go with a roast – the flavour is amazing. Croutons are also amazing cooked with duck fat. If you have any of the chilli jam left, you can keep it in the fridge – it adds a punch to lots of other dishes.

To make the chilli jam, put the ingredients into a saucepan over medium heat and cook until the chilli breaks down. Add a splash of water if the mixture becomes too dry and starts to stick to the pot. When the chilli is soft and look as though it will blend, remove from the heat.

Tip the mixture into a food processor and blend for 45 seconds until it is a slightly chunky paste, then set it aside.

Preheat the oven to 190°C.

Heavily season the skin side of the duck breasts. Put a large heavy-based frying pan on high heat, add the oil and when it is almost at smoking point, add the duck breasts, skin-side down. Fry until the skin is crisp and golden. Turn the breasts over and cook for a further 2 minutes. There should be a lot of fat rendered off the duck (save this for cooking other things!).

Place the breasts on a baking tray, smear 1 tablespoon of chilli jam on each breast, place in the oven and roast for 7–8 minutes. When cooked, remove the breasts, cover with foil, and leave to rest.

Peel the mango and finely shred the flesh with a peeler. In a large bowl, mix the mango, sprouts, onion, cherry tomatoes, coriander and mint. Add a good splash of nahm jim dressing and gently stir.

Slice the duck breasts into 3-mm thick pieces and toss through the salad. Sprinkle over the peanuts and shallots, squeeze over some lime and serve.

SERVES 4

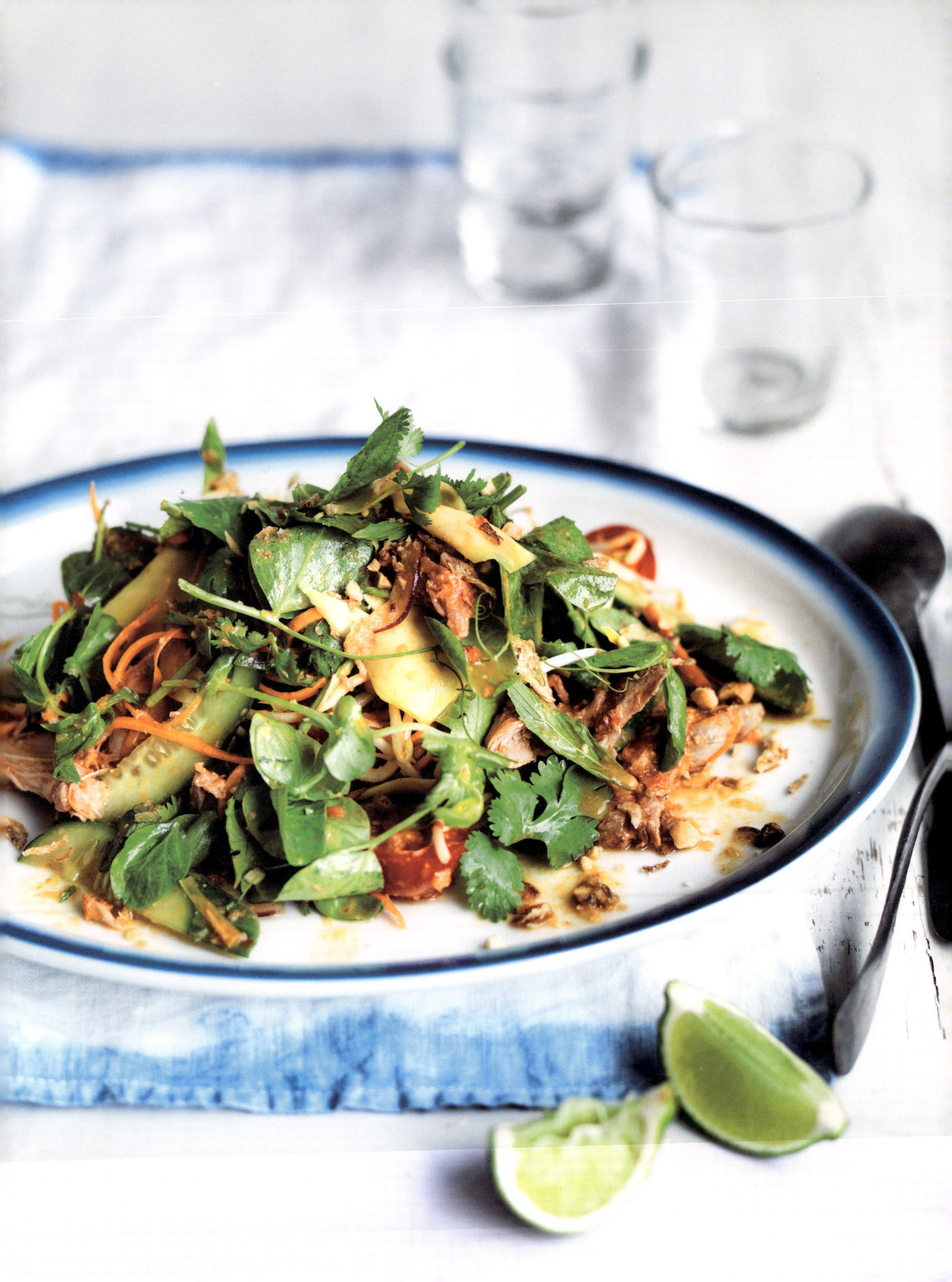

SLOW-COOKED LAMB SHANKS *for a* COLD DAY

6 lamb shanks
salt and white pepper
1 litre chicken stock
1 litre red wine
200 g can chopped tomatoes
1 sprig rosemary
2 garlic cloves, peeled
50 g Parmigiano Reggiano, grated
50 g toasted almonds
6 small leeks, washed, trimmed, white part only
4 zucchini, thinly sliced
juice and zest of ½ lemon
1 teaspoon honey
15 ml olive oil
1 small bunch of basil, and some mint leaves, torn

Lamb shanks are quite a cheap cut to buy, but slow-cooking them with tomatoes and herbs makes them a rich and satisfying meal. The crunchy almond and cheese topping is a bit of an unexpected twist.

Preheat the oven to 180°C.

Season the lamb shanks and fry in a pan over medium heat for a few minutes until golden brown. Place them in a casserole dish, add the stock, wine, tomatoes, rosemary and garlic and cover. Place in the oven and cook for 3 hours, checking occasionally.

Line a baking tray with baking paper. Sprinkle the Parmigiano on the tray, then put in in the oven for 5 minutes. Remove the cheese, let it cool, then blend in a food processor with the almonds until you get a coarse powder.

Put the char-grill on high heat.

Roast the whole leeks on the grill until blackened, then put them in a bowl, cover and leave them to steam for a few minutes. Remove the leeks and set aside.

Put the sliced zucchini into the bowl with the leek juices, lemon juice and zest and honey, olive oil and fresh herbs.

Cut the leeks in half lengthways and arrange on a platter. Place the slow-cooked shanks and a little of the cooking juices on the leeks, garnish with the zucchini salad and almond crumbs. Serve immediately.

SERVES 6

ONE-POT RABBIT STEW

Everything goes in one dish, the dish goes in the oven – and you relax until it's time to serve this up to friends or family. It's substantial but if you wanted to, you could serve a salad, or maybe just some good bread with it.

Preheat the oven to 200°C.

Put all the ingredients into a large baking dish, cover and bake in the oven for 2½ hours. Check after an hour or so, to make sure all the liquid hasn't evaporated. If it has, add a little more stock.

Remove the rabbit, pick the meat off the bone (it should come away very easily) and return the meat to the stew. Serve with crusty bread to mop up the juices.

SERVES 4

1 fennel bulb, trimmed and diced
2 red onions, diced
½ head of celery, trimmed and sliced
1 x 900 g–1.2 kg rabbit, cleaned, whole
2 punnets cherry tomatoes
4 garlic cloves, finely chopped
2 long red chillies, finely chopped
1 x 750 ml bottle Riesling
500 ml vegetable stock
1 bunch of rosemary, roughly chopped
1 bunch of thyme, roughly chopped
500 g purple potatoes, cut into wedges
salt and pepper
crusty bread, to serve

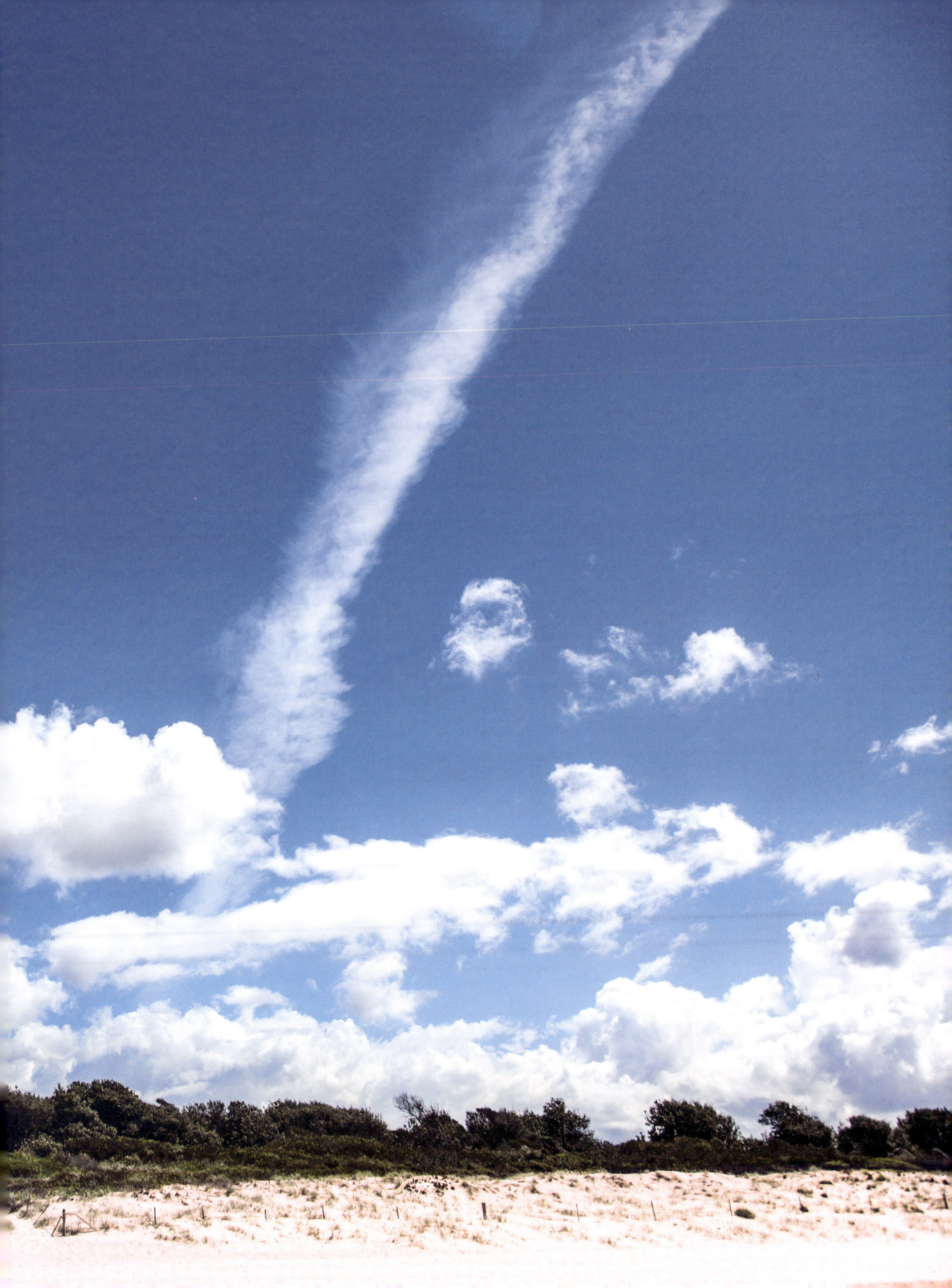

SPICED CHICKEN *in a* BROWN PAPER BAG

8 x 120 g chicken drumsticks
1 tablespoon grapeseed oil
2 tablespoons salt
1 brown paper bag

CAJUN SPICE MIX
1 teaspoon garlic powder
1 tablespoon smoked paprika
½ teaspoon white pepper
½ teaspoon dried thyme
½ teaspoon cayenne pepper

This is a great way of serving chicken at parties, and it's just as good made like this and eaten cold at a picnic. The spice mix here has a Cajun flavour but you can add different spices or herbs, or even replace the chicken with chunks of roasted sweet corn. Have a creamy mayonnaise, fresh coleslaw or chilli oil on the side.

Preheat the oven to 180°C.

Brush the drumsticks with a little oil and season with the salt. Roast for 15–20 minutes until golden brown and crispy.

To make the Cajun spice mix, mix all the spices together.

Remove the drumsticks from the oven, place in a brown paper bag, sprinkle in a good pinch of spice mix, close the bag and shake.

SERVES 4

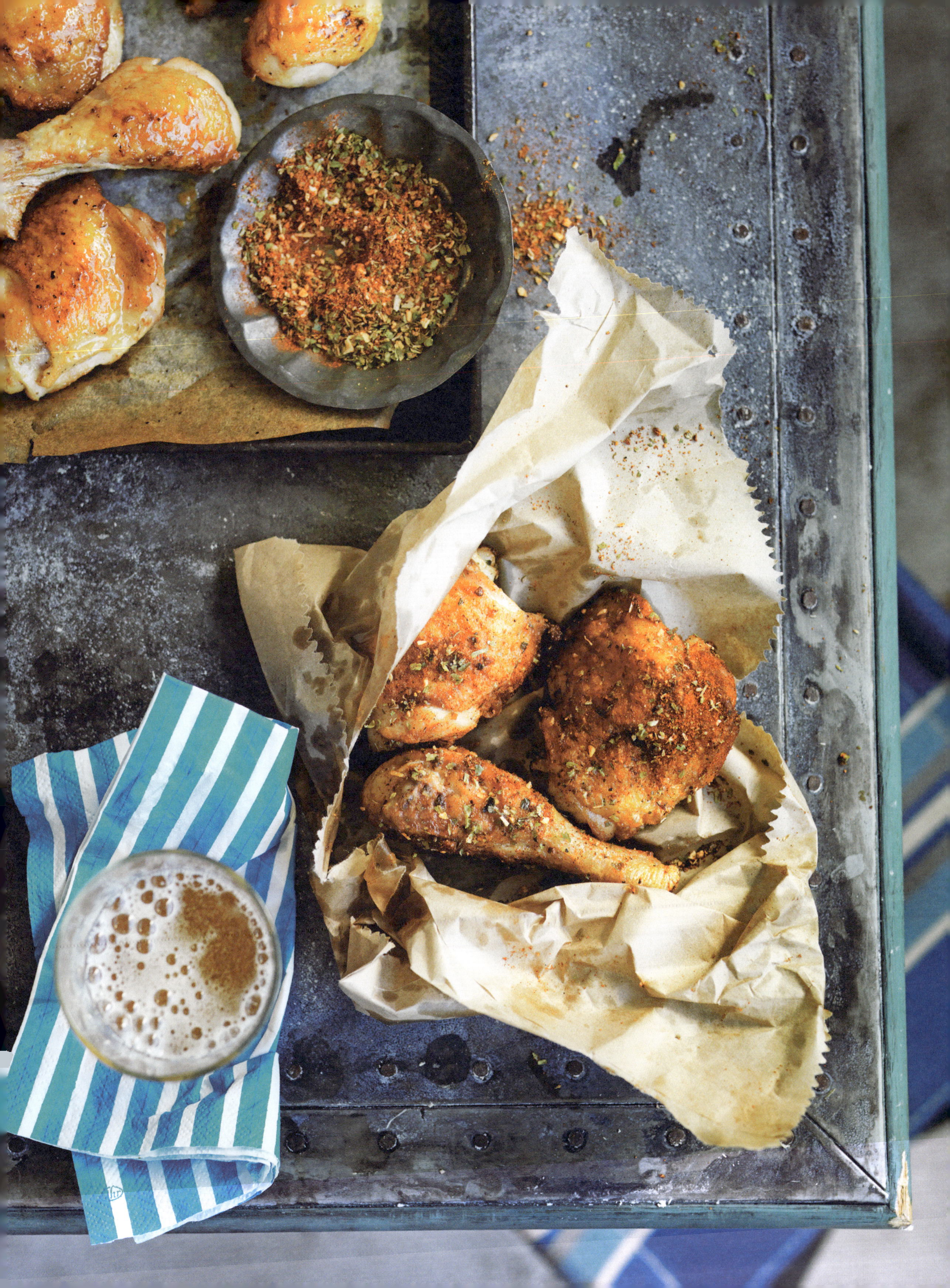

BRAISED and CHARRED OX TONGUE

1 x 2 kg ox tongue

BRINE
1 litre water
50 g salt
30 g sugar
1 bay leaf
1 teaspoon peppercorns
1 teaspoon juniper berries

POACHING LIQUID
1 carrot, peeled
1 celery stalk
1 medium onion, halved
200 ml red wine
1 teaspoon salt

You might have to order an ox tongue from your butcher, but it's worth going to the trouble. Ox tongue is still not used much in Australia, but those who cook with it know that it's a truly magical ingredient. It's also important to use the entire animal and not just the prime cuts. In the words of the great Fergus Henderson, known for his promotion of nose-to-tail eating, to not use the entire beast is disrespectful. So we encourage you to give this a go, you won't be disappointed. This recipe will need to be started two days ahead.

To make the brine, put all the ingredients into a saucepan, bring to the boil, then take off the heat and leave it to cool. Put the brine in the fridge until cold.

Put the tongue in the brine and leave for 48 hours.

Remove the tongue from brine, and put into another saucepan with all the poaching ingredients and just enough water to cover the tongue. Bring to simmering, then simmer, covered, on a very low heat for 3 hours. When it is cooked you should be able to push a fine skewer through the tongue with ease.

Remove the tongue from the pan, let it cool slightly, then peel away the outer skin and allow to cool in the fridge.

When the tongue is cold, you can slice it into 1-cm thick steaks, char-grill it for 1 minute on each side and serve with pickles or a little salad of chopped parsley, lemon and French shallots.

SERVES 8

HONEY-ROASTED BRINED DUCK BREAST

Brining changes the structure of the protein in poultry and meat, allowing it to retain more juice, making it much more tender and flavoursome. Drizzling the duck with honey before roasting gives a really crispy skin. Serve with a leafy green salad or an orange and fennel salad. This recipe will need to be started a day ahead.

To make the brine, put the water, sugar and salt in a saucepan, bring to the boil, then chill before using.

Place the duck breasts in the brine and soak for 24 hours. Remove and pat dry.

Preheat the oven to 170°C.

Heat the oil in a frying pan over low heat, add the breasts and cook, skin-side down, until the skin becomes golden brown and crisp. Put the breasts on a baking tray, drizzle over the honey and season with salt and pepper. Place in the oven and roast for 8–10 minutes.

Remove the breasts from the oven, rest for 8 minutes before carving.

SERVES 4

2 x 250 g duck breasts
1 tablespoon grapeseed oil
2 tablespoons of honey
salt and pepper

BRINE
1 litre water
100 g sugar
100 g salt

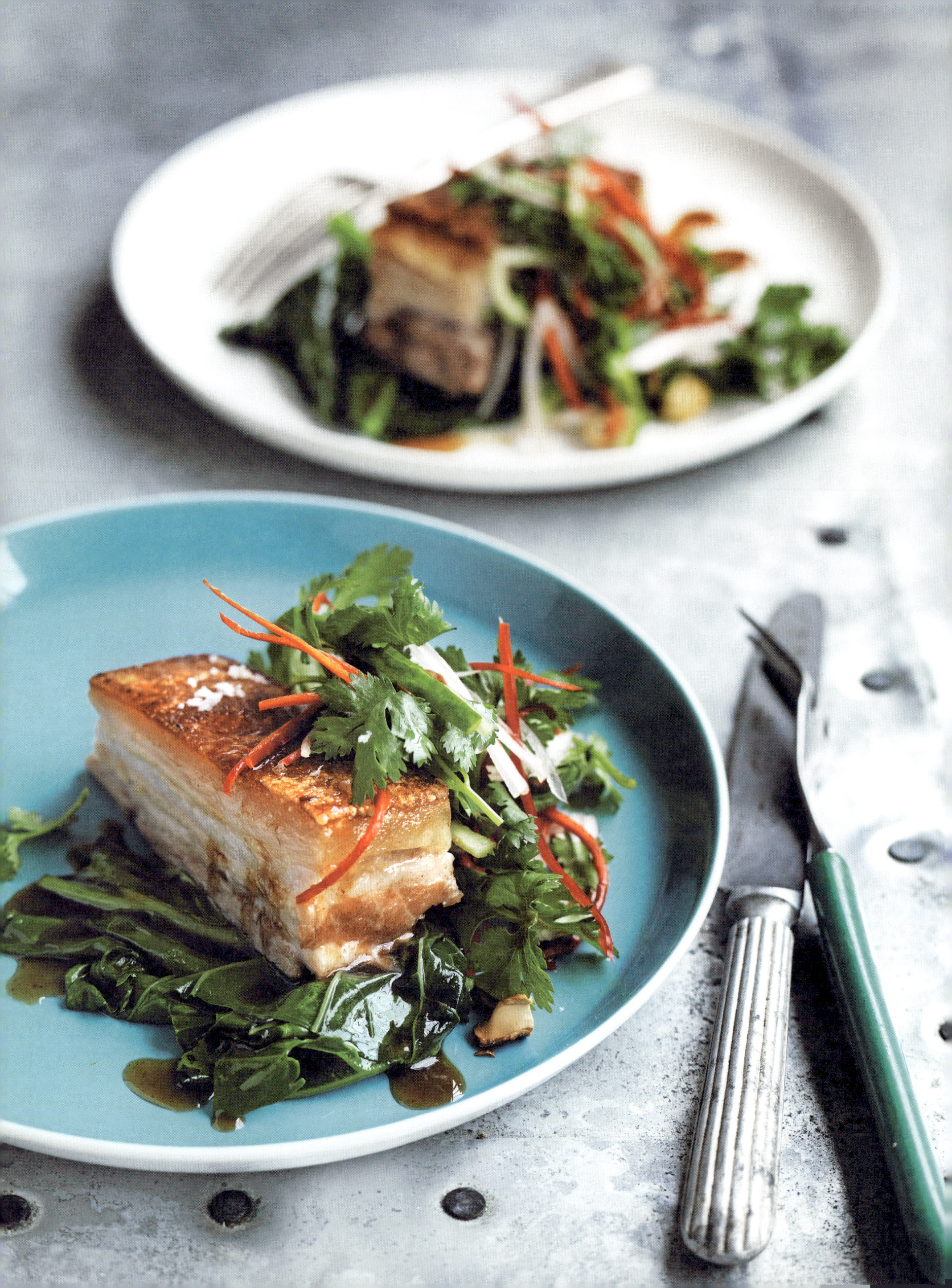

STICKY PORK BELLY

Pork belly is one of the most succulent cuts you can buy – tender, flavoursome and it's not hard to cook. Roast it with star anise and soy sauce for an Asian flavour, and coat it with some honey for that delicious sticky finish. It's great with steamed Asian greens to cut the richness, and maybe some shiitake mushrooms, chilli, coriander and steamed rice.

Preheat the oven to 175°C.

Score the skin of the pork belly, but don't cut through to the flesh. Brush the skin with a little vegetable oil and season with salt.

Mix all the other ingredients with the water in a bowl, and pour into a baking dish.

Put the pork in the dish, place in the oven and cook for 3 hours. Check it a couple of times and baste it.

Remove the pork from the oven, cover and leave to rest for 20 minutes before carving.

SERVES 4

1 x 800 g boned pork belly
1 tablespoon vegetable oil
1 teaspoon sea salt
2 star anise
1 cinnamon stick
5 tablespoons soy sauce
3 tablespoons honey
1 long red chilli, roughly chopped
1 tablespoon coriander seeds, roasted
1 teaspoon sea salt
60 g fresh ginger, chopped
1 bunch of coriander, roots only
1 litre warm water

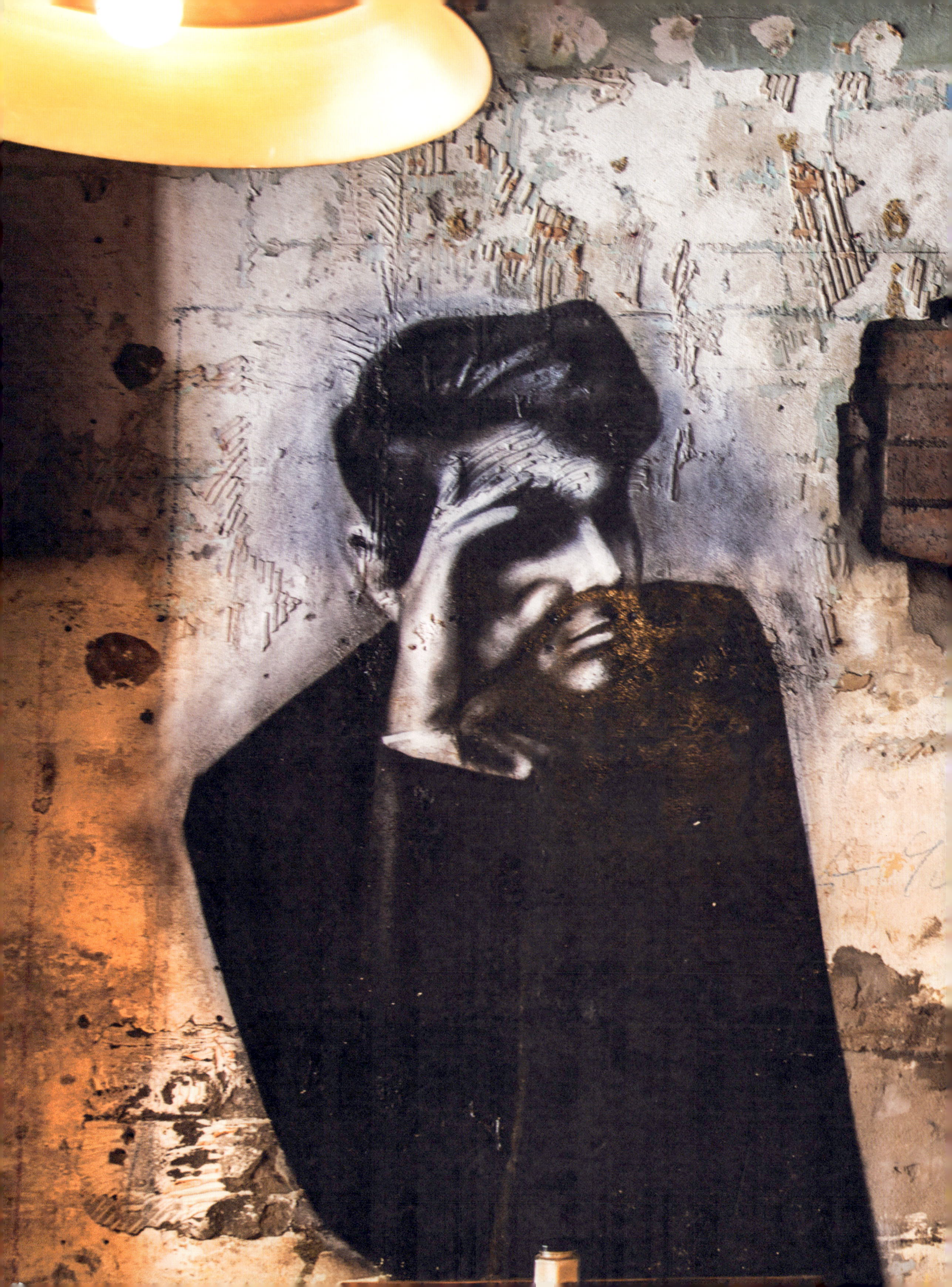

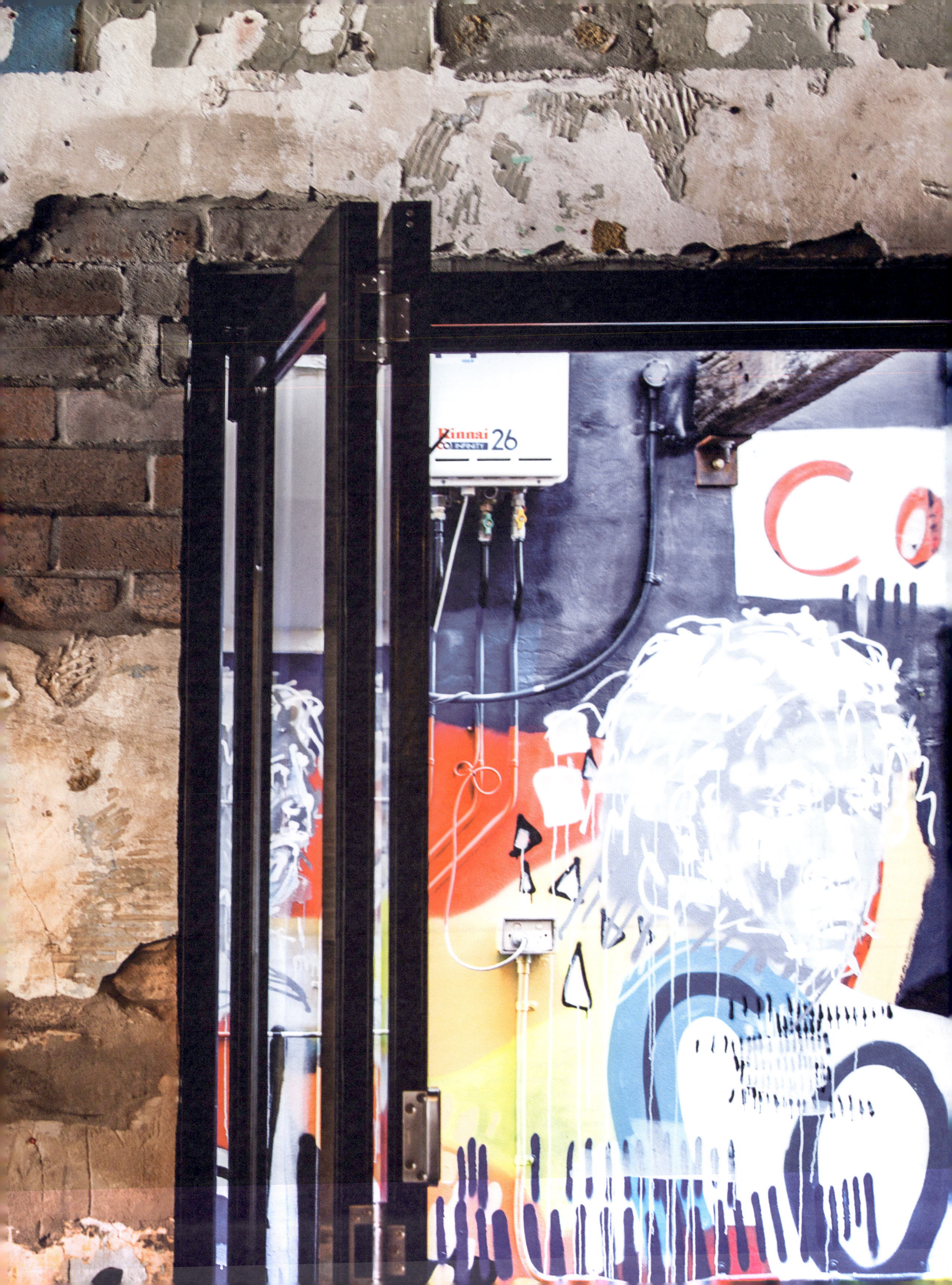
Rinnai
INFINITY 26

Know YOUR MEAT

So many of our most memorable meals involve meat. We love beef and lamb – fat with flavour and easy to cook. Whether you're frying salty beef patties on the backyard barbecue, trying to saw through a steak from the local RSL, or splurging on the $65 aged rib eye on your birthday, meat is gamey and exotic, earthy and piquant. It's bloody delicious.

Australia is one of the world's largest exporters of livestock and cattle. Only a small part of Australia is suitable for crop production so livestock farming is a really efficient use of the land. Australian cattle are tailor-raised for the wide variety of markets supplied, including grain fed, grass fed, organic, breed specific (for example, Wagyu and Angus) and market specific (such as for live export, manufacturing, domestic).

In Australia we have two types of beef available; grain fed and grass fed. Grass-fed cows graze on pasture, while grain-fed cows may start on pasture, but are later moved to feedlots and fattened on grain. Traditionally all cattle were grass fed and that is considered the most natural method of feeding them. A grain diet is said to interfere with natural digestion of ruminant animals such as cows. As well, many grain-fed cows are given feed additives and antibiotics to speed growth and reduce health problems. On the other hand, grain-fed cows use less land, water and energy, and produce less waste and fewer greenhouse gases. In Australia, there's not enough grass to sustain the number of cattle required to meet the demand for beef. Grain can be planted more densely to the acre than grass, grows more quickly, making the farmer less weather- and land-reliant and the product is less expensive and more sustainable.

There is also a difference in the flavour of grass-fed and grain-fed beef. Grain-fed cattle produce meat with more marbling, or deposits of intramuscular fat. It's that marbling, in meat such as Wagyu, that creates the tender juiciness. Certain breeds of cattle naturally have marbling, but nowhere near as much as if they are fattened on grain. In comparison, grass-fed beef is leaner, with a delicious earthy flavour. At the Ducks we use grass-fed beef for certain dishes and grain-fed for others, but we do try to make an informed decision when choosing our meat.

ORGANIC MEAT

The environmental and animal-welfare implications of eating meat make it important to know where your meat comes from. Conventional farming practice in Australia is predominantly factory farming, which involves raising livestock in confinement at high-stocking density. Recently, some farmers in Australia have championed an organic farming movement, yielding organic meat.

Organic meat comes from animals that have ranged free on pasture, been raised without the use of growth promoters (including growth hormones and antibiotics), eat chemical-free feed, and have no genetically modified inputs.

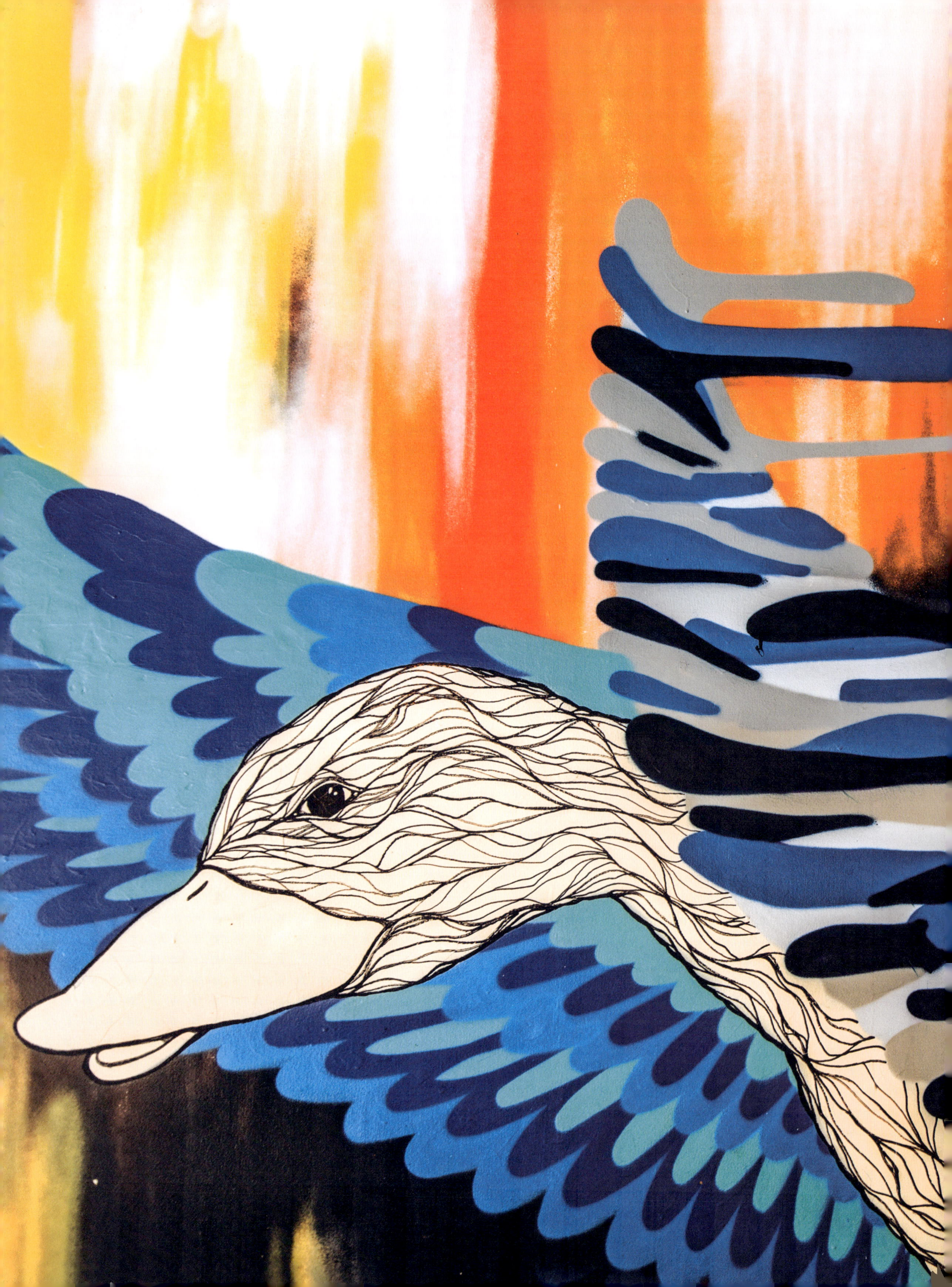

The truth is, anyone can use the word 'organic' to label their product. The only way to be certain meat is truly organic is to buy certified. Certification means the product complies with the national standard for organic and biodynamic produce. Look for the certification logo, or ask your butcher who certifies the meat you're purchasing. If he or she can't tell you, it may not certified organic. Organic meat is more expensive to produce so it is more expensive to buy than other meat.

SO, HOW CAN YOU SHOW RESPECT FOR MEAT AND HOW IT SHOULD BE CONSUMED, WHILE STILL ENJOYING IT?

- Change the way you shop to make sustainable choices. Where possible, purchase your meat at butchers or markets where you can find out where your meat is from, and if it was raised, slaughtered and handled ethically.
- Ask questions. Is it free range? Is it certified organic?
- Where you can, try to source and purchase free-range and organic options.
- Be wary if you're purchasing meat from supermarkets. Plastic packaging may hold pre-cut and pre-ground meat, fresh and frozen, with brightly coloured labels promising 'natural', 'cage free' and 'hormone free' products, however, many of these claims may be unregulated and meaningless. For information on labels and whether they can be trusted, check out greenerchoices.org.
- Use economical cuts of meat – most retailers receive their meat from large processing companies that break down animal carcasses into large 'primal' sections. The stores then break these down into retail cuts such as tenderloins, skirts and T-bones. Much of the remaining meat is discarded or used for sausage meat. Instead of always buying these cuts, try some economical cuts that will be super tasty and less wasteful.
- Practice 'nose-to-tail' eating, which involves avoiding wastage by using every part of the animal. For an everyday consumer, this means embracing typically under-appreciated parts such as bone marrow, kidneys, brains, snouts and trotters. It sounds scarier than it is!

It's all about being a mindful meat eater. Enjoy that juicy steak on your plate, but consider the responsibility you have as a consumer to purchase ethically raised meat.

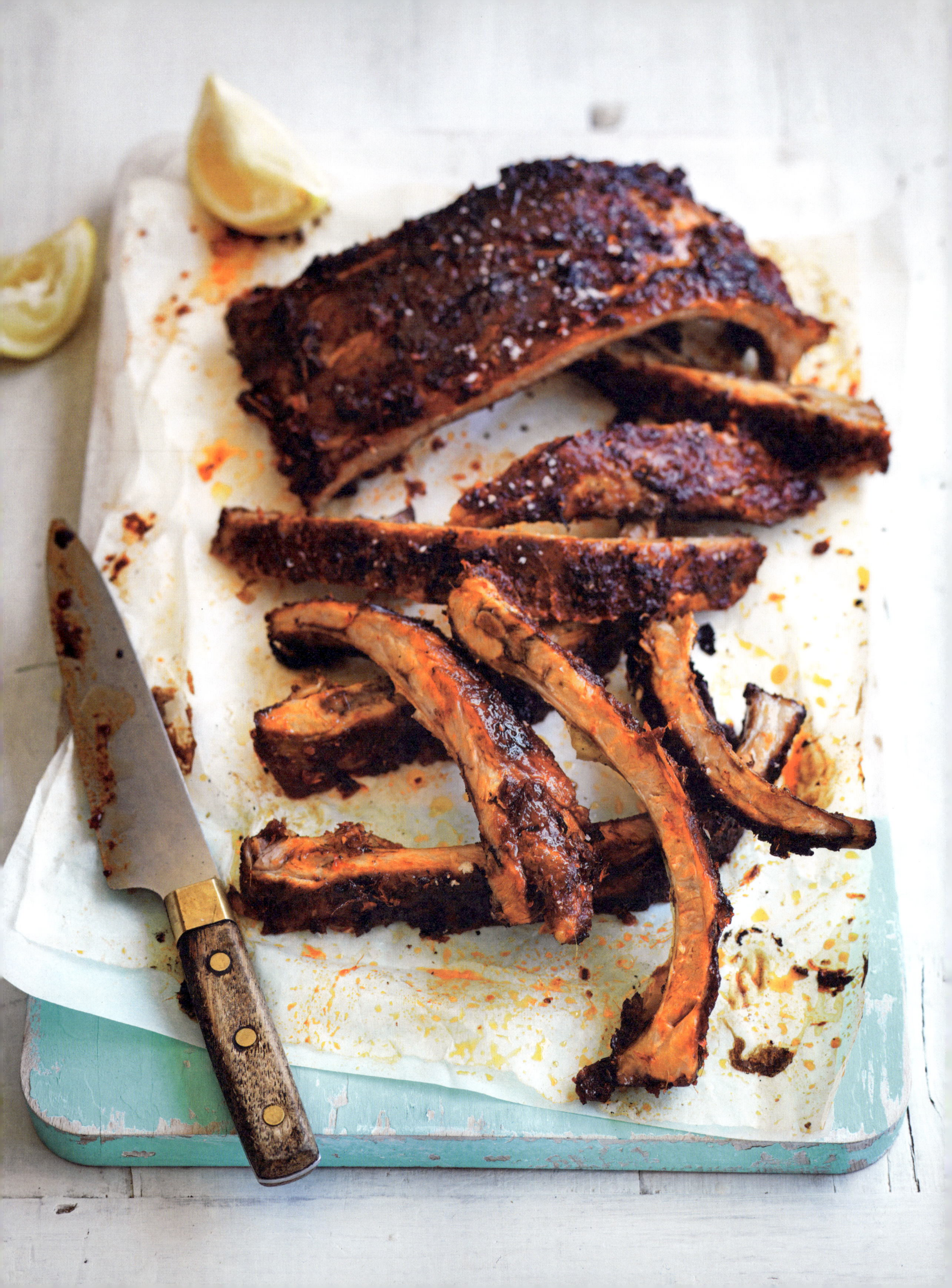

TWICE-COOKED STICKY PORK RIBS

Slow-cooking the ribs for an hour in the marinade and then caramelising them over the grill means you get the best of both worlds – soft, juicy flesh with plenty of subtle Asian flavours and a sticky outer skin.

Preheat the oven to 160°C.

To make the marinade, mix all the ingredients in a bowl.

Put the ribs in a roasting pan, pour over the marinade, keeping 100 ml to baste the ribs later. Cover the pan in foil, place in the oven and cook for 1 hour. Remove from the oven and leave the ribs to cool down for 30 minutes.

Heat the char-grill to high.

Baste the ribs with the remaining marinade and put on the hot grill for about 10 minutes, turning them to make sure they are nicely caramelised all over.

SERVES 4

2 racks of pork ribs
 (approx. 1 kg)

MARINADE
80 ml honey
2 tablespoons coriander seeds,
 ground and roasted
2 teaspoons cumin seeds, ground
 and roasted
1 garlic clove, minced
30 ml soy sauce
20 ml fish sauce
100 ml oyster sauce
1 teaspoon dark sesame oil
1 teaspoon cayenne pepper

PASTA with PANCETTA and TOASTED FENNEL SEEDS

3 tablespoons olive oil
200 g hot pancetta, minced
3 French shallots, peeled and finely chopped
1 teaspoon fennel seeds, roasted and coarsely ground
400 ml chicken stock
100 ml cream
50 g parmesan, grated
salt and pepper
500 g tagliatelle
1 tablespoon chopped chives

As soon as you smell the pancetta and fennel seeds frying, you know this is going to be a great pasta.

Pour the oil into a non-stick frying pan, fry the pancetta, shallots and fennel seeds over medium heat for 3 minutes. Add the chicken stock and cook on high heat for about 5 minutes to reduce to 150 ml. Stir though the cream, a little of the parmesan and season well with salt and pepper.

Cook the pasta in salted boiling water until al dente. Drain, then toss through the sauce. Add the rest of the parmesan, season with salt and pepper and serve, sprinkled with the chives.

SERVES 4

THE PERFECT STEAK

'How do you cook the perfect steak?' is a question we are often asked. There are so many opinions on this – some chefs like to colour the steak in a smoking-hot pan and finish it off in the oven, others cook it in the pan, turning the steak regularly. This recipe shows how we do it. The main points, really, are making sure you cook the steak from room temperature, that it is well-seasoned and it has a beautiful caramelisation. The internal temperatures should be 50°C for rare, 55°C for medium-rare and 60°C for medium.

1 garlic clove, slightly crushed
2 tablespoons grapeseed oil
1 x 250 g Wagyu sirloin steak, at room temperature
salt and pepper
1 lemon cheek

In a non-stick pan over medium heat, fry the garlic in the oil for 3 minutes.

Season the steak with salt and pepper and cook on medium heat for 5 minutes, turning every 30 seconds. Increase the heat to high for the last minute to caramelise. Remove from the pan and leave the steak to rest for 3 minutes.

Season with a little more salt and serve with a lemon cheek.

SERVES 1

CHICKEN LIVER PARFAIT

250 g chicken livers
salt and pepper
1 teaspoon vegetable oil
1 French shallot, peeled and thinly sliced
80 g butter, chilled, diced
1 small garlic clove, thinly sliced
40 ml port wine
40 ml Madeira
250 ml cream

The secret to a great chicken liver parfait is to use the freshest liver you can get your hands on. Serve this with pickles and good char-grilled sourdough.

Trim any sinew from the livers and season with salt and pepper.

Put a non-stick frying pan over high heat, add the oil and heat, then add the livers and fry for 10–20 seconds, moving the pan continuously. You want them to be brown on the outside but still pink and soft inside. Tip the livers onto a tray or into a bowl.

To the same pan, add a knob of butter, the shallot and garlic. Cook slowly over low heat for 4–5 minutes, stirring occasionally. Add the port and Madeira, increase the heat and cook for 3–4 minutes to reduce to a syrup.

Pour the syrup into a food processor. Add the livers, the remaining butter and the cream and blend to a smooth paste. Season to taste, then pour into a container, cover and refrigerate until chilled.

This should keep in the refrigerator for up to a week.

SERVES 8

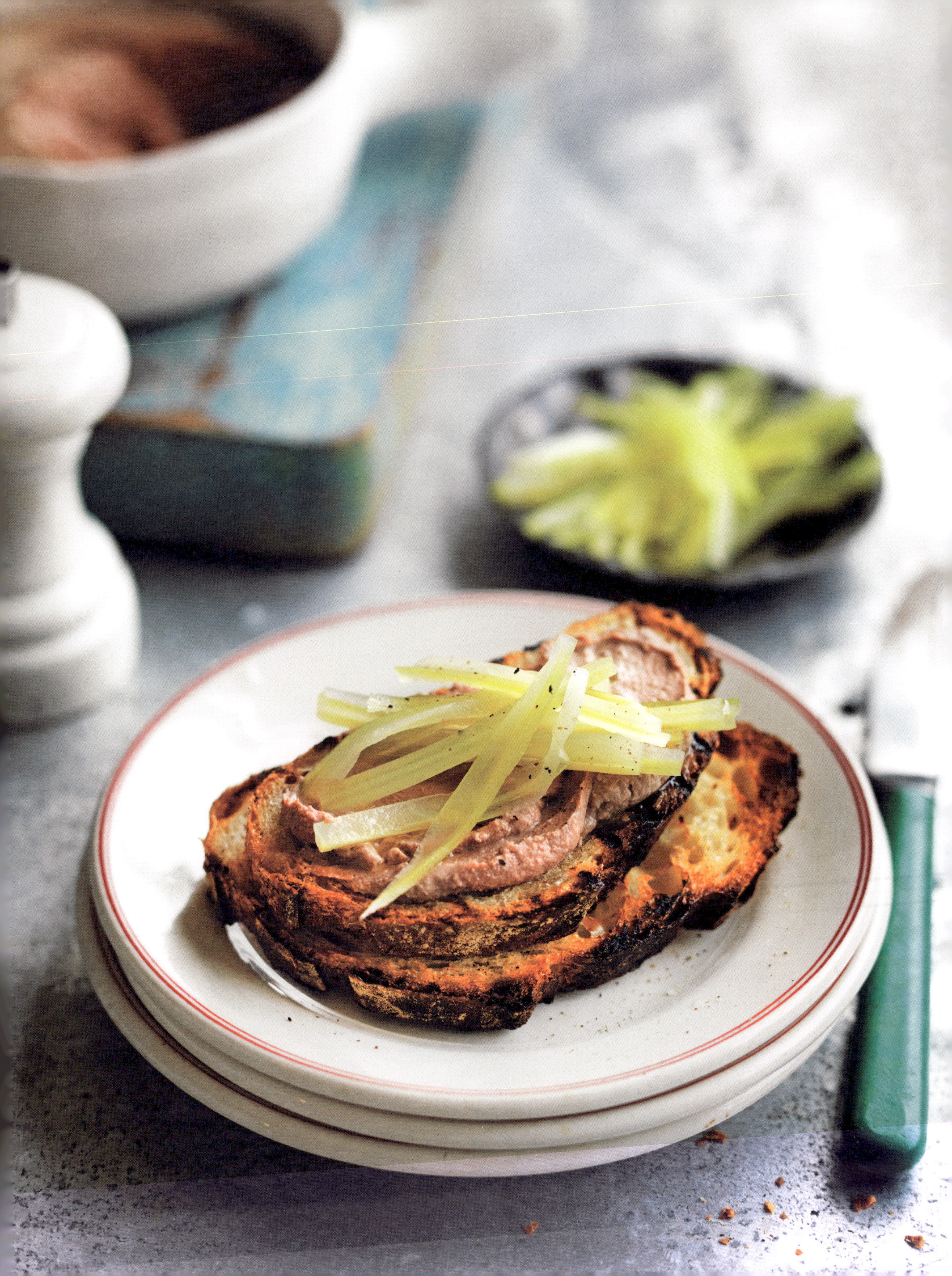

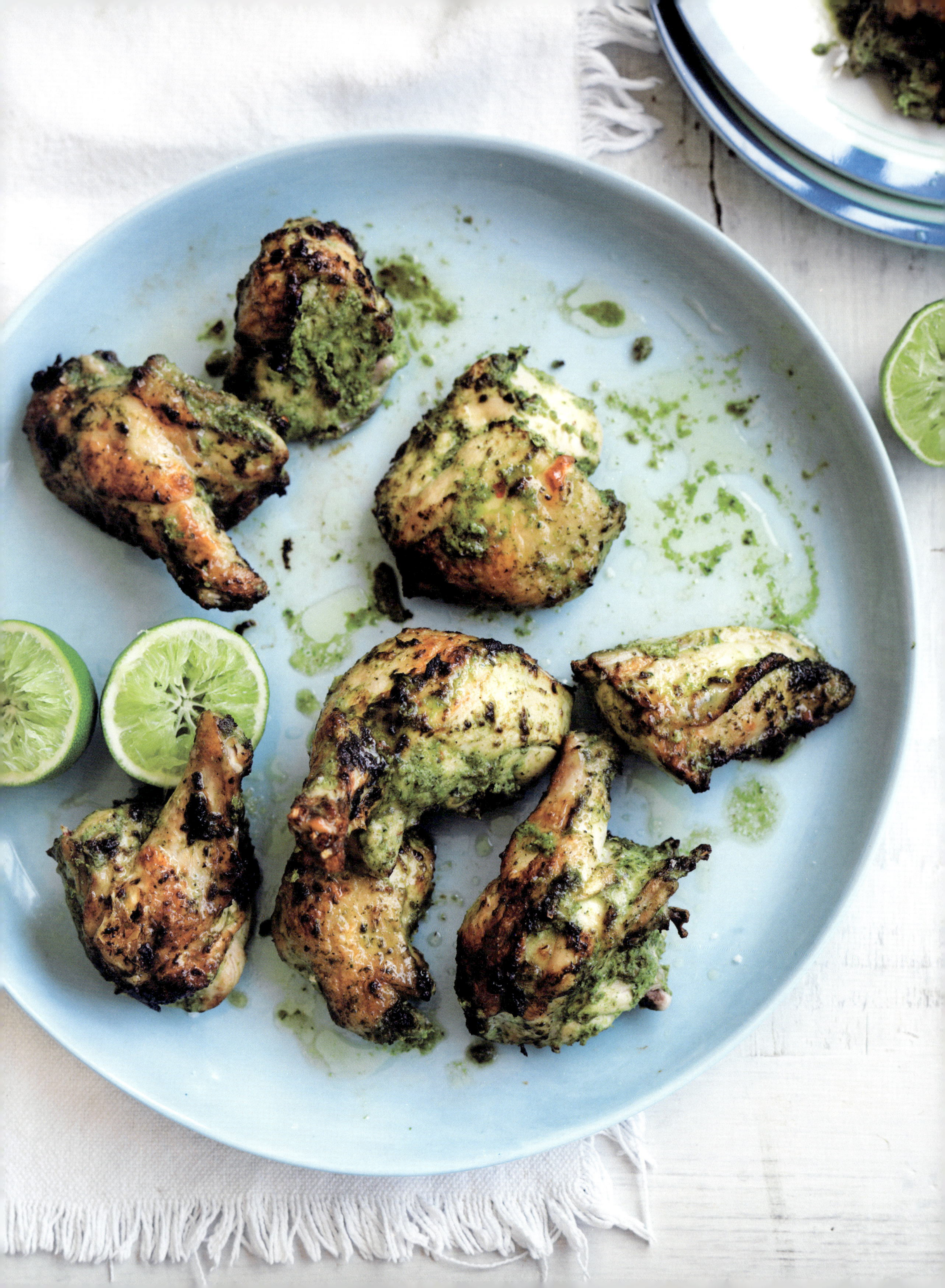

OUR GREEN CHICKEN

Our green chicken came about as another way to use up all the coriander and parsley stalks from our garden. Coriander and parsley stalks have loads of uses, plus they're full of nutrients and flavour. We pickle them, use them in chilli jams, hot sauces, pesto, stocks, salads, anything ... we never throw them away. So this is another ridiculously easy recipe, but one that transforms the plain old chicken to a bit of a crowd pleaser. Start this recipe a day ahead.

For the marinade, blend the ingredients in a food processor.

Rub the marinade onto the chicken pieces. Put the chicken into a dish, cover and refrigerate overnight. If you can't leave it overnight, at least marinate it for 3 hours for the flavours to get going.

Remove the chicken from the refrigerator 30 minutes before cooking.

Preheat the oven to 180°C.

Place the roasting chicken in a pan and roast for 20–25 minutes until cooked.

Remove the chicken from the oven, cover and leave to rest for 10 minutes. Season with a little more salt, pour over the lime juice, scatter with the lime zest and pan juices and serve.

SERVES 4

1 x 1.2 kg chicken, cut into 8 pieces
zest and juice of 1 lime

MARINADE
100 g coriander stalks
50 g parsley stalks
3 garlic cloves, peeled
50 g fresh ginger, peeled and chopped
100 ml grapeseed oil
1 long red chilli, halved
30 ml soy sauce

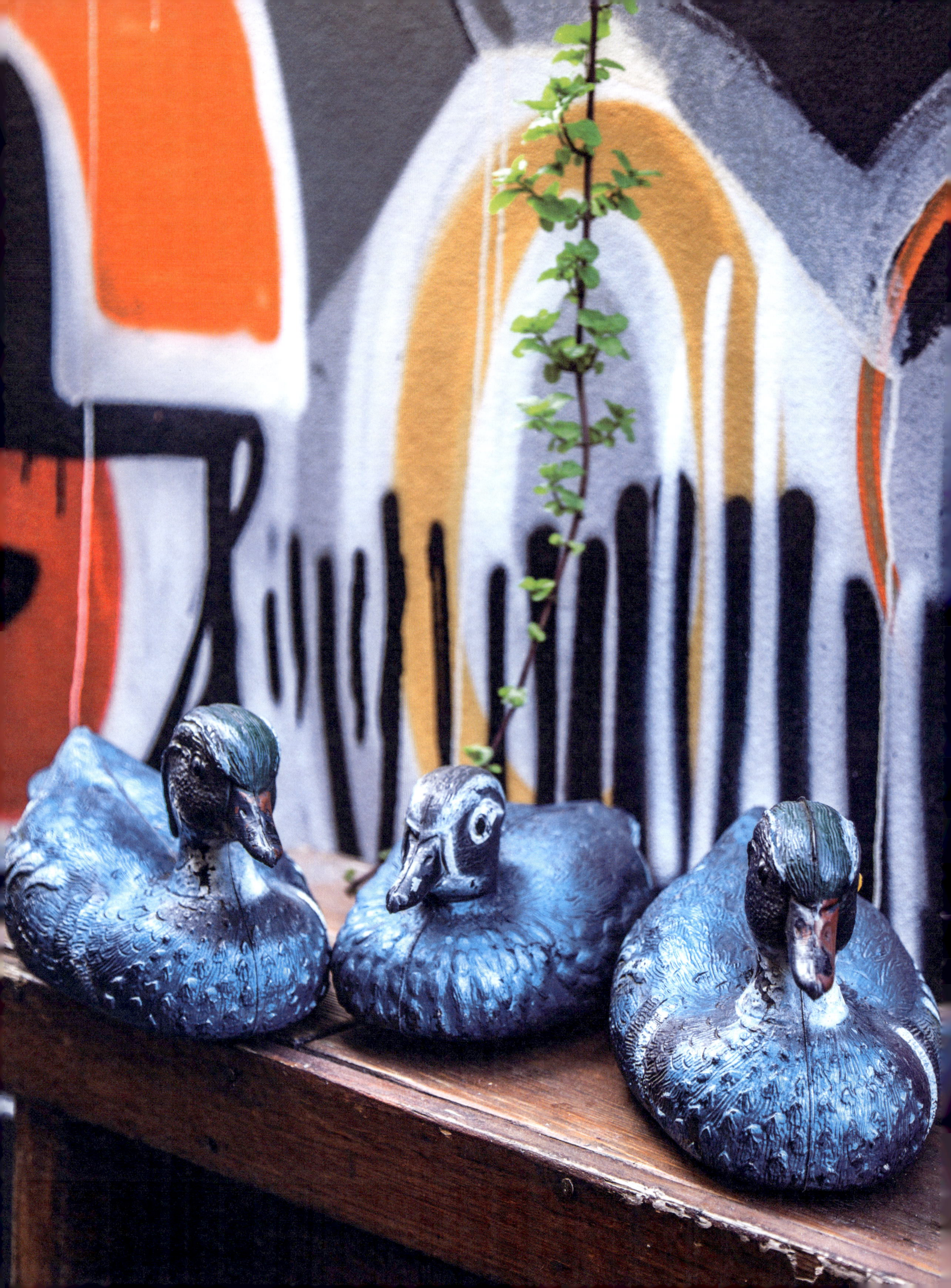

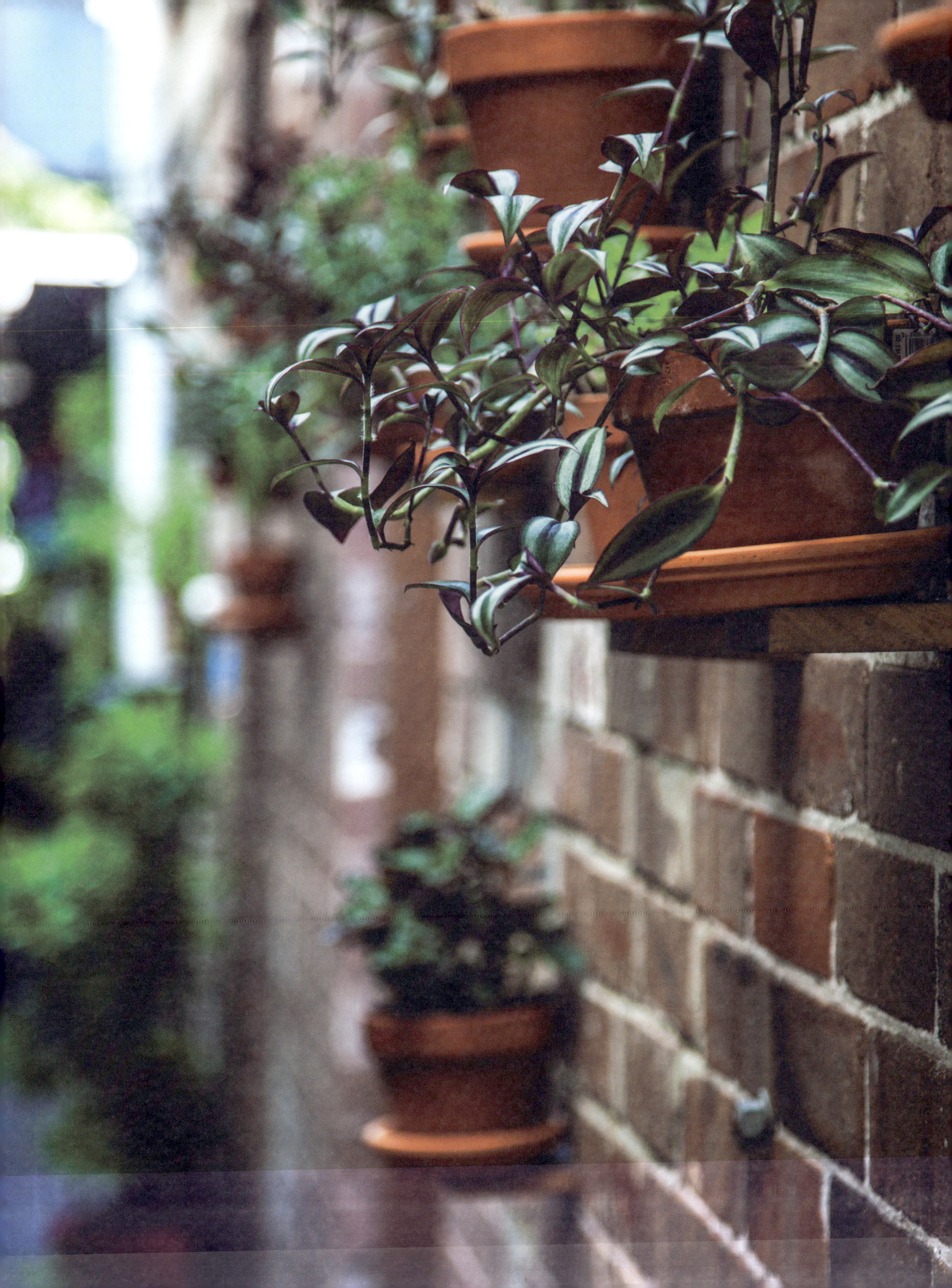

MIDDLE EASTERN LAMB with ZUCCHINI and LABNA

4 zucchini, halved lengthways
2 tablespoons olive oil
salt and pepper
8 x 120 g lamb fillets
1 teaspoon roasted, ground cumin seeds
1 handful of cherry tomatoes, quartered
¼ red onion, finely sliced
100 g labna
1 handful of mint and coriander leaves, torn
a pinch of ground sumac, to serve

Cumin, labna and lots of mint give this char-grilled lamb a Middle Eastern flavour. Labna is easy to make – if you haven't tried it, it's worth a go. Line a sieve with muslin or a thin clean tea towel and place it over a bowl. Pour in a large tub of natural yoghurt and tie the top of the tea towel. Place in the refrigerator to drain naturally overnight (don't press it, just leave it). You can season with salt and pepper or add herbs if you like. Or you can leave it and use it in sweet dishes too.

Put the char-grill on high heat.

Brush the zucchini with the oil and season with salt and pepper. Season the lamb with salt, pepper and cumin. Put the lamb and zucchini on the hot char-grill and cook for around 4–6 minutes, turning every minute.

Remove the lamb from the grill and leave it to rest for 3 minutes. Slice the lamb and zucchini into quarters and toss in a bowl with the cherry tomatoes, onion, a generous scoop of labna and then plenty of the fresh herbs. Sprinkle with sumac to serve.

SERVES 4

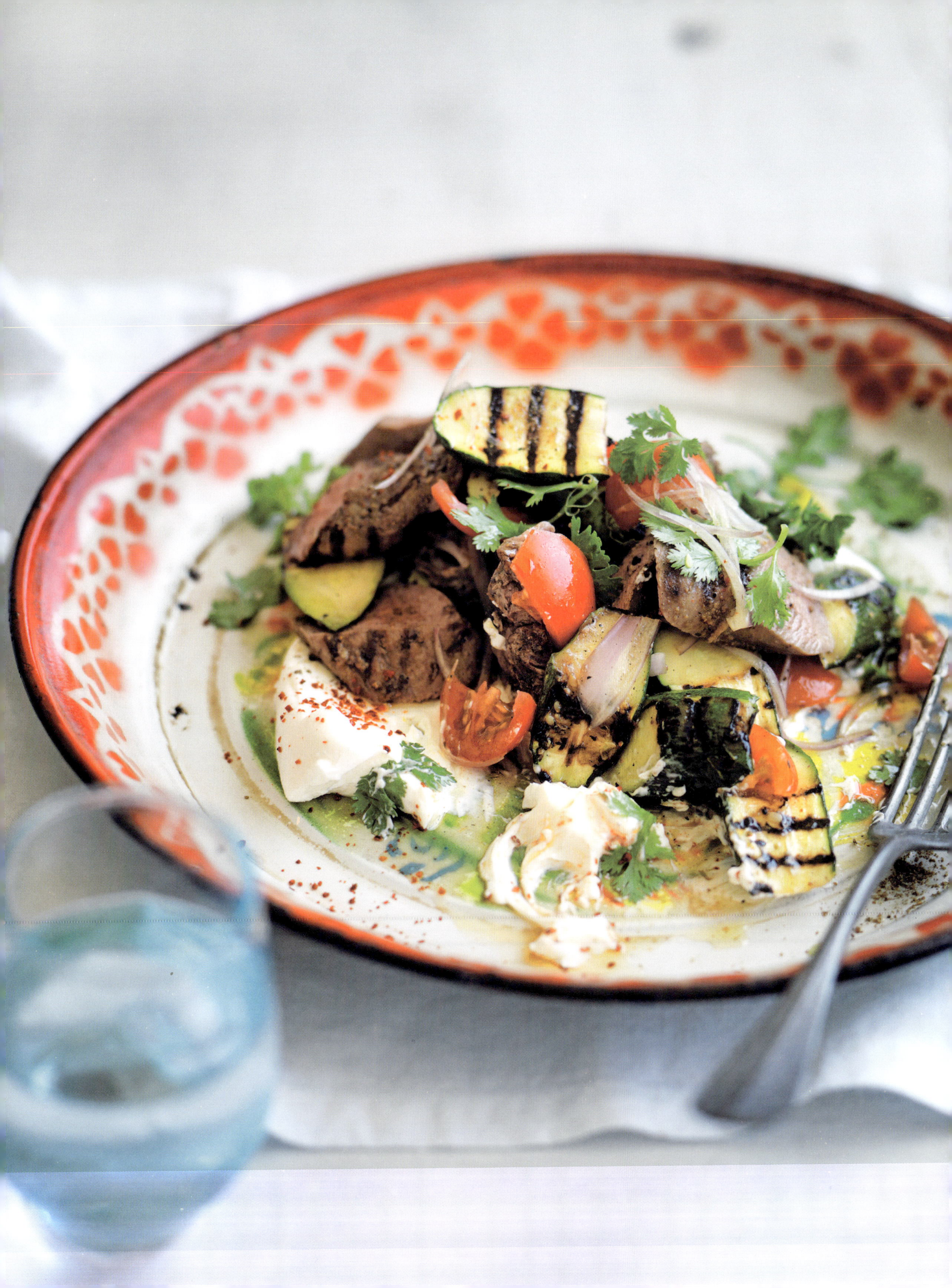

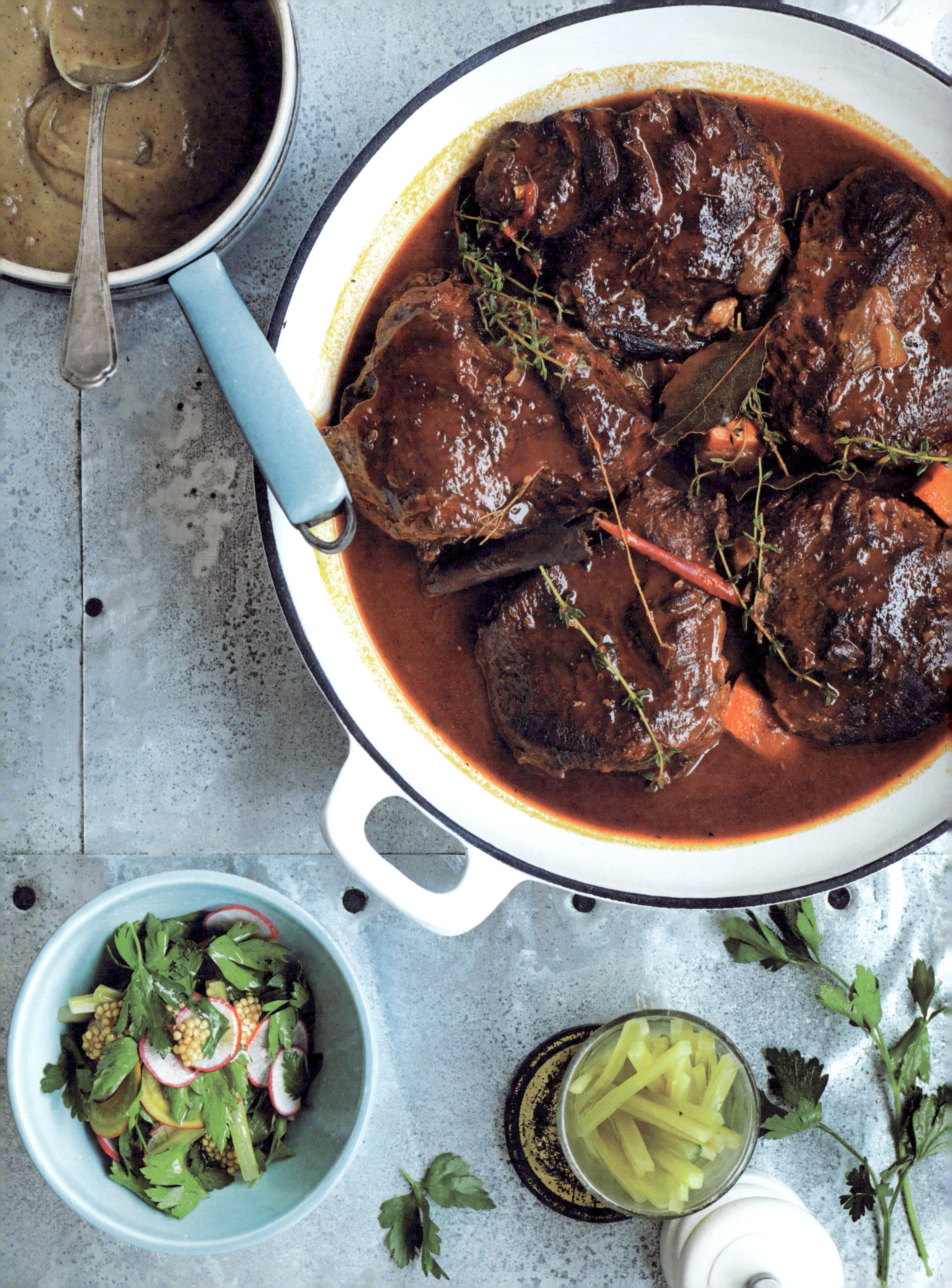

BRAISED BEEF CHEEKS, PICKLED CELERY and BURNT ONION PUREE

You need to start this recipe a day ahead to give the pickled celery time to develop flavour. The beef cheeks take a few hours to cook too, but it's worth the wait. Juniper berries are traditionally used to make gin, but they add terrific flavour for stocks and brines and work especially well with pork.

For the pickled celery, warm the sugar and vinegar in a small saucepan and add the coriander seeds. Leave to cool, then add the celery. It's best to leave this for 24 hours. If you don't have that much time, leave it for at least 4 hours for the flavours to develop.

Put the mustard seeds in a small saucepan and cover with water, bring to the boil and cook for 5 minutes. Strain the seeds and tip into a small bowl.

Shave the radish into the bowl, combine with the pickled celery, a little of the pickling juices, the olive oil, lemon juice and parsley. Season to taste with salt and pepper.

Preheat the oven to 180°C.

Heat the oil in a heavy-based saucepan, add the cheeks, season with salt and pepper, and cook until brown. Place the cheeks in a large casserole dish, cover with the veal stock, Shiraz, vegetables, spices and herbs. Place the casserole in the oven, cover and cook for 3 hours.

Strain half of the cooking liquid from the beef cheeks and reserve for the onion puree, then put the cheeks aside and keep warm.

For the burnt onion puree, cut the onions in half, put on an oven tray, drizzle with the oil, season with salt and pepper. Place in the oven and bake for 40 minutes until they are brown and caramelised. Remove from the oven, place in a saucepan, and add the sliced potato.

Pour the reserved strained cooking liquid and the same amount of water into the pan with the onion and potato. Cook over high heat until all the liquid has evaporated. Blend the onion mixture until pureed, adding butter and lemon juice. Season with salt and pepper to taste.

To serve, pile the onion puree into a large bowl, arrange the beef cheeks on top, pour a little sauce over the puree, then cover the cheeks with the pickled celery salad.

SERVES 6

---

2 tablespoons olive oil
6 beef cheeks
3 litres veal stock
100 ml Shiraz
1 carrot, roughly chopped
1 white onion, roughly chopped
½ long red chilli
2 garlic cloves
3 juniper berries
1 sprig thyme
1 bay leaf
1 cinnamon stick

PICKLED CELERY SALAD
2 teaspoons caster sugar
100 ml vinegar
6 coriander seeds, dry roasted
2 celery stalks, peeled and cut into 8-cm lengths
1 tablespoon mustard seeds
6 baby radishes, trimmed top and bottom
1 tablespoon olive oil
3 sprigs flat-leaf parsley, roughly chopped
juice of 1 lemon
sea salt and cracked pepper

BURNT ONION PUREE
4 red onions, trimmed
1 tablespoon olive oil
2 desiree potatoes, thinly sliced
1 tablespoon butter
juice of 1 lemon

CHAR-GRILLED LAMB KEBABS READY *for* WRAPPING

1 kg lamb rump, cut into 5-cm cubes
1 red onion, peeled and cut into 5-cm chunks
salt and pepper
200 g natural yoghurt
small handful of torn mint and coriander leaves, to serve
1 teaspoon ground sumac and lemon wedges, to serve
flat bread, to serve (page 83)

MARINADE
2 garlic cloves, crushed
1 teaspoon thyme leaves
1 teaspoon rosemary leaves
1 long red chilli, seeded and chopped
1 tablespoon chopped preserved lemon
1 teaspoon cumin seeds, roasted and ground
200 g natural yoghurt

These guys can marinate overnight if you have the time. They will definitely taste better for it and it means it's a great dish to make if you are cooking for large numbers as you can prepare ahead of time. For vegetarians, try replacing the lamb with chunks of pumpkin or eggplant prepared in exactly the same way. Try these with the flat bread on page 83.

To make the marinade, put the marinade ingredients into a large bowl and stir until well combined.

Add the lamb cubes to the marinade and mix until the meat is coated. Cover and marinate overnight in the refrigerator.

If using bamboo skewers, soak them in water for 30 minutes before using.

Assemble the kebabs using the lamb cubes and red onion. Season with salt and pepper.

Fire up the barbecue and cook the kebabs over hot coals for 4–6 minutes, depending how well you like your meat cooked.

Serve with a little yogurt, some fresh torn mint and coriander, sumac, lemon wedges and flat bread.

SERVES 6

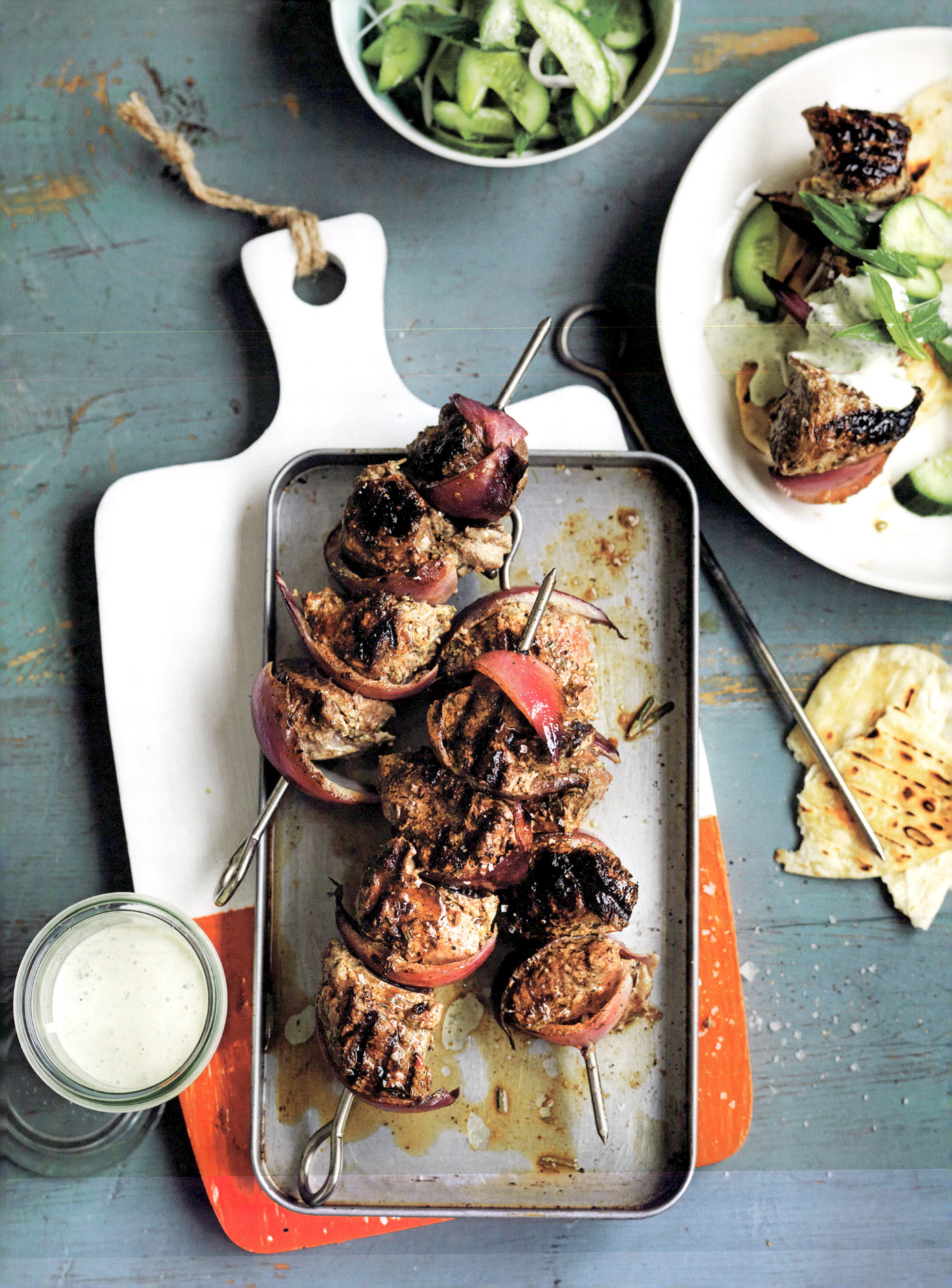

FRAGRANT DUCK SOUP

200 g daikon, peeled and cut into 5-cm rounds
200 g bok choy, chopped
100 g shiitake mushrooms, sliced
1 bunch of coriander, leaves picked
1 small bunch of spring onions, chopped
salt and pepper

steamed rice, to serve

BROTH
2 litres chicken stock
2 duck legs
80 ml soy sauce
30 ml fish sauce
2 garlic cloves, peeled
30 g fresh ginger, grated
2 star anise
1 long red chilli, chopped
1 cinnamon stick
1 teaspoon Sichuan peppercorns
1 tablespoon grated palm sugar

This looks like a long list of ingredients, but don't be put off. It's simple enough to make – it just takes a while to simmer away, extracting all the flavours and goodness. When the fragrance starts to fill your kitchen you'll be wondering why you didn't make it sooner.

Put all the broth ingredients in a large saucepan, bring to the boil and simmer for 2 hours. After 2 hours, add the daikon and cook for another 30 minutes.

Using tongs, take out the duck legs and pick off the meat. Return the duck meat to the broth. Finally, add the bok choy, mushrooms, coriander and spring onion, then adjust seasoning.

Serve in a large bowl with steamed rice on the side.

SERVES 4

COCONUT, LIME *and* LEMONGRASS CHICKEN SOUP

This soup recipe has quite a history to it. Jeff came over to get the recipe for Marks' famous chicken soup. A few hours later, and he'd become a Blue Duck. It's a great soup for business mergers.

Put a heavy-based frying pan over high heat and add 2 tablespoons of oil. Heavily season the chicken with salt and pepper and then fry in the pan for about 6 minutes on either side until it is crispy and dark in colour.

Put the lemongrass, the chopped ginger, 1 chopped chilli, and 3 garlic cloves, into a large saucepan with the water. Add the stripped corn cobs and the chicken and bring to the boil. Simmer over medium heat for at least 30 minutes. Keep adding water if you need to, so that there's always 2 litres of stock.

When the chicken starts to break down, remove it from the liquid. Pick all the meat off the carcass and set aside. Then remove the corn cobs, strain the broth through a sieve so that there are no chunks of ginger or stray bones, and set aside.

Give the pan a quick rinse and dry, and pour in the remaining oil, then add the remaining 3 chopped garlic cloves, the onion, grated ginger, the other 2 chopped chillies and the coriander stalks. Cook until the onion is soft, and then add the corn kernels and fry for another 3 minutes. Add the sweet soy sauce and stir. It will start to caramelise and go sticky.

Add the strained chicken broth that you made, as well as the chicken meat and coconut milk, then bring to the boil and turn off the heat.

To serve, ladle the soup into bowls, top with the bean shoots and sprouts, a good sprinkle of coriander leaves and lime zest and a generous amount of lime juice.

SERVES 4

5 tablespoons vegetable oil
1 large chicken, approx. 1.6 kg
salt and pepper
2 stalks of lemongrass, roughly chopped
1 big knob of ginger, the size of 2 golf balls, peeled, with half chopped and half grated
3 mild, long red chillies, seeded and finely chopped
6 garlic cloves, chopped
2 litres cold water
2 corn cobs, kernels cut off, but keep the cobs
1 red onion, thinly sliced
1 bunch of coriander, leaves roughly chopped, keep the stalks and finely chop them
3 tablespoons sweet soy sauce (kecap manis)
1 x 330 ml can coconut milk
250 g bean shoots
100 g snow pea sprouts
zest of 1 lime
juice of 3 limes

the COMMUNITY

The Ducks have been made to feel very welcome in the Bronte community. Two of us, Sam and Chris, grew up in Bronte and both still live here. They've been earning their stripes since they were in primary school – they spent their juvenile years at Bronte beach, working their way up the ranks of the local hierarchy.

The boys recall being given money and sent to the top of Macpherson Street to get the older guys pies for lunch. The system turned particularly feudal when the older boy didn't have cash, so the grommets would have to catch a bus or walk the 2 kilometres up the hill from Bronte beach to the ATM in Charing Cross to withdraw money before making their way to Bronte bakery to collect the pies. As adults, and as new business owners, Sam and Chris found themselves back at the pie shop, but with more to prove. They weren't just answering to the older boys at the surf club, but to the whole community of Bronte.

When we started doing the fit-out of the shop, everyone could see how hard we were working, and we felt the local support from the moment the old chicken shop sign was hauled down. The first morning we opened Iggy and Ludmilla of Iggy's Bread came over with a big wheel of sourdough and a bottle of grappa. We sat down, had a shot and they gave us a kiss and a hug, congratulated us and told us to get on with it.

In the beginning, we were all doing 100-hour weeks and Ian from the pharmacy would send over multivitamins. If anyone cut a finger or got a burn, they'd head across the road and Ian would administer ointment and a Band-Aid.

It's the irrepressible sense of community from the locals of Bronte and Macpherson Street that has made the Ducks such a happy workplace. We want people to drag themselves up from the beach, sand still blowing off their skin and use the Ducks as their local hangout. There's been the occasion where a local will come in for breakfast and leave at 4 pm when we close, after lunch and afternoon tea. That's a good day.

This year marked the second year of the Macpherson Street Christmas party. We wanted to block off the road and have a big trestle table running down the middle of the street. The council didn't take to the idea, however, so we settled for BYO plate and seat. We had music and food. It was a great way to connect with the other business owners. We want to invest in the future of the community. Along with Ludmilla, for example, we applied for a local council grant and were given some money to plant fruit trees and freestanding concrete planter boxes along Macpherson Street. The planters hold strawberries and herbs now. From behind the counter at the Ducks, we hope we'll soon see locals picking their own fresh fruit.

The Ducks has never claimed to be an ecologically sustainable restaurant, but we are making an effort, we're learning all the time and we're sharing what we learn with local communities. We're using the veggie patch as an

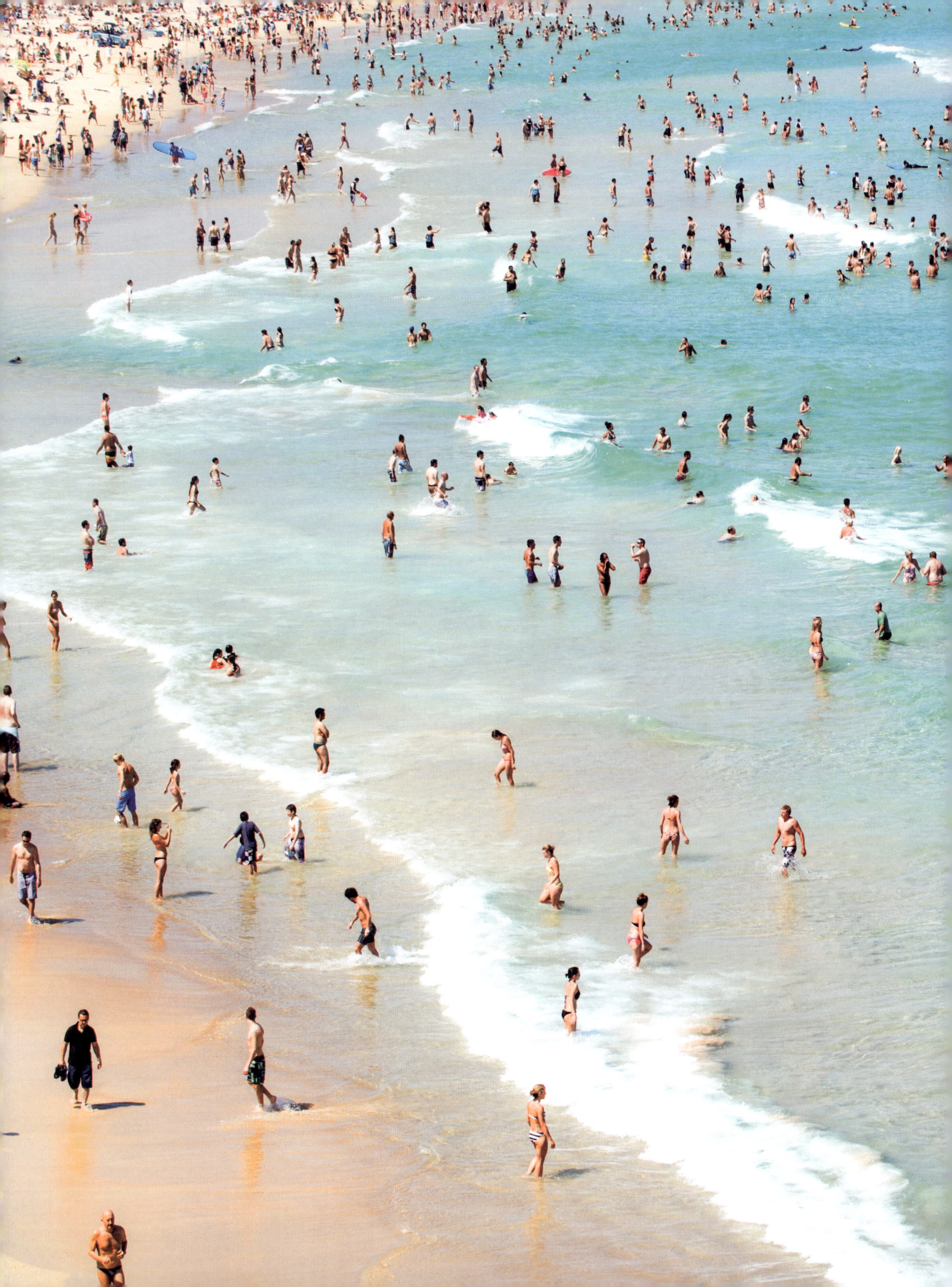

educational centre, a forum to teach people about backyard gardening. Permaculture Sydney South has had talks in the garden and the local preschool sends their kids over to learn about seedlings and to pick lettuce for their sandwiches. People are starting to embrace the idea of local gardens. We found out about the community gardens at 241 Bondi Road, Bondi, and were just stoked on the idea. It's a local initiative set up and maintained by residents who have started a sidewalk garden movement in Bondi. They run workshops and demonstrations – it's brilliant. A similar thing was done in Bronte, just down from the Ducks, a community sidewalk garden filled with salad leaves and tomatoes that locals can pick and use. It was disassembled this year however, because of complaints to local council that it was an eyesore. The community garden movement will take time to catch on, as people realise what it means, and what it can offer. Meanwhile, our little garden at the Ducks is flourishing.

The Grow it Local campaign has been another highlight where we have been able to engage with the community. Grow it Local is an initiative started in 2012, designed to encourage Sydney residents to grow their own vegetables and herbs, and register their garden patch on the organisation's interactive website. The organisers approached us with an idea: local residents would register and meet on a Saturday two months later, bringing in food from their garden to donate for a dinner, which they would then attend. We wanted to be involved, so we offered up the Ducks as the venue. We estimated that there would be about seventy people, which would be relatively easy to take care of. In the end, about 300 people turned up on the night. One guy had been fishing the day before in Sydney Harbour and brought in six bonitos he had caught and we made sashimi. It was busy, noisy and wonderful. The idea of sharing food is important to us. Food bridges the gap between people in a community. It's a way of spending time, of talking and sharing stories. The point of the Ducks is to treat the environment and people well. We want our staff to eat well and work hours that are conducive to a work/life balance, and we treat our food mindfully. This extends to our broader philosophy of creating a community. We're aware of the importance of being part of something bigger than just the shop and the local community has been a great place to start.

Three quick BREADS

ROTI

200 g bread flour
200 g wholemeal flour
250 ml water
1 teaspoon salt
1 tablespoon butter

Roti is a traditional flat bread, no yeast, no fuss, easy to make and even easier to eat. It's just the thing to mop up curries, chutneys, yoghurts – all the good stuff.

Put the flours, water and salt in a bowl and mix until a firm, sticky dough forms.

Put the dough on a lightly floured bench and knead it for a few minutes until it becomes smooth and springs back when touched. Put the dough on an oiled tray, cover with cling wrap and put it in the refrigerator for 1 hour.

Cut the dough into balls. Using a rolling pin, roll the dough on the floured bench into circles about 2 mm thick and 12 cm across.

Heat a heavy-based, non-stick frying pan over medium heat. Add some of the butter and start frying the roti in batches. When they start to bubble a little on top, turn them over. They need about 1–2 minutes on each side to be lightly browned. Repeat with the remaining butter and roti. Serve warm.

MAKES 16

SEEDY SODA BREAD

There's no yeast in this old-fashioned soda bread – a couple of spoons of bicarbonate of soda is all it takes to make it rise – so it's quick and easy to make. Eat it the same day, but if you do have any left over, it works well toasted.

Preheat the oven to 180°C. Line a baking tray with baking paper.

Sift the bicarbonate of soda and plain flour together into a bowl. Add the wholemeal flour, salt and buttermilk. Stir together until the mixture forms a soft dough.

Place the dough on a lightly floured bench and knead for 2 minutes until it feels smooth. Shape it into 4 balls and place them on the baking tray. Brush the tops with the buttermilk and sprinkle on the seeds.

Bake for 30 minutes until golden brown and the base sounds hollow when you tap it. Serve it with butter and home-made jam.

MAKES 1 LOAF OR 4 ROLLS

2 teaspoons of bicarbonate of soda
260 g plain flour
260 g wholemeal flour
2 teaspoons salt
440 ml buttermilk (leave a little for brushing)
2 teaspoons sesame seeds
1 tablespoon pumpkin seeds
1 tablespoon linseeds

FLAT BREAD

Serve with our lamb kebabs on page 74.

Mix the flour, salt and baking powder together in a bowl. Add 120 ml of the water and mix until it forms a dough – if it seems a little dry add more water.

Put the dough on a lightly floured bench and knead for 5 minutes until it is soft and pliable. Leave to rest for 10 minutes.

Cut the dough into golf ball-size pieces, and roll out to 3 mm thick. Brush a hot char-grill with a little oil and start cooking the flat bread (you'll need to do them in batches). As soon as they begin to puff up, flip them over. They take about 1–2 minutes to cook. Eat them warm.

MAKES 6-8 FLAT BREADS

500 g bread flour
1 teaspoon sea salt
1 tablespoon baking powder
about 140 ml warm water
2 tablespoons olive oil

THE LAND

Savoury Grains

MUSHROOMS and PEARL BARLEY with MACADAMIA BREAD SAUCE

200 g pearl barley
50 ml olive oil
1 pinch of chopped flat-leaf parsley
salt and pepper
200 g oyster mushrooms, sliced
200 g enoki mushrooms
200 g Swiss brown mushrooms, sliced
1 French shallot, chopped
1 tablespoon grapeseed oil
baby herbs, to serve
zest of 1 lemon, to serve

MACADAMIA BREAD SAUCE
300 g sourdough bread, roughly chopped
200 ml water
40 ml olive oil
1 tablespoon white wine vinegar
juice of 1 lemon
1 garlic clove, crushed
about 10 macadamia nuts

We really like the texture of barley – it's robust, nutty in flavour and slightly chewy. It's also healthy and high in B vitamins. If you wanted to, you could try this using buckwheat or quinoa. The bread sauce adds some extra nuttiness with macadamias.

To make the bread sauce, put the bread, water, olive oil, vinegar, lemon juice and zest, garlic and nuts in a food processor and blend until smooth. Season to taste and set aside.

Bring a saucepan of lightly salted water to the boil, add the barley, then simmer, uncovered, for 30 minutes. Drain, tip the barley back into the pan and add the olive oil and parsley and season with salt and pepper.

While the barley is cooking, sauté the mushrooms and shallot in the grapeseed oil for about 2 minutes until golden. Check the seasoning.

Spoon the barley into warm bowls, top with the mushrooms, add a small scoop of the bread sauce and sprinkle with the lemon zest and lots of baby herbs.

SERVES 6

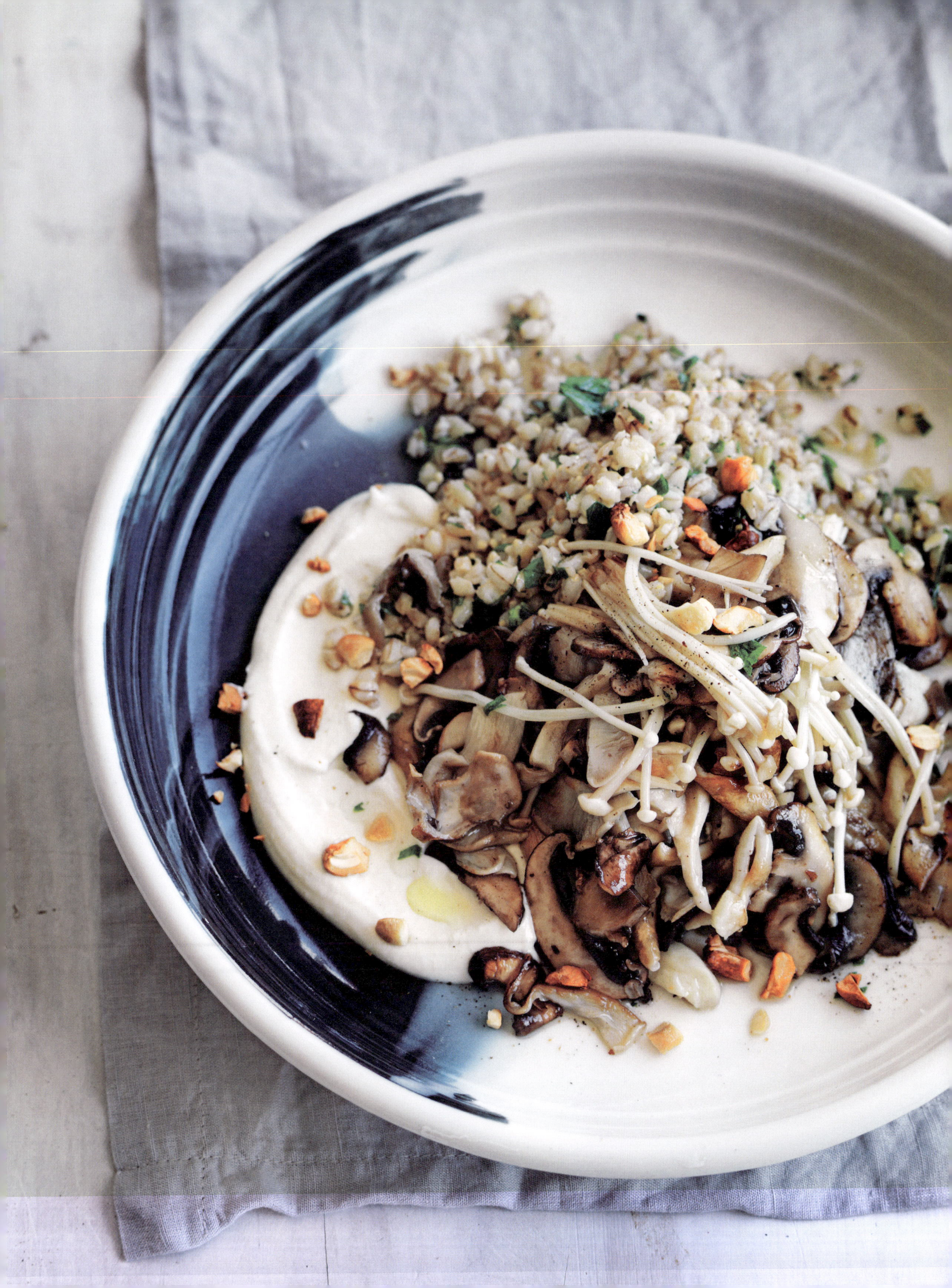

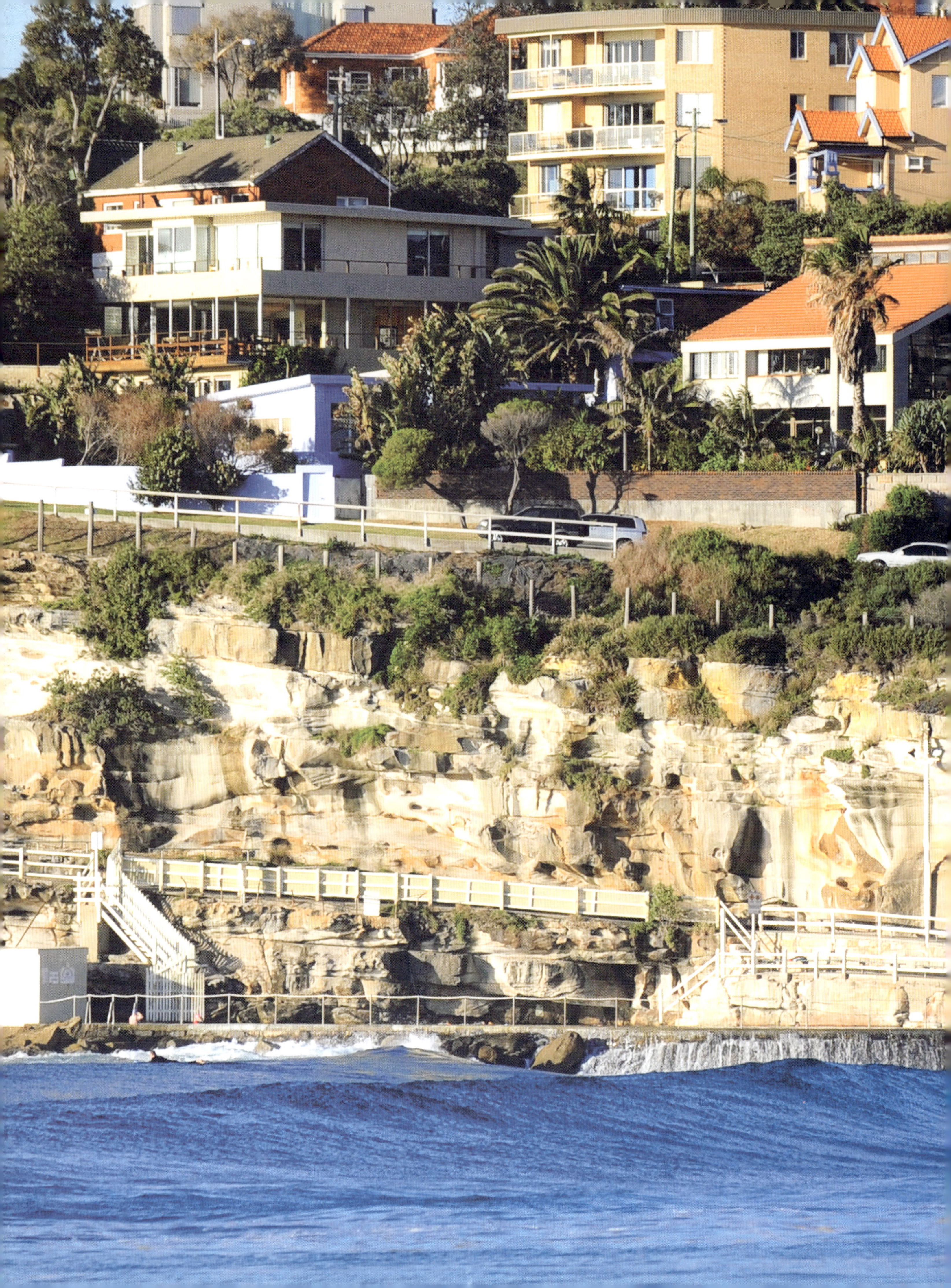

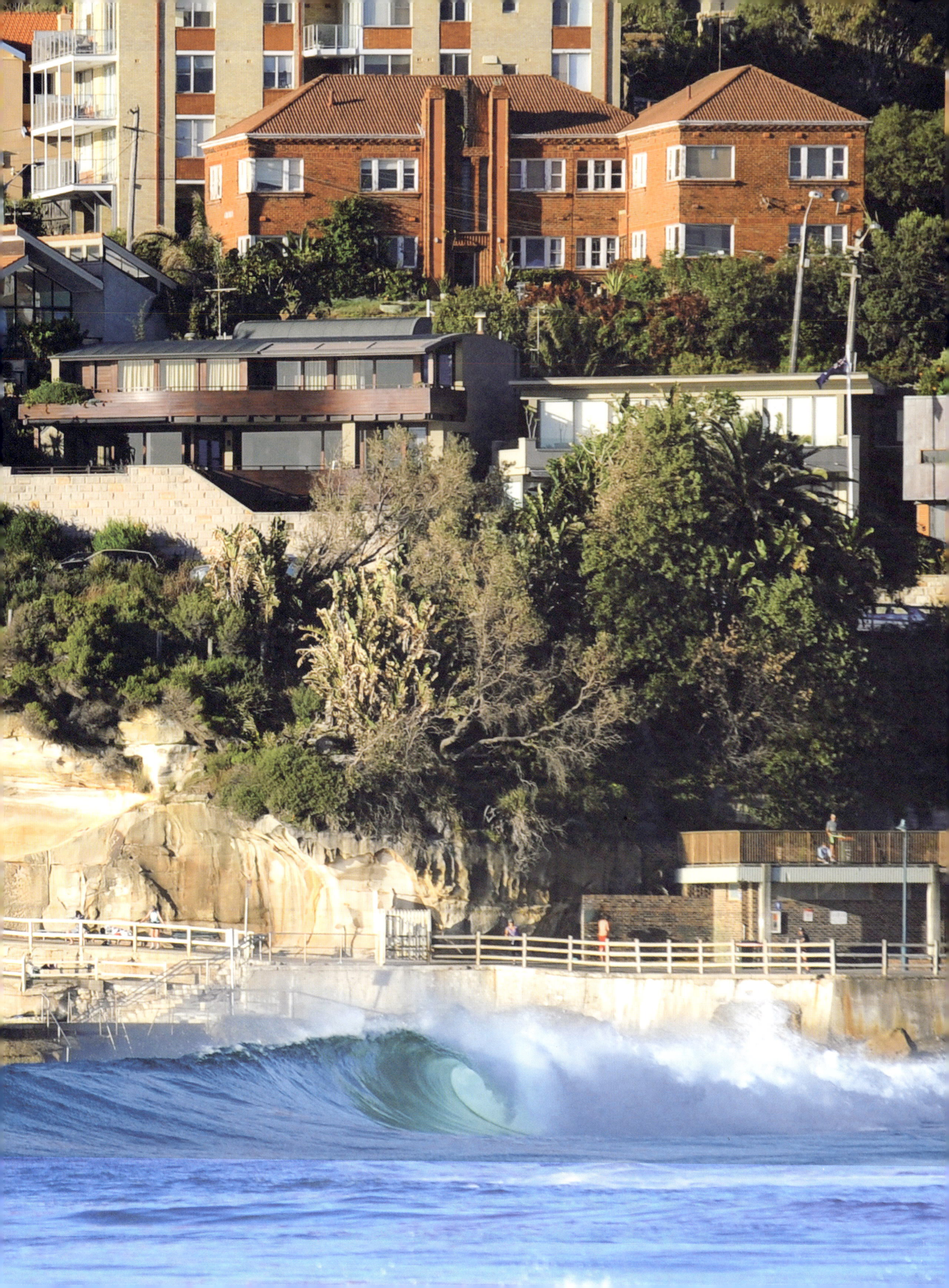

QUINOA, SMOKED EGGPLANT *and* YOGHURT SALAD

400 ml chicken or vegetable stock
100 g quinoa, rinsed
2 medium-sized eggplants
100 g natural yoghurt
1 red onion, sliced
½ a long red chilli, deseeded and chopped
1 handful mint leaves, torn
1 handful coriander leaves, torn
2 tablespoons of pomegranate seeds
salt and pepper

Burning the skin of the eggplant gives a lovely smoky flavour. Don't be afraid to really char the eggplant over an open flame or – even better – over hot coals.

Bring the stock to boiling, add the quinoa, cover and simmer over low heat for 15 minutes until cooked. The liquid will be absorbed and the quinoa should be light but still a have little pop to it when you bite into it. Stir it gently with a fork to separate the grains.

While the quinoa is cooking, put the char-grill on high.

Put the whole eggplants on the grill and cook for 10 minutes, turning occasionally, burning the skin to get a good smoky flavour.

When the eggplant feel soft and starts to collapse take them off the heat and leave them to cool. Then use a knife to peel away the skin, or scoop out the flesh and roughly chop.

Mix the eggplant in a bowl with the cooked quinoa, yoghurt, onion, chilli, fresh mint, coriander leaves and scatter with pomegranate seeds. Check the seasoning and serve.

SERVES 2

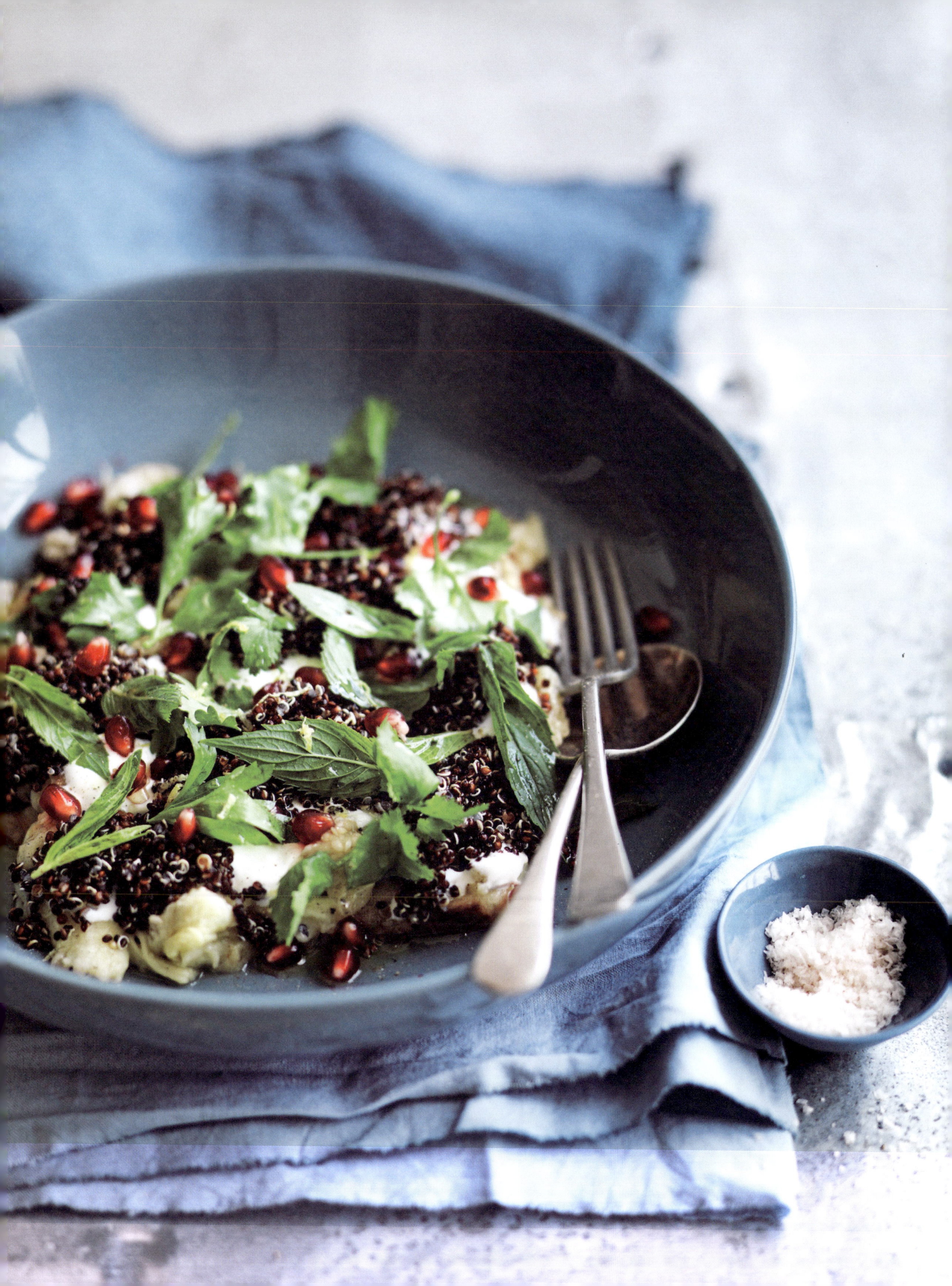

QUINOA and SPELT SALAD with ROASTED ALMONDS

2–3 tablespoons vegetable oil
2 red onions, finely diced
4 garlic cloves, chopped
2 long red chillies, finely diced
1 cup quinoa, rinsed
½ cup spelt
4 cups vegetable stock
1 punnet cherry tomatoes, halved
250 g baby spinach
1 bunch of flat-leaf parsley, roughly chopped
50 g currants
100 g almonds, toasted and roughly chopped
balsamic vinegar and good olive oil
salt and pepper

Quinoa is a grain-like seed originally from South America. Civilisations have been living off this high protein, slow-release carbohydrate for centuries. It makes a great foundation for a meal – nutty, textural, healthy and easy to prepare. Spelt is a cereal grain – you should be able to get it at health food stores and some supermarkets.

Place a large saucepan on high heat, add a splash of vegetable oil, the onion, garlic and chilli and cook for 5 minutes or so, stirring occasionally, until the onion is soft. Add the quinoa and spelt and cook for a further 5 minutes, constantly stirring (toasting the grains first gives them a more nutty flavour).

When the grains start to pop a little, add a good splash of vegetable stock and continue stirring. Lower the heat, continue adding the stock a little at a time and stirring, as if making risotto. When the grains are soft and fluffy and all the liquid is absorbed – it will take about 18–20 minutes – set aside to cool to room temperature.

When the grains are cool, add the remaining ingredients, toss well, season with salt and pepper and serve.

SERVES 4

THE BEST BANANA BREAD WE'VE EVER HAD – *Thanks Pauly!*

Pauly used to be our bread supplier, he had a business called Baker Friday. I tasted his banana bread and then hassled him for 6 months for the recipe. When he finally shared it, it was clear we were good friends. Pauly's banana bread is rich in flavour with the bananas and figs making it deliciously dense. Toasted or untoasted, with butter or without, it's epic.

Preheat the oven to 160°C.

Combine the flour, cornflour, cinnamon, baking power, bicarbonate of soda and salt into a large mixing bowl and set aside.

Whip eggs and sugar until white and fluffy.

Use a blender to puree the bananas and figs, leaving a few chunks if you prefer a little more texture in the bread, then add the oil, egg mix and butter.

Combine the wet and dry mixes together, taking care not to overwork it but making sure it's evenly incorporated.

Wipe the inside of a baking tin with a little oil, then sprinkle with the sesame seeds. Pour your bread mixture into the tin, being careful not to knock the seeds off the sides.

Chuck a whole peeled banana on top of the bread and sprinkle with the walnuts.

Place the bread in the oven and bake for 45 minutes until the bread is golden brown, or until a knife inserted in the centre comes out clean.

SERVES 8

200 g flour
10 g cornflour
1 teaspoon cinnamon
1 teaspoon baking powder
½ teaspoon bicarbonate of soda
pinch of salt
100 g eggs
170 g sugar
300 g bananas plus 1 extra for garnish
130 g fresh figs
45 g grape seed oil
40 g butter, melted
100 g black and white sesame seeds
100 g walnuts

Yum!

TOASTED MUESLI, THE WAY WE LIKE IT

You can add any dried fruit and nuts that you like, but this combination – with roasted coconut, almonds and apricots – is one of our favourites. Try it with some poached fruit or fresh berries and a big dollop of yoghurt.

Preheat the oven to 190°C. Line 2 baking trays with baking paper.

Melt the butter and honey together in a small saucepan. Put the rolled oats in a large mixing bowl, pour in the melted butter and honey and stir well to combine. The oats will start to soak up the liquid and become sticky.

Spread the oats on the baking trays, then place in the oven for 5 minutes. Remove from the oven, stir, then return the trays to the oven for a few more minutes until the oats are golden and toasted. Take the tray out of the oven and set aside to cool.

Put the remaining ingredients in a large bowl, mix well and then fold in the toasted oats.

When the muesli is at room temperature pour into glass jars. Store in a cool, dark place, such as a cupboard or pantry.

Serve with poached fruits or berries and yoghurt.

MAKES 2.7KG

150 g butter
150 g honey
1.5 kg rolled oats
150 g dried apricots, chopped
200 g toasted, slivered almonds
150 g currants
150 g pumpkin seeds
150 g desiccated coconut, toasted
100 g goji berries

BIRCHER MUESLI with HONEY for a CROWD

500 g rolled oats
500 ml orange or apple juice
1 apple, grated
250 g natural yoghurt
1 tablespoon honey

Soaking the oats overnight gives them a creamy flavour. This is satisfying just as it is, but in summer stone fruits such as peaches and nectarines, or whatever berries are in season, make it a bit more special. It's also good with some toasted nuts sprinkled on top.

Soak the oats in the juice overnight in a sealed container in the fridge. In the morning, stir the grated apple, yoghurt and honey through the oats … easy!

SERVES 6

SPICED BLACK QUINOA PORRIDGE

Black rice and black quinoa make a nutty porridge, especially with spices, toasted nuts and seeds. We started making this as a breakfast for our staff at the snowfields – when you're snowboarding all morning, a decent breakfast is vital. It goes really well with char-grilled or poached winter fruits.

Dry roast the quinoa over medium–high heat in a large saucepan for 1 minute, then add the black rice and roast for 30 seconds. Next, add 60 g of the sugar, the orange juice and zest, vanilla pod, star anise, cloves, cinnamon and salt and stir to mix. When the orange juice evaporates, pour in the milk and cream. Cook on low heat for 30 minutes, stirring occasionally.

Meanwhile, in a separate pan, dry roast the chia, linseed and pumpkin seeds over medium heat until just roasted. Keep your eye on them as the seeds can burn quickly.

When the rice mixture is cooked, serve in a warm bowl with the roasted seeds and the remaining brown sugar on top.

SERVES 6

50 g black quinoa, rinsed
100 g black rice
80 g soft brown sugar
zest and juice of 1 orange
1 vanilla pod, split lengthways
1 star anise
2 whole cloves
1 cinnamon stick
pinch of salt
3 litres milk
300 ml cream
1 tablespoon chia seeds
1 tablespoon linseeds
1 tablespoon pumpkin seeds

MUFFINS

Muffins are easy to make – just remember not to stir too much and overwork the batter or you will end up with a dense texture instead of light, fluffy muffins. Here's our basic recipe, plus a few of our indulgent favourites.

The Basic Recipe

350 g plain flour
3 teaspoons baking powder
75 g brown sugar
½ teaspoon bicarbonate of soda
135 ml grapeseed oil
3 eggs, lightly beaten
100 g natural yoghurt

Preheat the oven to 165°C, fan-forced. Lightly grease a ½-cup muffin pan and line with baking paper.

Place the dry ingredients in one bowl, the wet ingredients in the other. If you're adding dry flavourings, for example, chocolate bits, add them to the dry mix. If you're adding wet ingredients, such as fresh cherries, add them to the wet mix.

Stir the wet ingredients into the dry ingredients until just combined. Overworking the batter will result in a dense muffin, not a fluffy one.

Spoon the mixture into the prepared muffin pan and bake for 40 minutes. Check with a skewer – insert in the centre of a muffin – if it comes out clean, the muffins are ready.

MAKES 12 LARGE MUFFINS

Rocky Road

150 g marshmallows, torn
100 g pitted fresh cherries
100 g almonds, slivered and toasted
100 g milk chocolate, roughly chopped

Mix all the ingredients into the 'wet' muffin ingredients, keeping aside a little of each to put on top of the muffins when they are baked.

When the muffins have cooled, melt the reserved chocolate, put some on top of each muffin and add some marshmallow and almonds – as the choc cools it will stick there very firmly.

Pear and Ricotta

2 pears, diced
150 g fresh ricotta

Mix the pear and ricotta into the 'wet' muffin ingredients, keeping aside some pear to pop on top before you bake the muffins.

Salted Caramel-Banana

200 g sugar
1 tablespoon sea salt
2 bananas, sliced

Pour the sugar into a very clean, medium-sized frying pan over medium heat, and leave the sugar to melt (5–8 minutes) until a caramel forms. Don't stir it – be patient – just let it melt. Add the salt and most of the banana (save a few banana slices to go on top of the muffins before baking), and stir until the banana is just coated.

Add the caramel/banana mix to your 'wet' muffin ingredients. Save a teaspoon of caramel for each muffin, to be drizzled on top after the muffins are baked and cooled.

Chocolate and Macadamia

150 g milk chocolate, roughly chopped
150 g roasted macadamia nuts, halved

Add the chocolate and macadamias to the 'dry' muffin ingredients, keeping aside a little of each to decorate the baked muffins.

When the muffins are cool, drizzle some melted chocolate on top and sprinkle with the macadamias.

WHITE CHOCOLATE *and* VANILLA FRIANDS

350 g butter, melted
1 tablespoon almond essence
360 g egg whites, lightly stirred
250 g almond meal
420 g icing sugar, sifted
125 g rice flour
1 vanilla pod, split lengthways and seeds scraped
75 g white chocolate, finely chopped

These little cakes are moist, flecked with vanilla seeds and white chocolate, and they're gluten-free. You can pop a fresh strawberry or a couple of blueberries on top before baking. The recipe makes about 30, but keep the mixture covered in the fridge and you can bake some fresh daily for a week or so.

Preheat the oven to 170°C. Lightly grease 2 friand pans (or 2 small muffin pans).

Put the butter, almond essence and egg whites in a medium-sized mixing bowl and stir until just mixed. Add the almond meal, icing sugar, rice flour, vanilla seeds and white chocolate. Mix together until thick and smooth in consistency.

Spoon the batter into the friand pans and bake for 20 minutes until the tops are golden.

Remove the pans from oven. Leave to cool for a minute, then tip the friands onto a wire rack to cool.

MAKES ABOUT 30 FRIANDS

DARK CHOCOLATE, DATE and WALNUT BREAD

This bread looks great with chunks of chocolate and walnuts through it. We like it toasted with honey, home-made jam or maybe some fresh ricotta. Use good-quality chocolate – around 60 per cent cocoa fat is ideal – and good-quality walnuts.

Dissolve the yeast in 50 ml of the tepid water. In a bowl, mix the salt, the remaining water and the flours together, stir in the yeast mixture and bring together to form a dough.

Put the dough on a lightly floured bench or board and knead for several minutes until it becomes smooth and springs back when you push it lightly.

Mix in the chocolate, dates and walnuts. Place the dough in a bowl, cover with a clean cloth and leave in a warm place until it has doubled in size. It will probably take around 30 minutes.

Knock the air out of the dough and cut it into 4 pieces. Roll into balls. Put the bread onto a baking tray lined with baking paper and leave again until almost doubled in size.

Preheat the oven to 200°C.

When the oven is hot enough, put the bread in and bake for about 20 minutes. When the bread is cooked it should be golden brown and sound almost hollow when tapped on the base.

You don't have to make rolls — you could make any shape loaf you fancy – just remember the larger the loaf, the longer it will take to cook.

MAKES 4 BIG ROLLS

30 g fresh yeast (or 50 g dried yeast)
625 ml tepid water
1 tablespoon salt
500 g bread flour
500 g wholemeal flour
100 g dark chocolate, chopped
50 g dates, chopped
50 g walnuts, chopped

LIME, POLENTA and RICOTTA CAKE

110 g fine (instant) polenta
200 g almond meal
2 teaspoons baking powder
1 teaspoon sea salt
200 g unsalted butter, at room temperature
180 g caster sugar
3 eggs
zest and juice of 3 limes
250 g fresh ricotta

The ricotta in this cake means it's quite firm and moist. It's the type of cake you could take on a picnic, or you could serve it up with some fresh berries or ricotta as a dessert.

Preheat the oven to 160°C. Grease a 23-cm x 13-cm x 8-cm loaf pan and line the base and sides with baking paper.

Mix all the dry ingredients in a bowl.

Beat the butter and sugar in an electric mixer until it turns white. Still beating, slowly add the eggs until completely mixed. Then fold in the dry ingredients by hand. Finally, fold in the zest, juice and ricotta. Try to keep the ricotta fairly chunky.

Spoon the mixture into the prepared pan and bake for 40 minutes, or until golden brown. To check if it's cooked, insert a skewer in the centre – if it comes out clean, the cake is ready.

SERVES 10-12

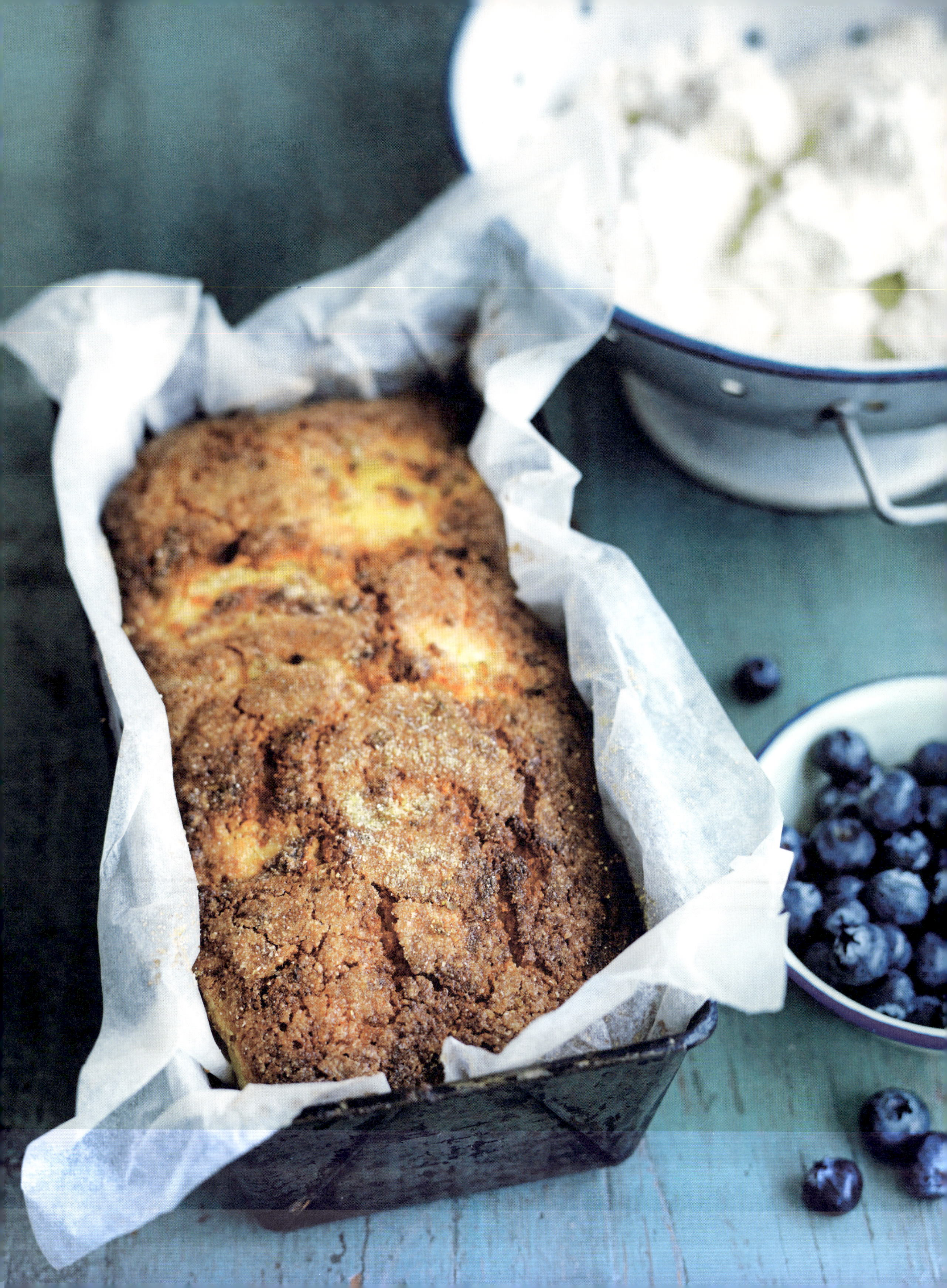

BREAD and BUTTER PUDDING with a FEW HERBS

3 tablespoons brandy
80 g sultanas
400 ml full cream milk
200 ml cream
3 sprigs rosemary
1 bay leaf
½ teaspoon allspice
1 vanilla pod, split lengthways, seeds scraped
100 g unsalted butter, soft
10 slices bread
5 eggs
50 g raw sugar, plus a little extra for topping

Bread and butter pudding is a classic British recipe. It gets full marks for being a great way to use stale or excess bread, it's super easy to make, and very, very comforting. We use sourdough for ours but you could try plain white, and fruit loaf is especially good. Or, if you really want to push the boat out ... try using brioche. For a twist on this classic, we often infuse the milk with herbs before cooking to give it an extra depth of flavour. Give it a go with rosemary, thyme or bay leaves.

Warm the brandy and pour over the sultanas.

Place the milk, cream, rosemary, bay leaf, allspice, vanilla pod and seeds in a saucepan, heat to 80°C, or until almost boiling, take off the heat and leave to infuse for 20 minutes.

Butter a baking dish or a deep tray, then butter both sides of the bread and arrange in the baking dish with the sultanas between each layer.

Whisk the eggs and sugar, pour the spiced milk over the eggs and whisk to combine. Pour the mixture over the bread and leave to soak for 30 minutes.

Preheat the oven to 180°C.

When the bread has soaked up the custard, sprinkle the extra sugar on top and bake for 35 minutes until golden brown. This goes very well with fennel ice cream (page 184).

SERVES 6

RICE PUDDING with CINNAMON, HONEY and LIME

Rice pudding is an old family favourite, usually served with some brown sugar or even strawberry jam when we were kids. This version has a slight twist, using Arborio rice, a short-grained rice used to make risotto, which makes for a little extra creaminess. Then we add some lime to wake the whole thing up. Serve it in a big bowl in the middle of the table and another bowl with some poached fruit or berries when they're in season.

Put the milk, spices, honey and sugar in a large non-stick saucepan, bring the milk to a simmer, then stir in the rice. Cook gently over low heat for 40 minutes, stirring occasionally. Remove from the heat and stir through the lime zest.

Serve with poached fruits, berries or just sprinkle with a little more brown sugar.

SERVES 8

1.2 litres full cream milk
1 bay leaf
1 cinnamon stick
pinch of freshly grated nutmeg
½ a vanilla pod
50 g honey
50 g soft brown sugar
200 g Arborio rice
zest of 1 lime
poached fruit or berries, to serve

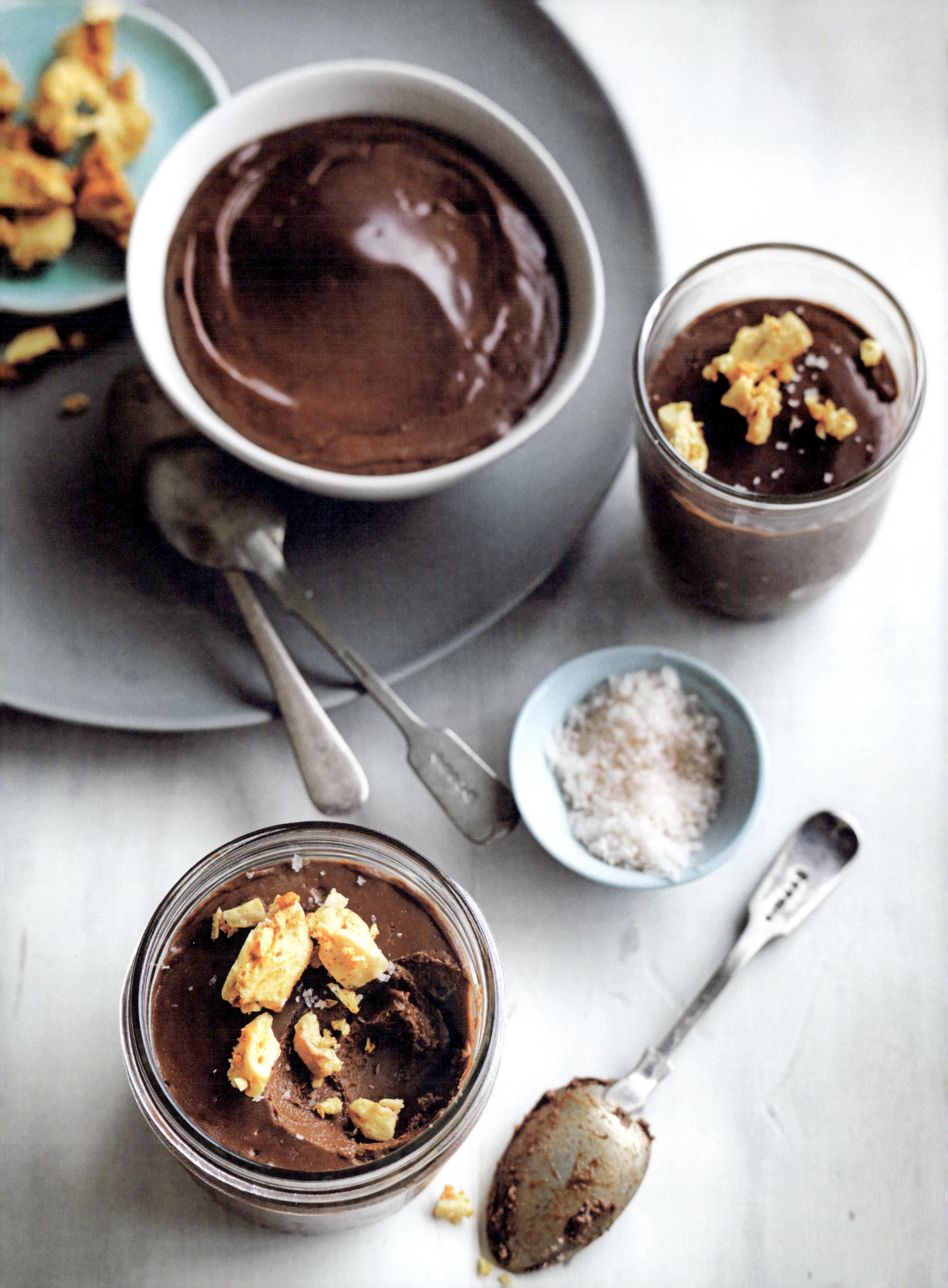

CHOCOLATE POTS *with* WHATEVER YOU FANCY

The better quality the chocolate in these, the richer and more delicious they are. Once you've made the basic recipe, you can add whatever takes your fancy … honeycomb, blueberries, walnuts, hazelnuts, chilli powder, sour cherries or even a little whisky. Or you can leave them plain.

Put the cream and glucose in a small saucepan and warm to 80°C (check this with a sugar thermometer if you want to, or wait until just before the cream comes to the boil).

Remove the pan from the heat, add the chocolate and salt, stir until the chocolate completely melts. Now add whatever flavouring you like and stir through.

Pour into some of your favourite little pots or ramekins and chill in the refrigerator for at least 3 hours before serving.

SERVES 4

300 ml cream
1 tablespoon liquid glucose
250 g dark chocolate, at least 68 per cent cocoa fat, chopped
a pinch sea salt
your choice of flavouring – honeycomb, blueberries, walnuts, hazelnuts, chilli powder, sour cherries, whisky

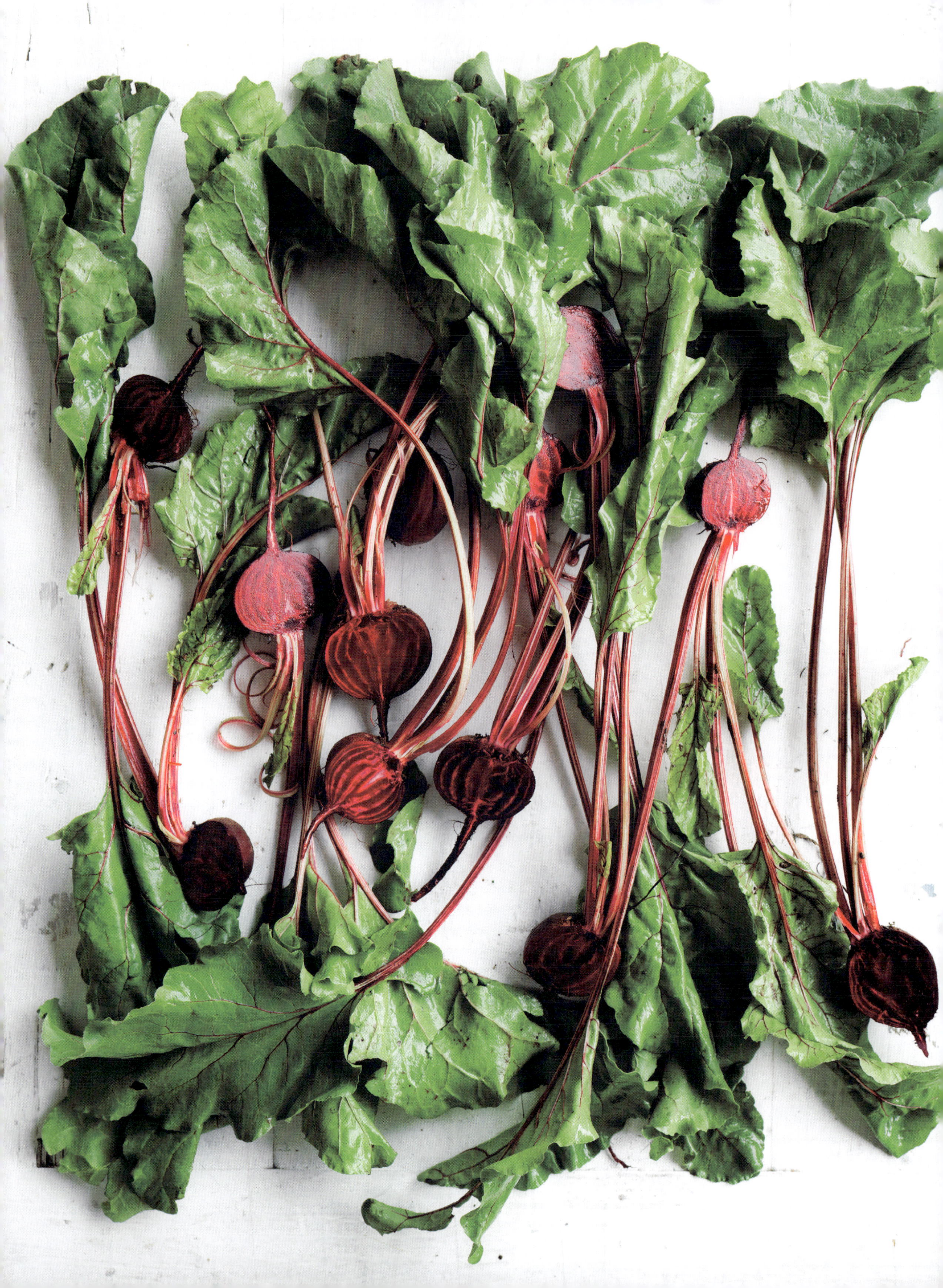

THE GARDEN

Vegetables · Honey
Savoury preserves
Sweet preserves
Eggs · Desserts

TOMATO and TORN MOZZARELLA SALAD

6 medium-sized ripe tomatoes, diced
1 red onion, finely diced
1 long red chilli, finely chopped
½ bunch of basil, leaves torn
¼ bunch of mint, leaves torn
5 tablespoons good olive oil
3 tablespoons balsamic vinegar
sea salt and cracked pepper
pinch of sugar
6 large buffalo mozzarella balls, ripped into quarters
zest and juice of ½ lemon
6 slices of toasted sourdough, to serve

Summer is the time to make this salad, when tomatoes are at their best. We've been lucky enough at the Ducks to grow vegetables in our garden, so we can pick home-grown tomatoes as well as fresh herbs like basil and mint. If you can't find buffalo mozzarella, buy fior di latte mozzarella, but make sure it's really fresh.

Put the tomato, onion, chilli, basil, mint, 4 tablespoons olive oil and vinegar in a medium-sized bowl, stir well, season with salt, pepper and a pinch of sugar, and leave to sit for 10 minutes.

Preheat the oven to 180°C.

Put the mozzarella, lemon juice and zest, a good splash of olive oil and plenty of sea salt and cracked pepper in a stainless steel bowl. Put the bowl in the oven for 3–4 minutes – just enough to warm the mozzarella and let the lemon and seasonings infuse the cheese.

Put the tomato/herb mixture into a serving bowl, arrange the warmed mozzarella on top, drizzle over the juices and serve with the toasted sourdough.

SERVES 6

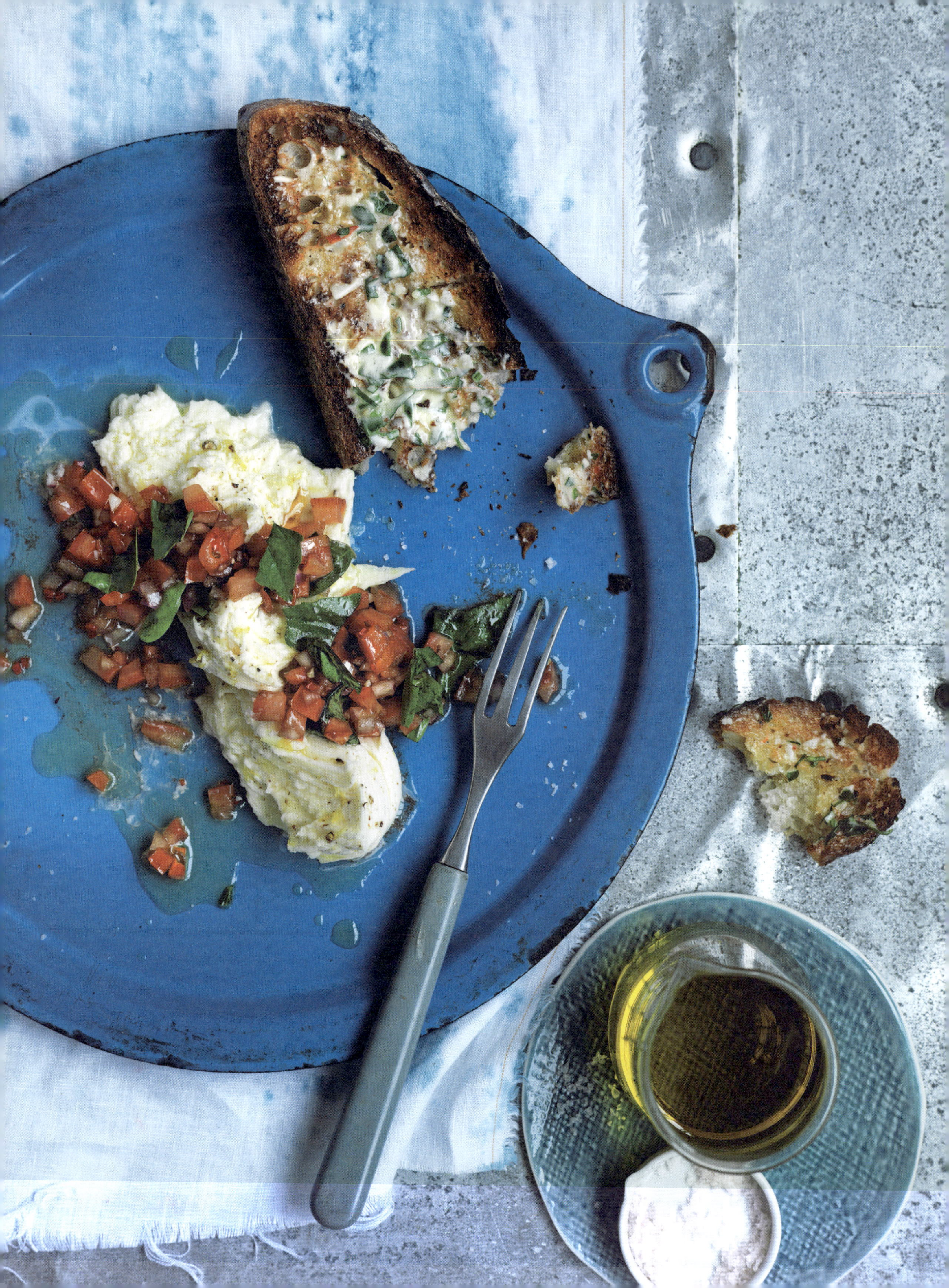

DRESSINGS

Dressings are the key to any good salad. Spend the time and money on nice ingredients and you will have amazing results. Here are some of our favourites.

Apple-balsamic

Great with tomatoes and roasted lamb.

**1 litre apple juice
350 ml balsamic vinegar
500 ml extra virgin olive oil
salt and pepper**

Pour the apple juice into a large saucepan over high heat and reduce until you have around 100 ml of juice (about 10 minutes). Cool, then add balsamic vinegar and oil, then season with salt and pepper.

Pour the dressing into a clean bottle, seal the top and store in the refrigerator.

The dressing will last indefinitely if you keep it in the fridge.

MAKES ABOUT 1 LITRE

Honey, mustard and citrus

Great with fennel, spinach and green beans.

1 tablespooon Dijon mustard
2 tablespooons honey
100 ml lemon juice
150 ml grapeseed oil
salt and pepper

Place mustard, honey and lemon juice in a bowl, and whisk until smooth. Then slowly add the oil until the dressing thickens, and season to taste.

MAKES ABOUT 250 ML

Nahm jim

This is super fragrant and great with oysters, duck and herb salads.

1 punnet cherry tomatoes
3 long red chillies, seeded and roughly chopped
75 g grated palm sugar
200 ml lemon juice
1 golf ball-sized knob of ginger
2 kaffir lime leaves, thinly sliced
1 bunch of coriander root
40 ml fish sauce
30 ml soy sauce
4 peeled French shallots

Place all the ingredients in a blender, and mix for a couple of minutes until smooth.

MAKES ABOUT 600 ML

Soy-mirin

This is a perfect dressing for a freshly shucked oyster or a wakame salad.

4 tablespoons soy sauce
1 granny smith apple, peeled and finely grated
1 x 20-cent piece-sized knob of ginger, finely grated
1 long red chilli, seeded and finely chopped
¼ bunch of coriander leaves, stalks and roots, finely chopped
1½ tablespoons honey
zest and juice of 1 lime
juice of 2 lemons
2 teaspoons sesame oil
2 teaspoons mirin

Add all the ingredients to a bowl and mix. Taste, and if it needs a little more salt, add soy, if it needs to be sweeter, add more honey.

MAKES ABOUT 250 ML

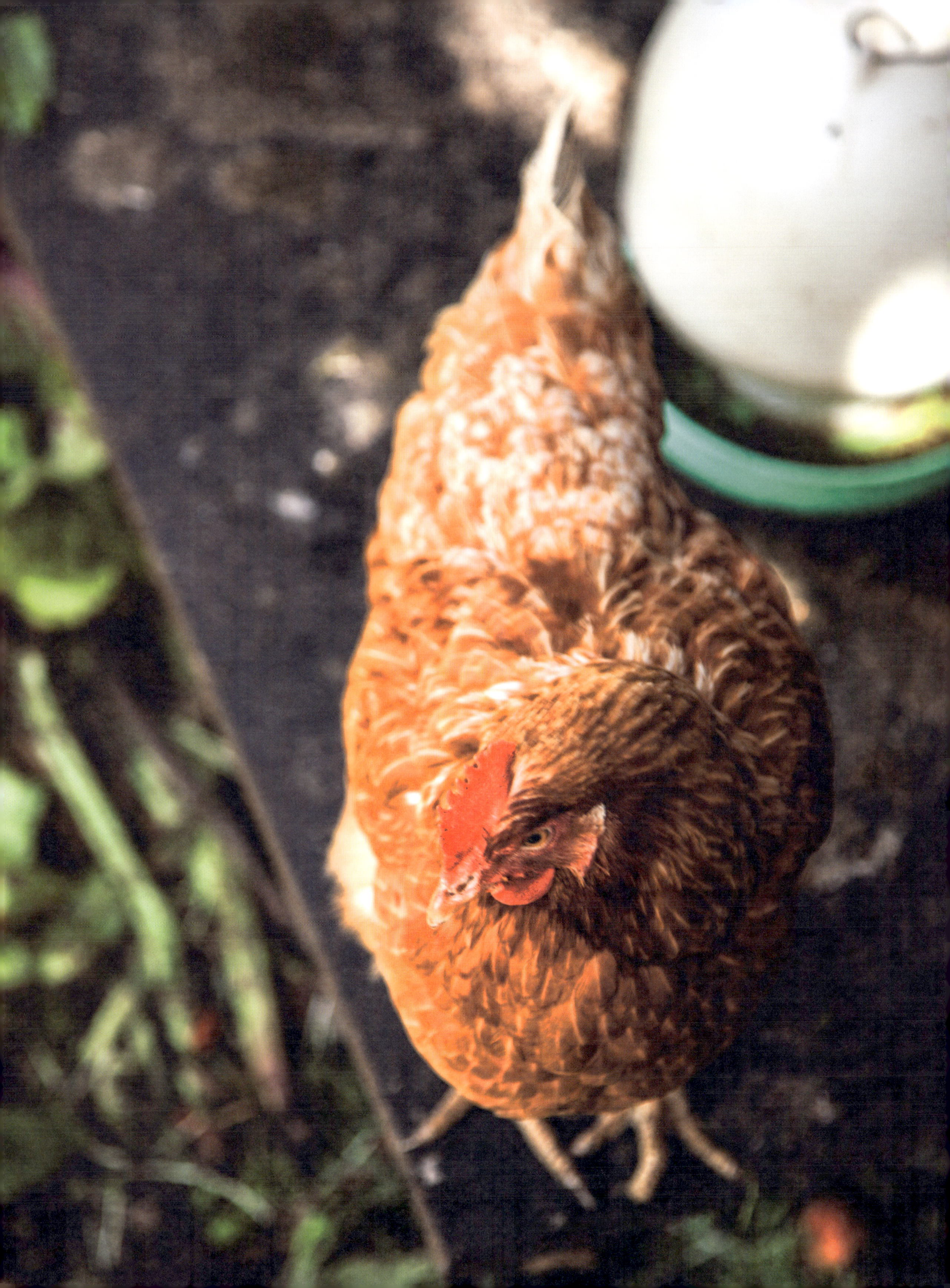

MAYONNAISE

This is a recipe for basic mayo, but the list of possible additions is almost endless. You could add wasabi, lemon juice, Tabasco and tomato sauce (for a classic cocktail sauce), capers and cornichons. If the mayo becomes too thin, add more oil; if it's too thick, add a little warm water, vinegar or lemon juice. Don't be tempted to replace grapeseed oil with olive oil or you will have a bitter-tasting mayo. You could use a good-quality vegetable oil if you really wanted to though.

Place the eggs yolks, mustard and vinegar in a food processor and process on high speed for 5 minutes. Then slowly – very slowly – pour the oil into the mixture as you continue whisking until the mayo is until thick, pale and glossy. If you add extra lemon juice, or any liquid that is thinner than the mayo, you will need to add some more oil to thicken it up again.

When the mayo is the consistency you want, season it with salt and pepper and store in a covered container in the fridge. It should last about 2 weeks.

MAKES 500 ML OR A TOUCH MORE

3 egg yolks
¾ heaped tablespoon Dijon mustard
50 ml apple cider vinegar
500 ml grapeseed oil
salt and pepper

PARSNIP and JERUSALEM ARTICHOKE SOUP

1 kg parsnips, tops removed
1 kg Jerusalem artichokes
10 ml grapeseed oil
2 sprigs thyme
salt and white pepper
100 g butter
6 French shallots, peeled and sliced
1 garlic clove, peeled and sliced
2.5 litres chicken stock
200 ml cream
250 g Parmigiano Reggiano, grated
zest of 1 lemon and 2 teaspoons of juice

Roasting the parsnips and artichokes involves a bit of extra work but it also makes the flavours much more intense. If parsnips and artichockes aren't in season, try replacing them with cauliflower, potatoes, celeriac or kohlrabi.

Preheat the oven to 180°C.

Scrub and dry the parsnips and artichokes, then chop them into 2-cm cubes, leaving the skins on. Drizzle with the oil, scatter over the thyme, season with salt and pepper and roast for 30 minutes.

While the vegetables are roasting, put a little oil and the butter in a large pan or stockpot over low heat, add the eschalots and garlic and cook for 8 minutes, then pour in the chicken stock.

When the parsnips and artichokes are roasted, remove them from the oven and add to the chicken stock. Cook for a further 10 minutes, or until the vegetables are soft. Take the pan off the heat.

Now add the cream, cheese, lemon zest and juice. Using a hand-held blender, blend until smooth, adding a little water if the soup is too thick.

Season to taste with salt and pepper and serve.

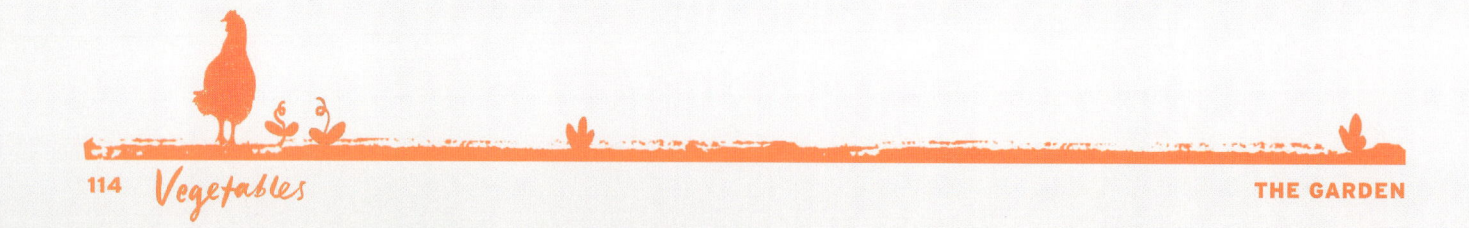

SERVES 8

CHICKEN and CHARRED LEEK SOUP

One of the benefits of roasting a whole chicken is the variety of dishes you can make with the leftover carcass. Soup is a great way to use up the bones and adding charred leeks and spinach makes this soup an absolute cracker.

Remove any remaining chicken from the carcass and set aside. Put the chicken carcass in a large saucepan, cover with cold water, add the garlic, bay leaf, a little salt and pepper, the potato and thyme.

Put the char-grill on high heat.

Add the leeks and grill them until golden brown on both sides. Chop the leeks and add to the pan with the chicken. Bring to the boil, then turn down to a simmer and skim the top. Cook, uncovered, for 50 minutes.

Use tongs to remove the carcass, and discard. Add the reserved chicken meat, the spinach and lemon zest to the pan. Blend with a hand-held blender until the soup is smooth.

Check the seasoning and serve with plenty of crusty bread.

SERVES 6

1 chicken carcass (left over from Sunday lunch)
1 garlic clove, thinly sliced
1 bay leaf
salt and pepper
400 g desiree potatoes, sliced on a mandoline
1 sprig thyme, leaves picked
4 leeks, trimmed and halved lengthways
300 g spinach leaves, well washed
zest of ½ lemon
crusty bread, to serve

THE GARDEN

GROWING *your own* VEGGIES

As our garden at the Ducks got going, our ambitions grew too – we imagined an urban mini farm that could also moonlight as a backyard fruit and vegetable emporium. However, despite our fantasies of rambling aisles of organic produce waiting to be picked from stem, stalk and pod, we were limited by space and time. We knew a little about permaculture and it appealed to us because it's about using available space to create gardens that are ecologically and economically sustainable.

Permaculture methodology suggests closely observing the space intended for your garden before you actually plant. You need to consider the utilisation and design of the space, the ease of access to the plants and the layout. You need to work with your local climate; for example, gardens in the eastern suburbs of Sydney won't produce stone fruit that requires a frost. Another consideration is the aspect of your garden: where the sunlight is coming from, and which direction the garden faces. Dappled shade protects the garden from the heat of the day, so deciduous trees are ideal as in winter they will drop their leaves and let more sun through. Wind is a potentially destructive force as it dehydrates the soil, as well as removing important nutrients by blowing topsoil away. Trees can be used as a natural barrier to block out the wind and sun. You have to consider the scale of your garden: is it only suitable to grow herbs and salad leaves, or do you have the space for fruit trees and other perennials? Consider the structure: will you plant against walls, or will there be freestanding plants that require stabilising by staking or trellising. Is the area protected from local predators? The most common predator in the garden at the Ducks is the fruit fly – our tomatoes in particular suffer terribly. To combat the destruction, Mark's brother, Grant has stopped growing large tomatoes because they have a thinner skin. Smaller cherry-sized tomatoes have a thicker skin that the fruit fly can't pierce. A perfect, natural solution.

By observing the area before planning and planting the garden, you can save yourself time, effort and even a little heartbreak. However, ultimately, you will have to wait to see how your garden grows, how it deals with the local environment and the forces of nature.

STARTING FROM THE GROUND UP – COMPOSTING AND BUILDING SOIL

Every week, the Ducks produces 80–100 kg of organic waste, including coffee grounds, and fruit and vegetable scraps. Before the garden, there was no alternative than to bin the waste, sending it to the Mordor of landfill. A common misconception is that because food waste is biodegradable it decays naturally in landfill. However, when waste is sent to landfill it is buried and cut off from a source of oxygen, making it unable to decompose aerobically. As the waste breaks down it creates methane, a toxic greenhouse gas. In comparison, above-ground home composting produces very little methane.

Composting alters the soil structure, helping it to retain water and nutrients, balances the pH level, and prevents plant disease. The way it works, bacteria join with fungi and protozoa (single-celled organisms), as well as centipedes, millipedes, beetles and earthworms, and this band of cheeky brutes acts as decomposers. The more decomposers, the faster the compost will break down. Decomposers use carbon in brown 'woody' waste like dried leaves, sticks, wood chips and straw, as an energy source. They also use nitrogen from green 'grassy' materials, like vegetable and fruit scraps, grass and manure, as protein to grow and multiply. To make good compost, use both brown and green materials, as well as water for moisture. Then just walk away. Other than adding to it, and turning it every couple of weeks, walk away and watch it get more potent than a dead wombat in a heatwave. Your soil will show its thanks by giving birth to leafy heads of lettuce and fecund pumpkins.

A compost pile takes care of garden waste, produces plant fertiliser, and acts as a great breeding place for earthworms. Worm and compost tea provides liquid fertiliser for the garden, and the surrounding frame of the compost can support climbing plants like tomatoes and corn. At the Ducks, we put our compost pile under the canopy of the loquat tree. The pile acts as a fertiliser for the tree, and when it rains water runs off the compost pile and into the surrounding area, carrying nutrients to the rest of the garden. Use the naturally occurring systems of the garden to your advantage.

Healthy soil yields healthy plants. It is worth spending time building your soil, or nourishing impoverished soil back to health. New gardeners often get caught up in the excitement of having a garden, plant in haste, then wonder what went wrong when everything dies. You need to invest in the soil. Over time, you will create a rich layer of organic matter, manure and rotted vegetables. When used by itself, local hardware-store potting mix lacks nutritional value and is fairly inert for plants. Commercial soil is a good starter, but it is just that – a starter. Because of its proximity to the coastline, the sandy soil at the Ducks is gutless. It is free-draining, but struggles to hold onto moisture and nutrients. Grant, our resident garden expert, mixed cow, chicken and horse manure, lucerne, mushroom compost and commercial potting mix. He let it ripen for four weeks and then used it as potting mix.

WHAT TO PLANT
If you are a first time gardener, start with a small herb garden and once you have mastered that, you can move onto lettuce and other vegetables. Then perennials, and on you go until you are confident enough to grow whatever you want to eat. If something is hard or tedious, then it's not going to be enjoyable to get out there and tend to. Just as we read for interest,

plant for eating. What you eat most, grow more of. If you love tomatoes, plant them everywhere, in teapots, old tyres, broken furniture and disused laundry baskets. If pesto quickens your pulse, then basil up your courtyard. If snow peas are your thing, wallpaper your patio with them.

SEED SAVING AND PLANTING

The idea of long-term investment in the soil is extended to the issue of seed saving. Seed saving refers to the collecting and storing of virgin seeds from plants, to be used for re-planting. For example, drying the seeds of a tomato plant, and re-planting those seeds to create a new tomato plant. For the purpose of seed saving, heirloom and open-pollinated seeds are the two best varieties. Open pollination occurs when plants are pollinated by insects, birds, wind or other forces of Mother Nature. They are free from chemicals, pesticides, growth hormones and other types of human genetic modification. Because of this, there is greater genetic diversity of the plants. Also, plants that reproduce through natural means adapt to local conditions and evolve over time. If you use hybrid plants they will produce seeds, however, the plant that grows from them will not be identical to the plant you harvested the seed from. Open pollinated and heirloom plants will yield a more true seed.

HOW TO SAVE SEEDS

There are two main methods of seed saving – the dry method and the wet method. The dry method, the most common, involves harvesting the head of a plant that has gone to seed and leaving it to dry, before crushing the head to release the seeds. You would use this method for lettuce, beans, leeks, onions, peas and cauliflower. The wet method is for plants with no seed head, and involves collecting the seeds from the fully mature fruit or vegetable, scraping out the seeds, and washing them in a sieve before laying them out to dry. You would use this method for tomatoes, zucchini, cucumbers and pumpkins.

SOME TIPS FOR SEED SAVING

- Collect seed from your garden before midday and after the dew has disappeared.
- For herbs, pull the root out of the soil and hang the whole plant upside down in a cool, dry place. Cover the plant with a paper bag so the seed doesn't drop off onto the ground.
- Gather the seed from your choicest plants. The most productive, those with the best tasting fruit, those most resistant to diseases and pests.
- To dry your seeds, don't use an oven or direct sunshine, as this will damage the seed.

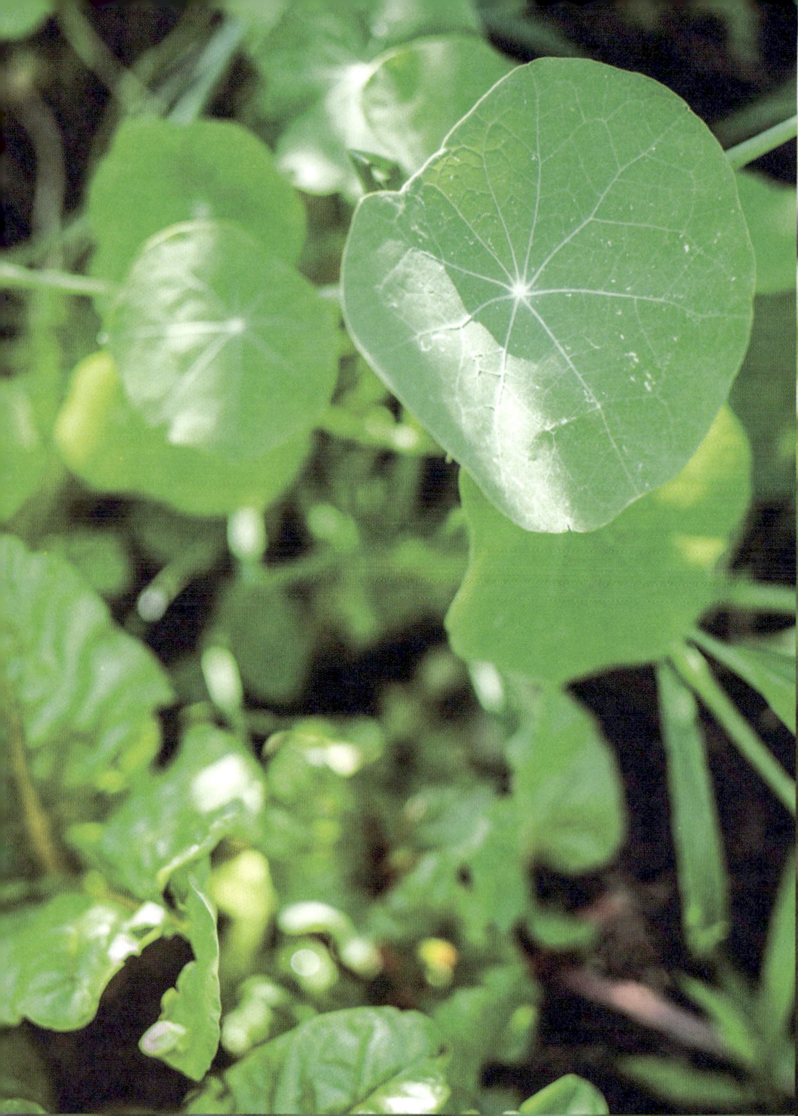
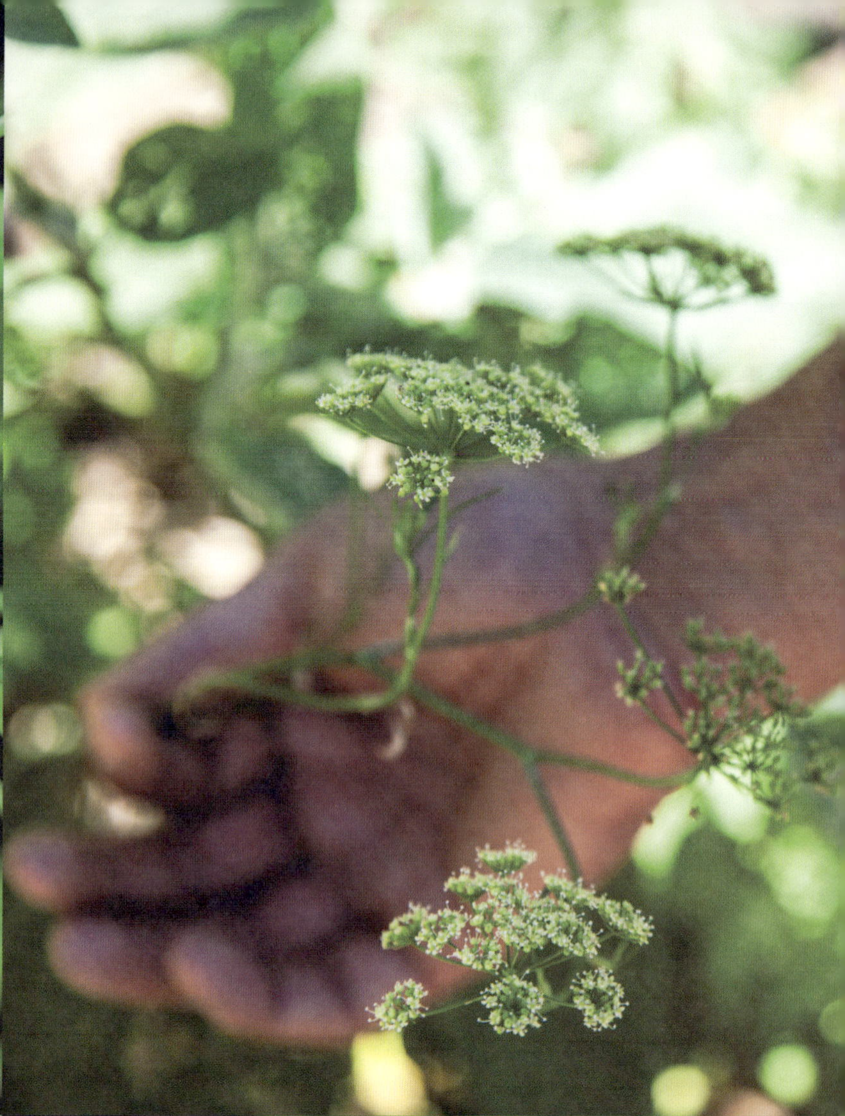
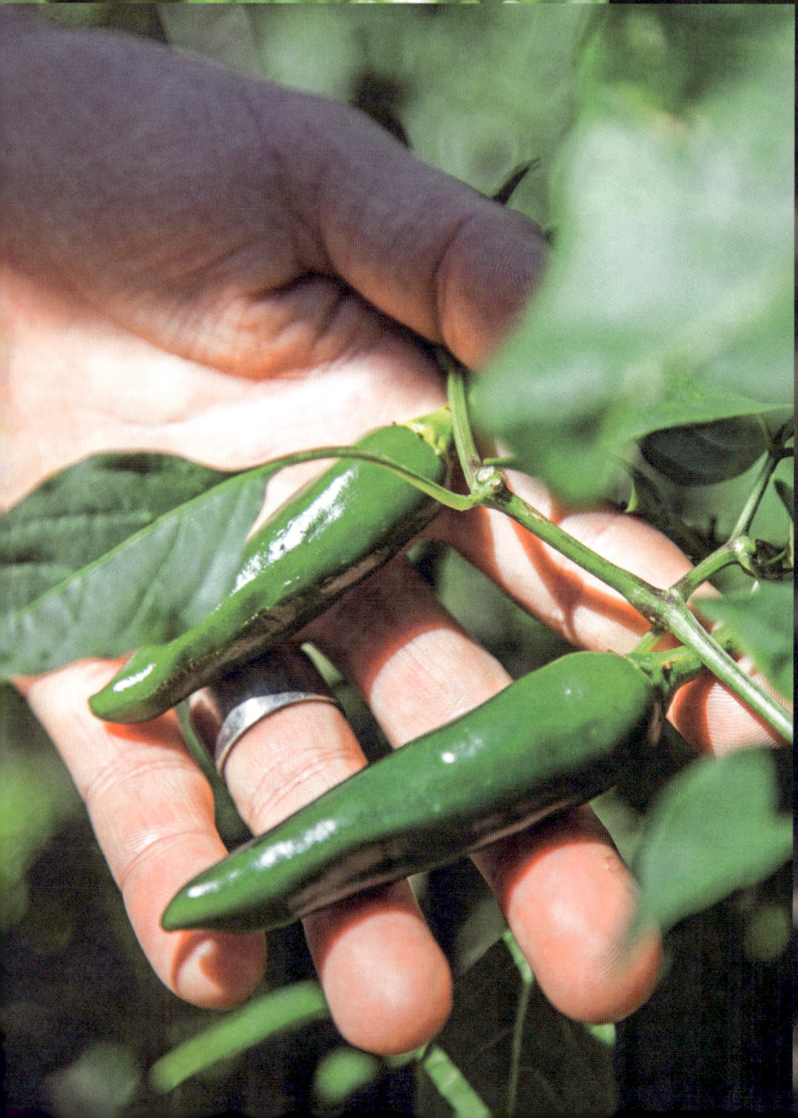
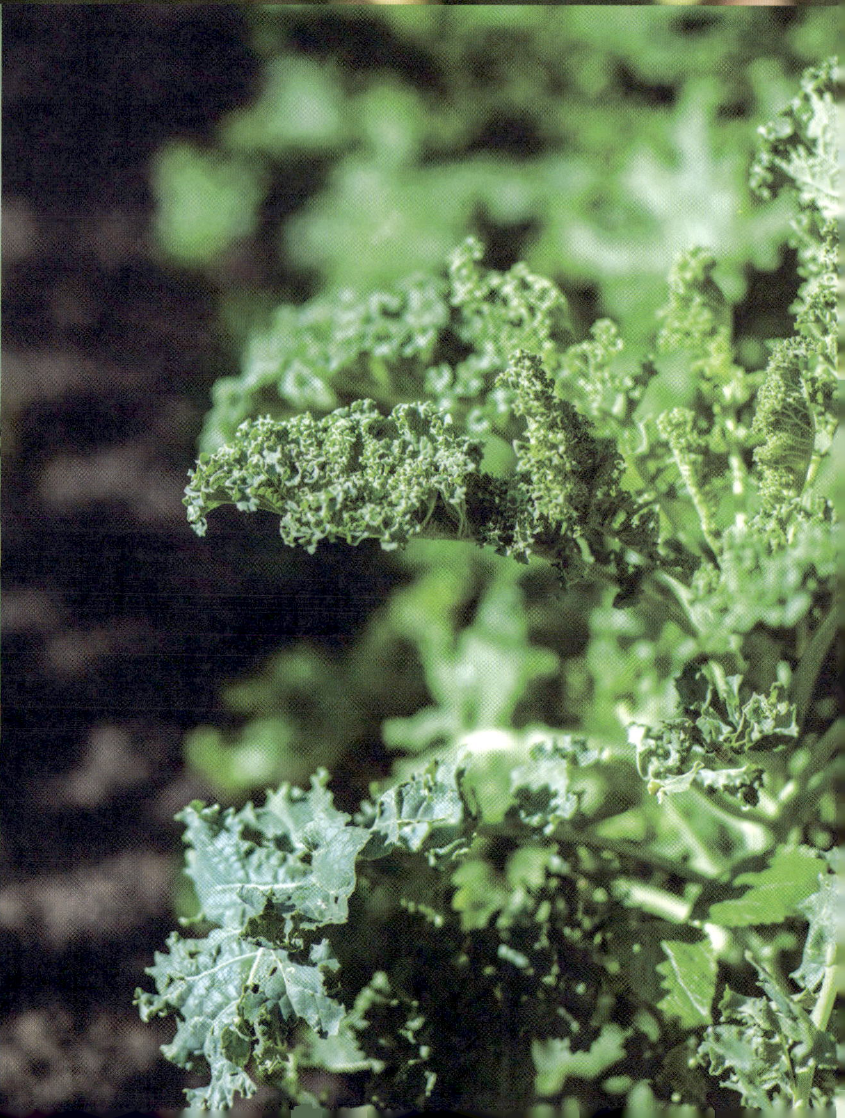

Seed saving is a global issue. Historically, seed saving has allowed local farmers to maintain a livelihood, as well as healthy crops, by regenerating their seed season after season. However, in 1998 a US patent was passed to prevent unauthorised seed saving by farmers. The patent allowed seed companies to genetically alter seed so that it will not germinate if planted a second time, forcing farmers to buy new seed every season. The problem is that half of the world's farmers are too poor to buy new seed every season, yet they are feeding almost a quarter of the world's population. This technology patent treats the earth as a corporate asset instead of a natural resource for everyone.

For raising seeds, you need quite a sandy mix to force root growth – typically 1:4 compost to sand mix. That's a good way to start seeds as it gives them a lot of space for the roots to spread and grow. You keep the seedlings in that mix for about four weeks, then transplant them to more nutritious soil. Aerated soil is best. Compacted soil becomes extremely acidic and it makes it hard for plants to flourish, so don't stamp down the soil around your plants too hard.

WORM-FARMING

Every home gardener should have a worm farm. Worms act as primary decomposers and add nutrients to the soil. As plants grow, they draw out nutrients and if the soil isn't nurtured or supplemented in some way, it becomes exhausted and inert. Worms act as a pH balancer, leaving the soil with a relatively neutral pH level, and their manure, or vermicast, is a rich organic fertiliser.

Talk to your local garden centre, or cruise the Internet to find the type of worm farm that suits your needs. Find a suitable location, as worms don't like direct sunlight or heat. The size of your worm farm will depend on how much space you have and how much organic waste you produce from your kitchen. Before introducing the worms to your worm farm, ensure the bedding is wet enough. Squeeze a handful of the bedding and if it is adequately moist, a few drops of water will run between your fingers. Put the worms on top and they will burrow deep into the bedding quite quickly. Put your food scraps into the worm farm but be wary of overfeeding. If the worms can't eat the waste before you add more, acid builds up, which can be deadly. Overfeeding is the most common way to kill your worms. Generally, worms can eat up to their own body weight in food per day. So one kilo of worms is going to need around one kilo of food scraps.

You can make worm tea by rinsing the worm farm once a week with water; as the water washes through the farm it collects the broken-down green material. You can use the worm tea as fertiliser. Dilute it 1:10 with water and spray it or just sprinkle it on garden beds. Worm tea adds nutrients to the soil, and is also full of worm eggs, so you're distributing worms as well.

ALTERNATIVE GARDEN SYSTEMS

After learning about – and putting into practice – permaculture techniques, Grant discovered aquaponic garden systems and vertical growing walls. Both are ideal for urban gardens, as they take up little space. Aquaponics involves the symbiotic cultivation of fish and edible plants together. The water is re-circulated through the system, being cleansed as it passes through, and acting as a source of nutrients for the plants. Aquaculture is becoming increasingly important as whole communities, particularly in Asia, base their food and fish production on it. In our research on aquaponics, we read about communities in China that raise carp in ponds that are surrounded by mulberry bushes. The rich pond sludge fertilises the mulberry plants, and the leaves are picked and fed to silkworms that produce silk which the locals sell. The silkworm droppings feed the carp and the communities eat and sell the carp. It's a totally sustainable system. We wanted to experiment with aquaculture and sustainability. We bought the system and planted it with kale, lettuces and herbs. Pretty much anything except root vegetables. However, if the power is accidentally switched off, the water stops running, the clay dries out, and the microorganisms inhabiting the clay, die. Ironically, we need a more hands-off approach for the system, so it isn't repeatedly turned off.

The vertical growing wall is another story. We have watched with delight as a colony of herbs and plants swells our vertical growing system. It's a great solution for growing produce in an urban setting, as all you need is a wall. You can make a growing wall from almost anything: old pots or tyres stacked on top of each other, fruit boxes, or plumbing pipe that runs up the wall. However, the most common way is to purchase kits or purpose-built equipment from a supplier. We use black geotextile felt fabric but it needs to be watched carefully on a hot day, as it loses moisture and dries out quickly. We have another one made out of aluminium, which isn't a sustainable material, but works a lot better and doesn't lose too much moisture. At the moment our vertical growing wall is full of herbs, but it is possible to put most plants in, as long as they are sure to receive proper light, water and nutrients.

The first relationship is between the plant and soil.

The other essential relationship is that between the gardener and the site.

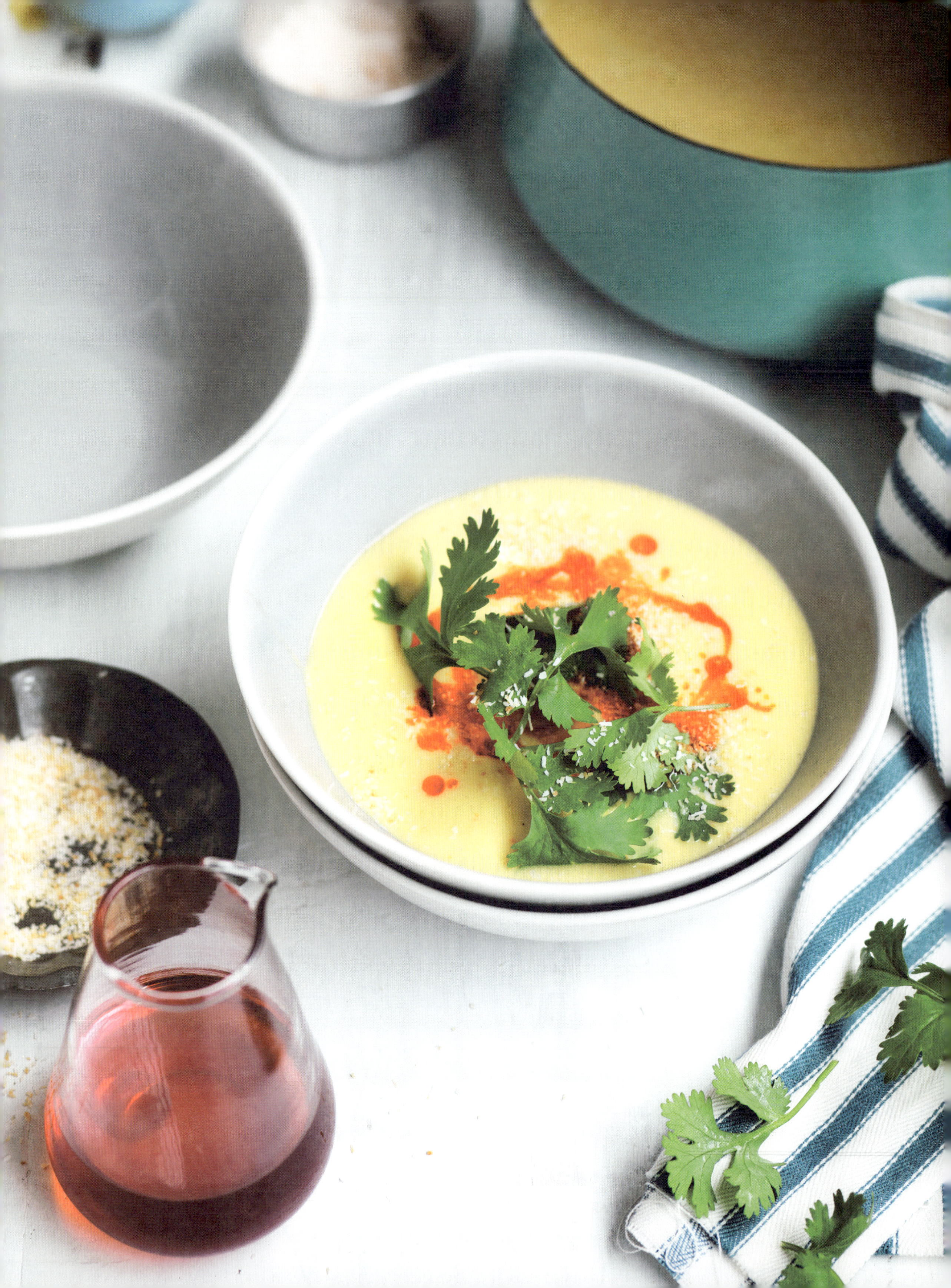

SWEET CORN SOUP with TOASTED COCONUT and CHILLI

We use sweet corn at the Ducks raw in salads, char-grilled with chilli and melted cheese, or just boiled and served with sea salt and plenty of butter. This corn soup is pretty punchy – you can make it as hot as you like by adding the chilli oil, or leave the oil out completely. Use the cobs when making the soup as they're packed with flavour and slow cooking extracts all the goodness.

You can buy chilli oils, but we make our own – it's a good chance to use all the chilli seeds we have, and it's great for giving things a kick.

To make the chilli oil, put all the ingredients in a small saucepan, bring to the boil, then simmer until the water has evaporated. This should take around 40 minutes. Strain and chill before using.

To make the soup, put the oil in a large saucepan over low heat, then add the garlic, chilli, onion and ginger and fry for 5 minutes, without letting it colour. Add the corn kernels (and corn cobs, if you want to), lime leaves, cinnamon and chicken stock, bring to the boil and simmer for 10 minutes.

Remove the corn cobs, cinnamon stick and the lime leaves and blend the soup with a hand-held blender until it's smooth. Season with salt and pepper, lime juice and serve with the coriander leaves and toasted coconut sprinkled on top. Then drizzle on as much, or as little, chilli oil as you like.

SERVES 4

2 tablespoons grapeseed oil
2 garlic cloves, chopped
1 long red chilli, chopped
1 red onion, chopped
20 g fresh ginger, grated
4 corn cobs, corn removed from the cob, but keep cobs
2 kaffir lime leaves
1 cinnamon stick
1 litre chicken stock
salt and pepper
juice of 1 lime
1 bunch of coriander, leaves picked
4 tablespoons shredded, dried coconut, toasted

CHILLI OIL
100 g chilli seeds
1 teaspoon smoked paprika
1 garlic clove, sliced
200 ml grapeseed oil
200 ml water

WARM SALAD of KIPFLER POTATOES

1 kg kipfler potatoes, scrubbed
sea salt
1 French shallot, chopped
1 tablespoon capers
2 tablespoons chopped flat-leaf parsley
zest and juice of 1 lemon
30 ml olive oil
2 tablespoons grain mustard
1 anchovy fillet
cracked pepper

Kipfler potatoes are a knobby-looking finger-shaped potato with a thin skin, yellow flesh and a smooth waxy texture. They hold their shape and are definitely one of the best potatoes for salad. If you haven't tried them, this is a good dish to start with.

To make the dressing, put all the ingredients, except the potatoes, in a small bowl and mix well.

Put the potatoes in a saucepan with some salt, bring to the boil and simmer for 25 minutes until soft. Drain, then pour on the dressing while the potatoes are still warm and toss.

Serve warm or at room temperature.

SERVES 6

CHARRED ASPARAGUS with CODDLED EGGS and BUTTER SAUCE

Making this butter sauce takes a little bit of practice but you will be surprised how quickly you can learn to do it. It's best to use coddled eggs but you can use poached eggs if you prefer. Watercress is quite peppery so check before adding any extra pepper.

To make the butter sauce, put 5 cm water in a small saucepan, place a small bowl over the top to create a double boiler. The water should not touch the base of the bowl. Put the double boiler over medium heat, add the egg yolk and vinegar and whisk until it becomes thick. Be careful not to overheat the mixture or you will scramble the eggs. (If this happens just start again.)

When the mixture has almost doubled and is thick and velvety, start to slowly add the butter while constantly whisking. Your mixture will become thick and buttery, just be careful not to add the butter too fast or else you will split the mixture. If it splits, start again (it may seem difficult at first but you can do this ... once you have made it a few times you will be surprised how easy it is to make).

Take the butter sauce off the heat, add the chives and salt and pepper to taste, set aside in a warm place.

Heat the barbecue or put the char-grill on high heat.

Place the asparagus on and grill until it starts to blacken. Remove from the grill, slice each asparagus stalk into 3 pieces and scatter over a serving platter.

Put the watercress in a bowl, add the lemon juice, a good splash of oil, season with sea salt and toss. Arrange the watercress on top of the asparagus, make a nest for each egg, then place a coddled or poached egg at the centre of each watercress nest. Spoon some butter sauce over the eggs, scatter with the shaved parmesan and serve.

SERVES 4

16 stalks asparagus
1 bunch watercress (about 4 handfuls), washed
juice of 1 lemon
good splash of olive oil
4 coddled or poached eggs
about 50 g parmesan cheese, shaved

BUTTER SAUCE
1 egg yolk
3 tablespoons white balsamic vinegar
100 g butter, melted but not too hot
1 bunch of chives, finely chopped
sea salt and pepper

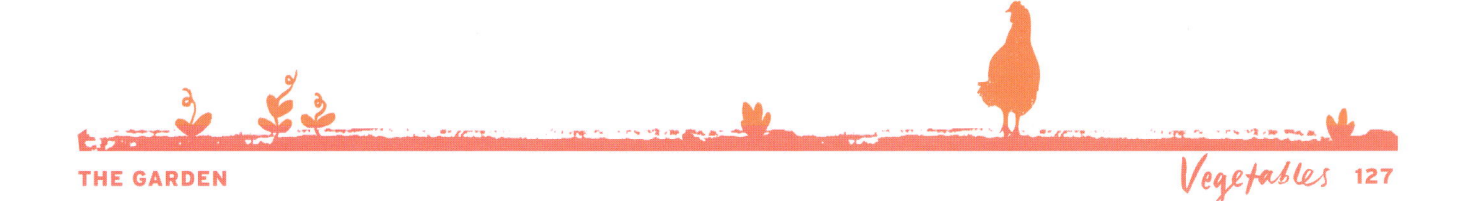

CAULIFLOWER CHEESE, OUR WAY

1 cauliflower
30 g duck fat
2 French shallots, peeled and diced
1 garlic clove
1 teaspoon mustard seeds
50 g sourdough breadcrumbs
500 ml milk
100 g parmesan cheese, grated
zest of ½ a lemon
salt and pepper

One of the best things about this dish is the contrast between the creamy cauliflower and the crispy bits on top. It's the ultimate veggie comfort food.

Separate the cauliflower florets from the stems.

Heat the duck fat in a frying pan over medium heat, add the cauliflower florets and cook on high heat for 2 minutes, reduce the heat, add the shallots, garlic, mustard seeds and breadcrumbs, cook for a further 2 minutes. Remove from the pan, put onto paper towel and set aside.

Roughly chop the cauliflower stems. Put the cauliflower and milk in a medium-sized saucepan. Bring to the boil, then reduce the heat to low and simmer for 5–10 minutes until soft.

Strain off a little milk, then pour the remaining milk and cauliflower into a food processor. Add the parmesan and lemon zest and blend until smooth like thickened cream. Season with salt and pepper to taste.

Serve in a large bowl with the crispy goods on top.

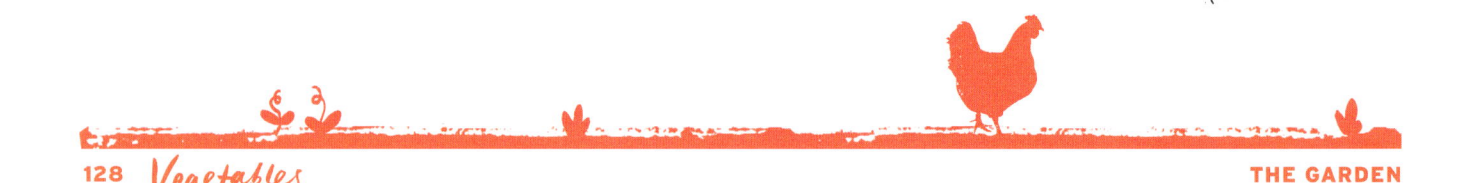

SERVES 6

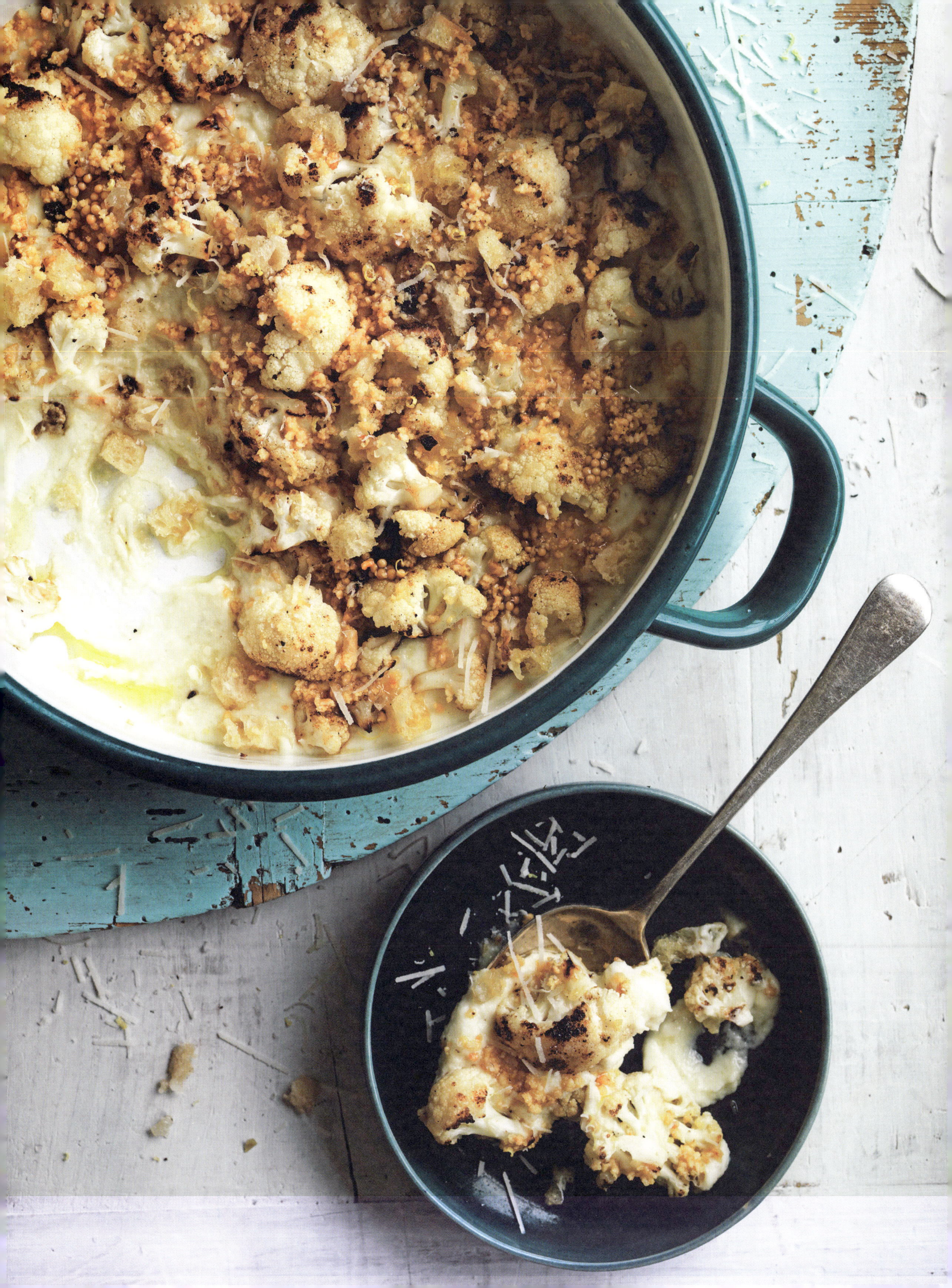

Hey PESTO!

A classic pesto is made from pungent fresh basil leaves and pine nuts. But, if you follow the basic guidelines, you can use almost any flat-leaf herb you like, for example, peppery rocket, nasturtium, even carrot tops. And you can change the nuts too.

The Basic Recipe

250 g green herbs (basil, rocket, or even carrot tops or nasturtium leaves)
100 g pine nuts or almonds, toasted
zest and juice of 2 lemons
2 garlic cloves, peeled
75 g good-quality parmesan cheese
at least 100 ml extra virgin olive oil, to achieve desired consistency
salt and pepper

Put all the ingredients into a food processor and process until you have a chunky pesto. Adjust the consistency using olive oil. Be sure not to over-blend the mixture or it will go brown.

Heavily season with salt and pepper and spoon into small containers. Cover the top with at least a 5-mm layer of olive oil, which will seal the pesto and keep out bacteria. Put a lid on the containers and store in the refrigerator.

This should keep well for a few weeks if you keep it in the fridge and always make sure there is a layer of olive oil over the top creating an airtight seal.

MAKES 500 ML

Rocket

carrot tops →

Nasturtiums

ROASTED VEGETABLE SALAD

600 g baby beetroots, scrubbed and quartered
½ bunch of spring onions, cut into 4-cm lengths
3 red onions, cut into wedges, skin on
1 butternut pumpkin, cut into 5cm x 2cm wedges, skin on
½ bunch of rosemary, roughly chopped
½ bunch of thyme, roughly chopped
2 long red chillies, roughly chopped,
seeds and all
1 garlic bulb, cloves peeled
1 bunch of Dutch carrots (baby carrots) – keep carrot tops to make pesto
2 tablespoons paprika
salt and pepper
good olive oil
1 quantity of carrot-top pesto (page 130)

This is a really easy salad. You can throw it all on a baking tray, pop it in the oven and go off and do something else for half an hour – perfect!

Preheat the oven to 190°C.

Put the beetroots, spring onions, red onions, pumpkin, rosemary, thyme, chilli, garlic, carrots and paprika in a bowl, season with salt and pepper and mix well. Add enough oil to lightly coat all the vegetables.

Tip the vegetables onto a baking tray, place in the oven and roast for 30 minutes.

When roasted, the salad is delicious served with a drizzle of carrot-top pesto (see previous page).

SERVES 6

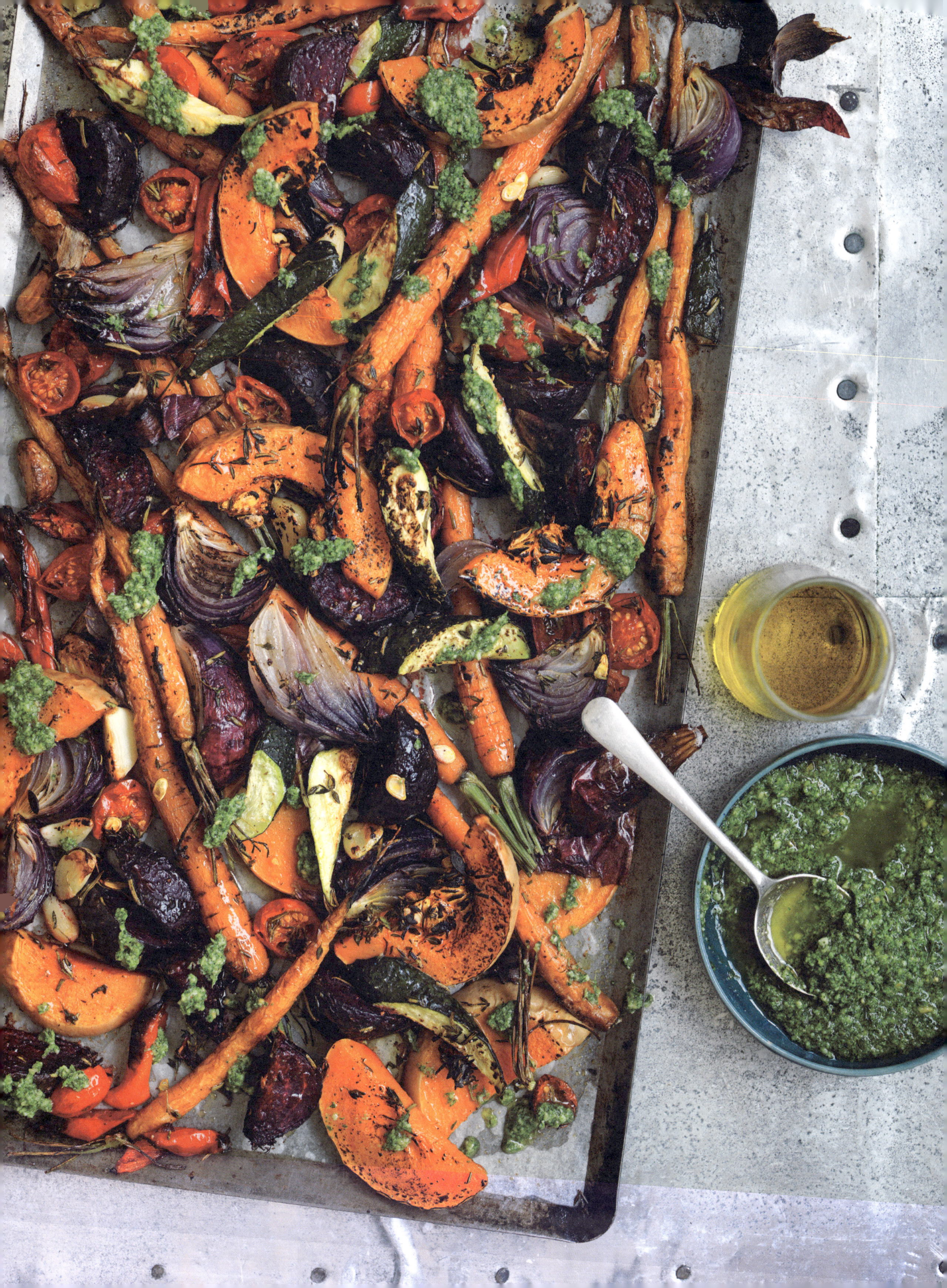

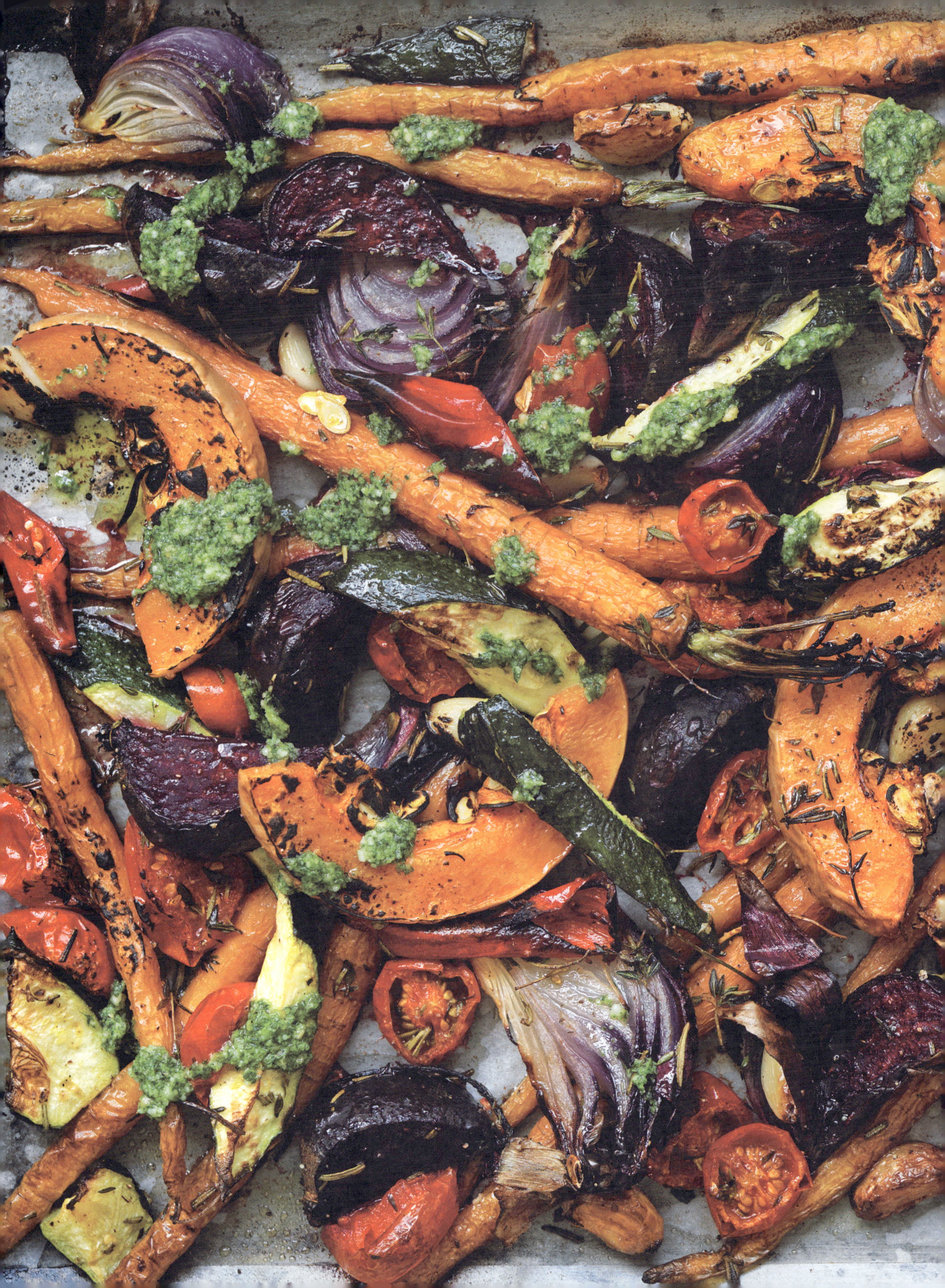

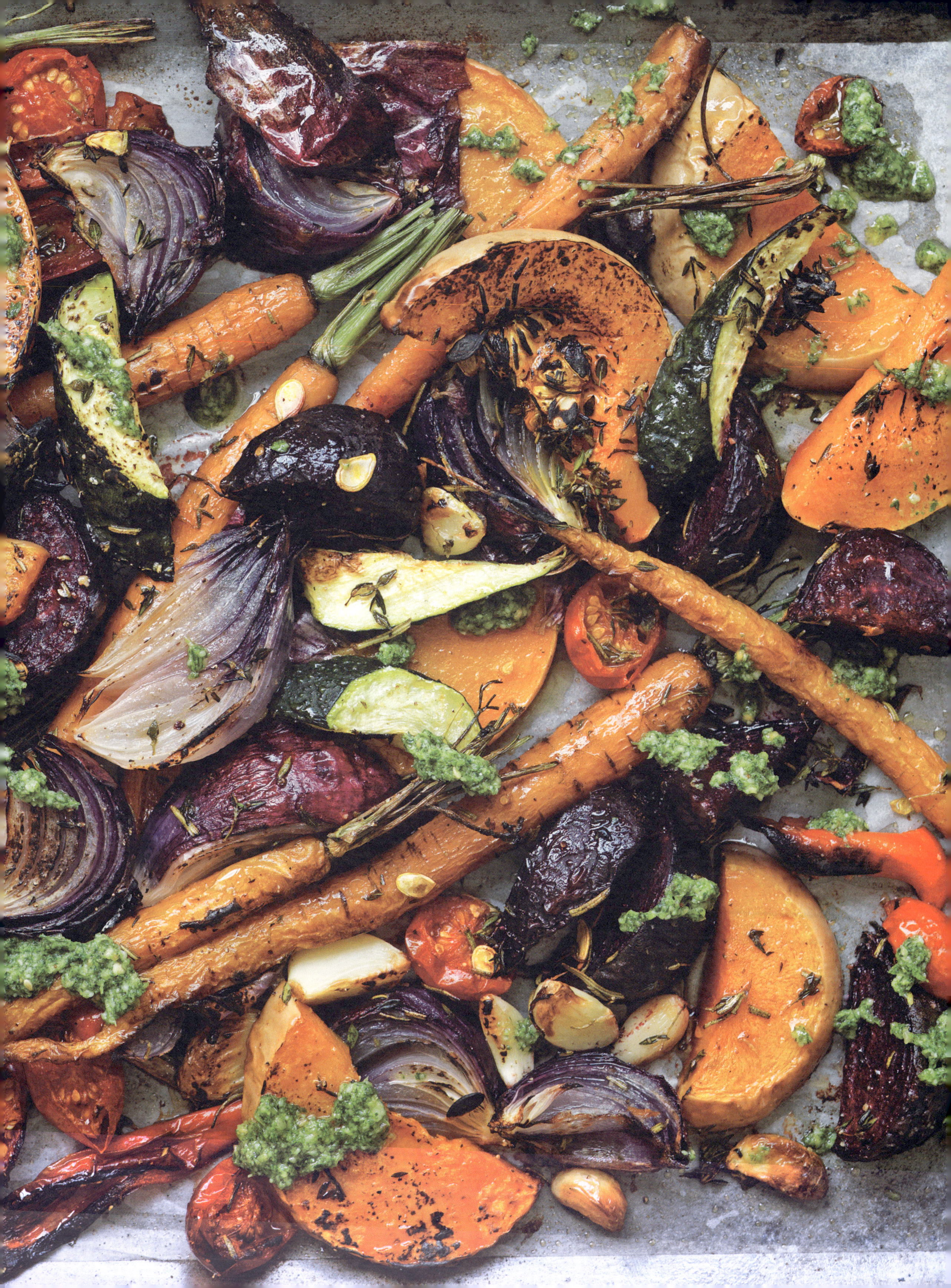

in the GARDEN

Before it was a garden, the backyard of the Blue Ducks, was a rubbish dump. An industrial nachos, stuffed with timber offcuts, chipped bricks and waste from the construction of the restaurant. Initially, we wanted a little patch of garden where we could put a table for twelve to use as additional seating. It was an aesthetic initiative to change the ugly space into a communal area.

If there had been a 'frequent dumpers' card issued by the local tip, we'd be up for a free visit. Even now, a session of weeding dredges up pieces of metal and old bottles. A few friends began pottering and planting and it quickly became a heaving bed of seedlings. The garden really changed shape, however, in the hands of Mark's brother, Grant LaBrooy. He'd been building steak sangas in the kitchen for about a year before a natural interest led him to the study of gardening and permaculture. Grant took over the garden and immediately saw the potential of the space, first as a natural composter of the green waste coming out of the restaurant, and then later, as an urban mini farm. The philosophy behind this fitted in with our desire for the restaurant to become more sustainable.

The Ducks' backyard garden is about 15 x 8 metres, and north facing, so the sun shines on it for most of the day. The garden design definitely changed as Grant's knowledge increased. The beds that featured in the very first layout were scuttled in favour of a whole garden plot that takes up virtually the entire space, and is divided into beds by wooden sleepers. This design has more space and is easier to access. For a while it seemed that every new permaculture course Grant took saw the upheaval and re-design of the garden. He remained steadfast in his loyalty to his own process though, and five re-re-landscapes later, he's got a fat green thumb and we have a backyard oasis.

Overlooking the garden is a big cow skull we found on a farm in Grafton; it sits high over the tomatoes at the end of the patch and keeps an eye on things. We had a small hope that it would scare off predators on the hunt for a leafy snack or a chook, but in reality it probably scares the staff more than the birds. Undeterred by the skull, foraging animals nibble through the garden at leisure while flocks of rosellas are concealed by the fertile camouflage of strawberries, rainbow chard and Warrigal greens.

We wanted to extend the garden to the restaurant, to make it feel wild and untamed, so we went to the local hardware store and bought about thirty little terracotta pots and planted basil, coriander, rosemary and micro herbs in them and then fastened the pots to the brick walls. A few Saturdays later, I watched a woman pick leaves of basil from one of the pots, tear it into slivers, and sprinkle it on her scrambled eggs. Either we have created a new phenomenon of interactive dining, or we didn't season the eggs enough!

The grand plan for the garden

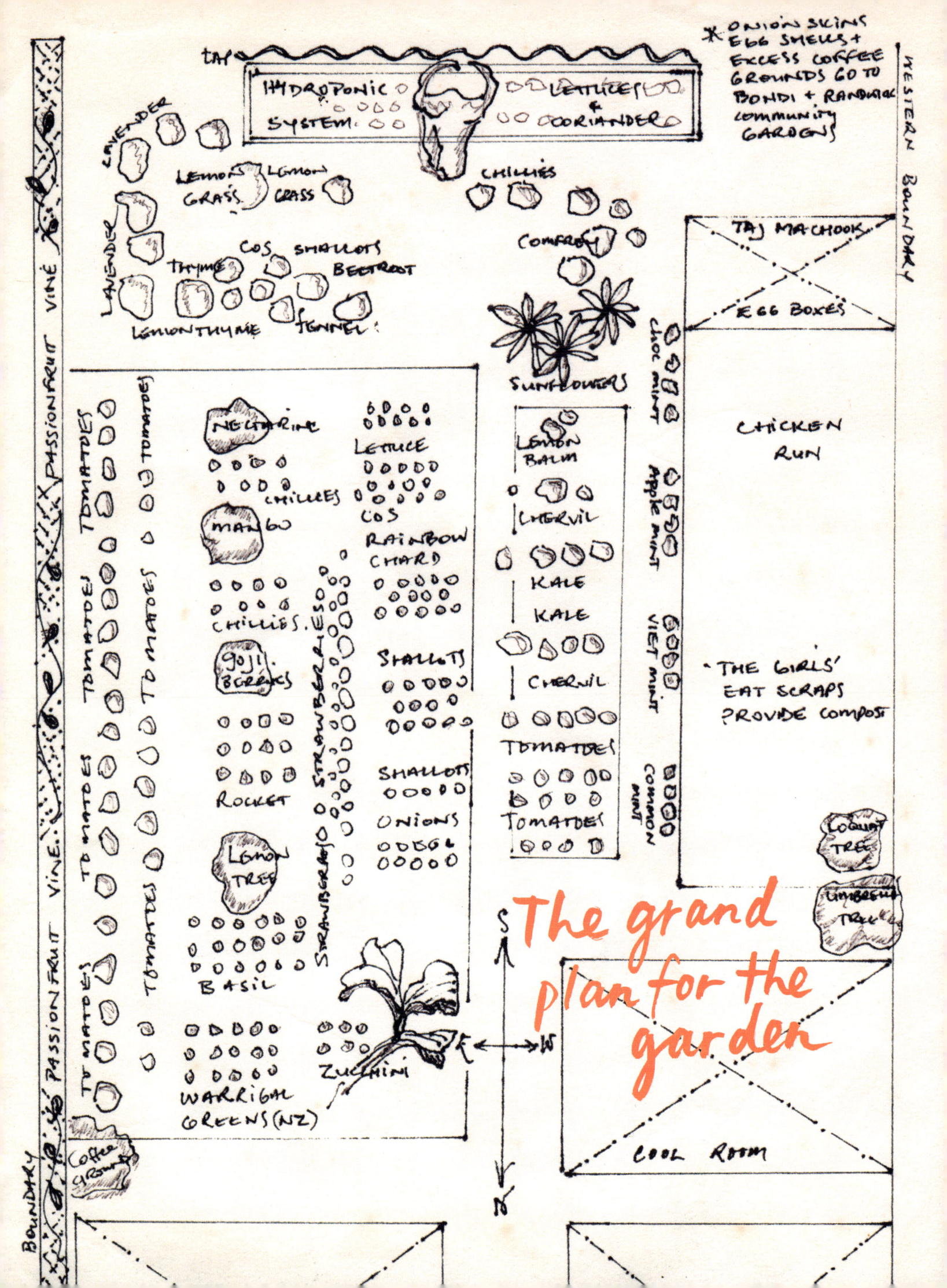

Of course, for all undercover plants, there is the responsibility to water them regularly. In the beginning, we put empty buckets along the ground underneath the roof, so that when it rained the water ran off the drains into the buckets and we could droozle it on the garden and into the pots. Now, we have tanks that we can use to water all the plants.

PLANT AND SOIL, GARDENER AND SITE
The first essential relationship in gardening is between the plant and the soil. The other essential relationship is that between the gardener and the site. Whether it is acreage, a small backyard patch, a balcony, a windowsill or a single terracotta pot, the gardener has to make decisions about what to plant, where and when to plant. The gardener uses the site, as well as the science of soil, sun, shade and season to design a plot that balances function and beauty. But the relationship between gardener and garden is ultimately an experiment.

Grant has spent months getting to know the garden, befriending it, working out its quirks. He has coerced kale and reasoned with strawberries; however, like a lot of relationships, it remains unpredictable. For example, we have a broad bean trellis at the front of the garden, but it faces directly north and so acts as a shadow barrier to the plants behind it. Instead, we need them running in lines north to south, so they only cast shade on each other. We want it to become a solid self-sustaining system, capable of maintaining itself by its own efforts. That is the endgame. Of course, for a while the inputs will far outweigh the outputs.

In the beginning, we spread organic waste from the kitchen with abandon. We assumed it was rotting into potent fertiliser sludge, but we underestimated how delicate the balance is. We'd been using the garden as a composter for the excess coffee; however, 50 kilograms of coffee grounds a week started to contaminate the garden. Instead of sustenance it became a pollutant. We've started sending coffee grounds, like our excess green restaurant waste, to local community gardens.

We use the garden every day. We pick fennel pollen, nasturtium and zucchini flowers for garnishing, and basil for pesto. If the season is right and the stars and worms align, we'll yield a proper bounty of produce. A while back the rainbow chard went crazy and we put a dish on the menu with rainbow chard and beetroot puree with blue-eye. Two years ago, the tomatoes ran rampant and we made a huge batch of green tomato relish that went on the steak sandwiches. It seems right making the most of what's in season, and the food is always tastier too.

FIG, WALNUT *and* GOAT'S CHEESE SALAD

4 handfuls of baby spinach
½ red onion, finely sliced
400 g green beans, topped, tailed and blanched
150 g walnuts
sea salt and cracked pepper
8 figs, cut into quarters
150 g goat's cheese, crumbled

LEMON DRESSING
1 teaspoon Dijon mustard
2 teaspoons honey
juice and zest of 2 lemons
about 75 ml grapeseed oil

This is a great summer salad and looks amazing. Figs only have a short season so take advantage of them when you can. If you're buying them, choose fruit that's plump and soft. Better still, ask if any of your friends have a fig tree and pick them fresh.

To make the dressing put all the ingredients into a bowl and whisk together. Taste and add more oil if you need to.

Put the spinach, onion, beans and walnuts in a large bowl. Season with salt and pepper, add a good splash of lemon dressing and toss until coated.

Arrange the salad on a platter, scatter the figs and goat's cheese on top and serve.

SERVES 4

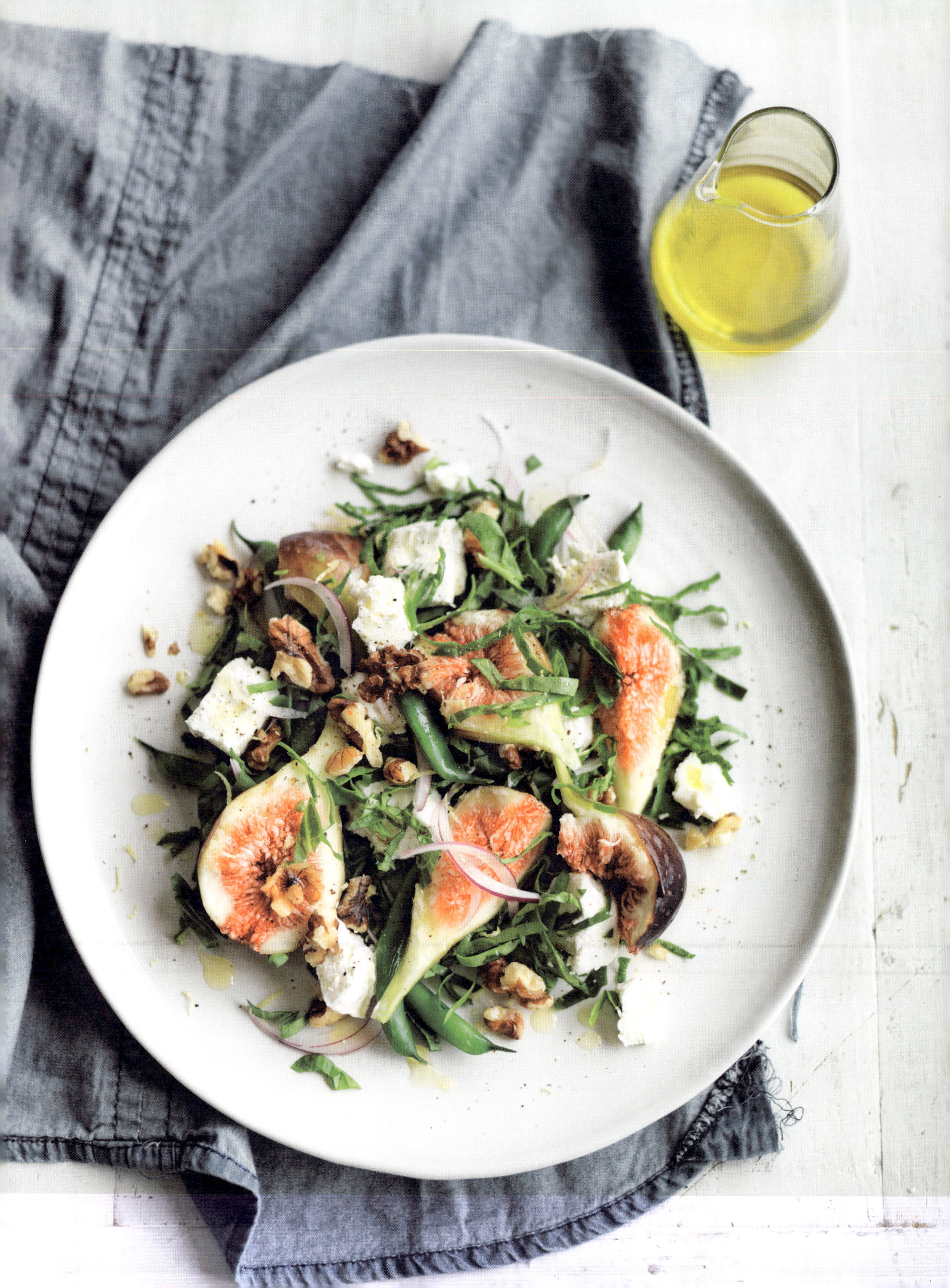

WINTER BRUSSELS SPROUTS *with* ROASTED CHESTNUTS

4 garlic cloves, roughly chopped
2 medium-sized red onions, finely chopped
6 rashers bacon, diced
1 kg Brussels sprouts, trimmed and halved
1 tablespoon olive oil
salt and pepper
1 tablespoon balsamic reduction (available from supermarkets)
200 g peeled roasted chestnuts
1 bunch of flat-leaf parsley, roughly chopped

This is a really nice dish to have in winter when Brussels sprouts are at their best. The chestnuts remind me of winters in Switzerland, where you can buy freshly roasted chestnuts on the street. Choose the smaller sprouts as they are usually a bit sweeter in flavour. Try serving this with crisp-skinned barramundi – it's a top combination.

Put the garlic, onion and bacon in a large heavy-based frying pan over medium heat and stir-fry until the onion is soft and the bacon starts to have some good caramel tones and is starting to go crisp.

Preheat the oven to 200°C.

Toss the sprouts in the olive oil, season with salt and pepper, place on a baking tray, drizzle with the balsamic reduction, add the chestnuts and bake for 15 minutes, or until the sprouts are soft in the middle and a bit crispy on the outside.

Remove the sprouts and chestnuts from the oven, tip them into a serving bowl, add the onion and bacon, fold in the parsley and serve.

TO ROAST CHESTNUTS
Heat the oven to 180°C. Pierce the chestnuts and put in the oven for 5 minutes, toss, then put them back in for another 5 minutes. Let them cool a little then peel.

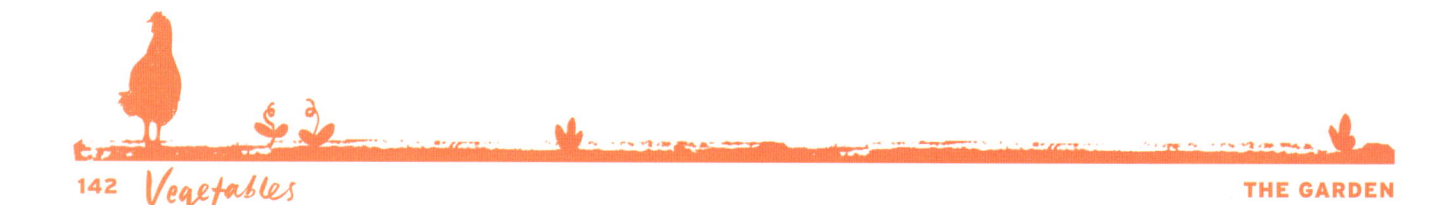

SERVES 6

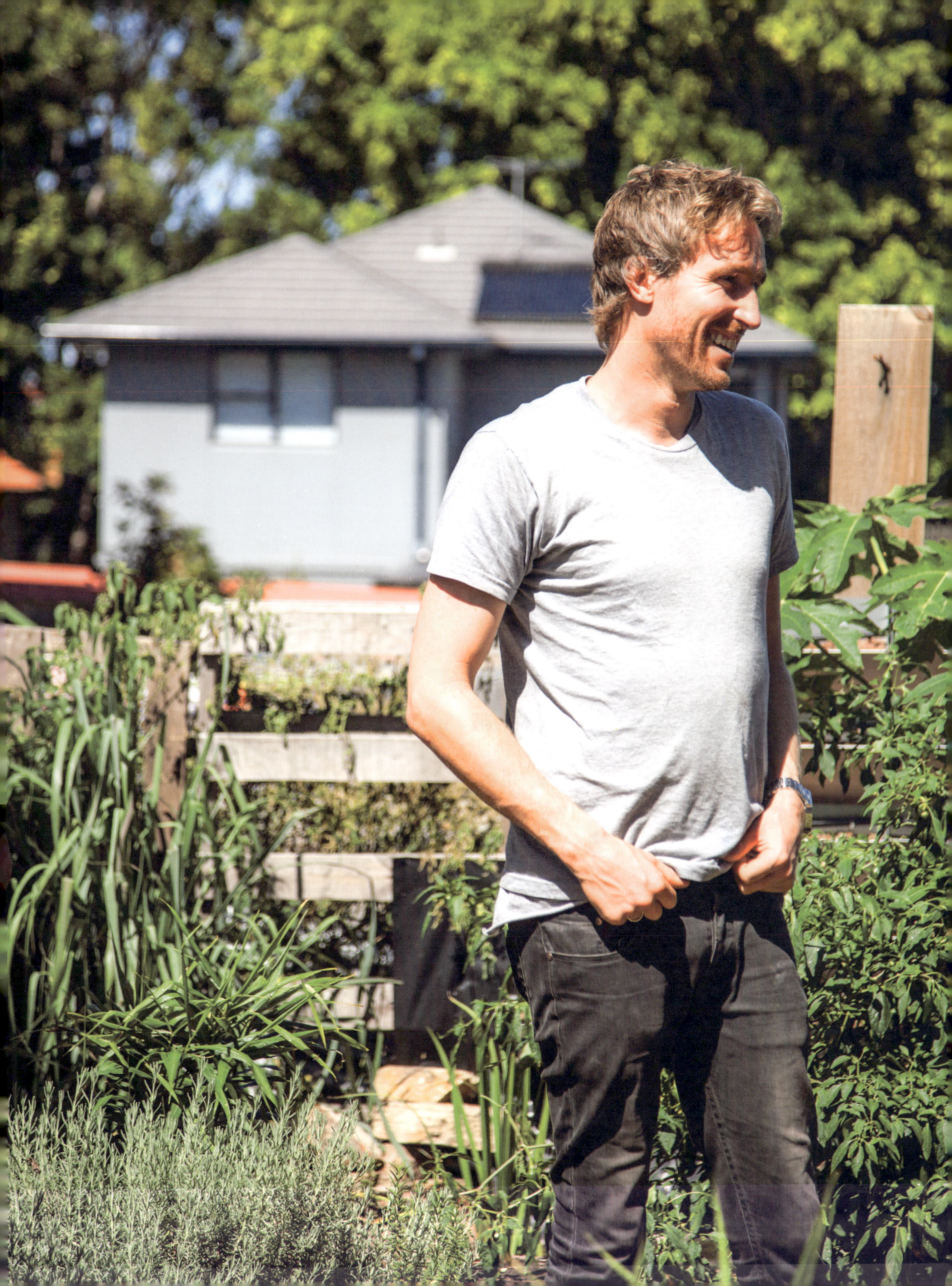

Keeping BEES

Bees are much maligned, which seems unfair as they are industrious and diligent, not aggressive by nature, and produce delicious golden honey and beeswax. They are also essential for cross-pollination. In fact, bees carry out almost 80 per cent of all pollination, playing a key role in agriculture, creating robust food crops and flourishing backyard gardens.

In a relatively recent phenomenon referred to as Colony Collapse Disorder, which has occurred since 2001, whole colonies of bees have literally disappeared. It's been speculated that one possible reason is the increased use of pesticides and chemicals on rural crops. As bees collect pollen from plants that have been sprayed, they also collect minute amounts of the chemical pesticides. The poisoned material is gradually built into their hive and stored in their wax. Eventually the hive becomes toxic to the bees and they die. As people in the city are less likely to spray their gardens with chemicals, urban areas are, ironically, the ideal place to have honeybees. Sydney in particular is prime humming terrain, as it has trees bearing flowers all year round. A single female bee can visit as many as 17 flowers per minute! Bees gather pollen in a 10 kilometre radius from the hive, so in suburban gardens bees tend to be exposed to a wider variety of plants than they would in rural areas on single-crop acreage. Urban honey reflects this multitude of flowering plants with a surprisingly delicate and full flavour.

We knew we had the space at the Ducks, and we had a sense of responsibility hearing about the current fate of bees, so we acquired a hive, put it in the garden of the restaurant, and introduced a swarm to it.

If you are interested in keeping bees yourself, you can source a beehive and its components from local and rural suppliers. Your local beekeeping association will be able to give you information, or you can check out publications such as the Australasian Beekeepers Journal. Creating a bee-friendly environment in your own backyard simply means planting a variety of species that flower at different times. Generally, native plants attract native bees and introduced species attract honeybees. However, a bounteous backyard is not essential, because the beauty of urban beekeeping is that far from requiring helicopter parenting, bees have an inherent wanderlust and seek out pollen and nectar outside the backyard.

There are local council laws restricting the number of hives, so we started with one, to be safe. If you keep one or more hives of honeybees in New South Wales you are required to be registered as a beekeeper with the NSW Department of Primary Industries. Another consideration, particularly with urban beekeeping, is your neighbours. Almost everyone can recall a time when they were stung by a bee, maybe as a child running through the grass, or maybe like Mark, playing cricket in the front yard and picking up a stinger on the way through a fast bowl. A concerned neighbour can usually be turned with an olive branch in the form of raw honey delivered to their doorstep!

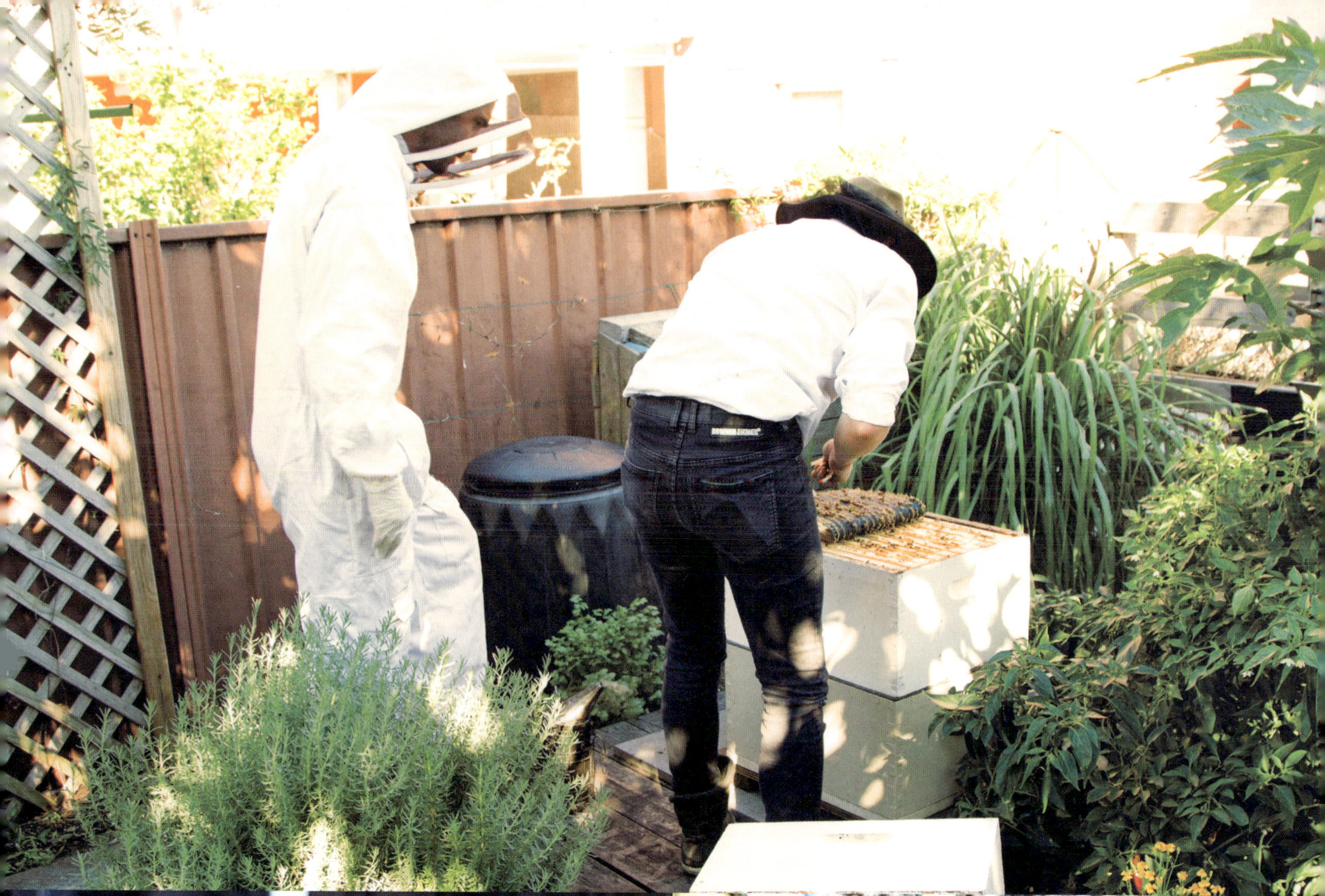

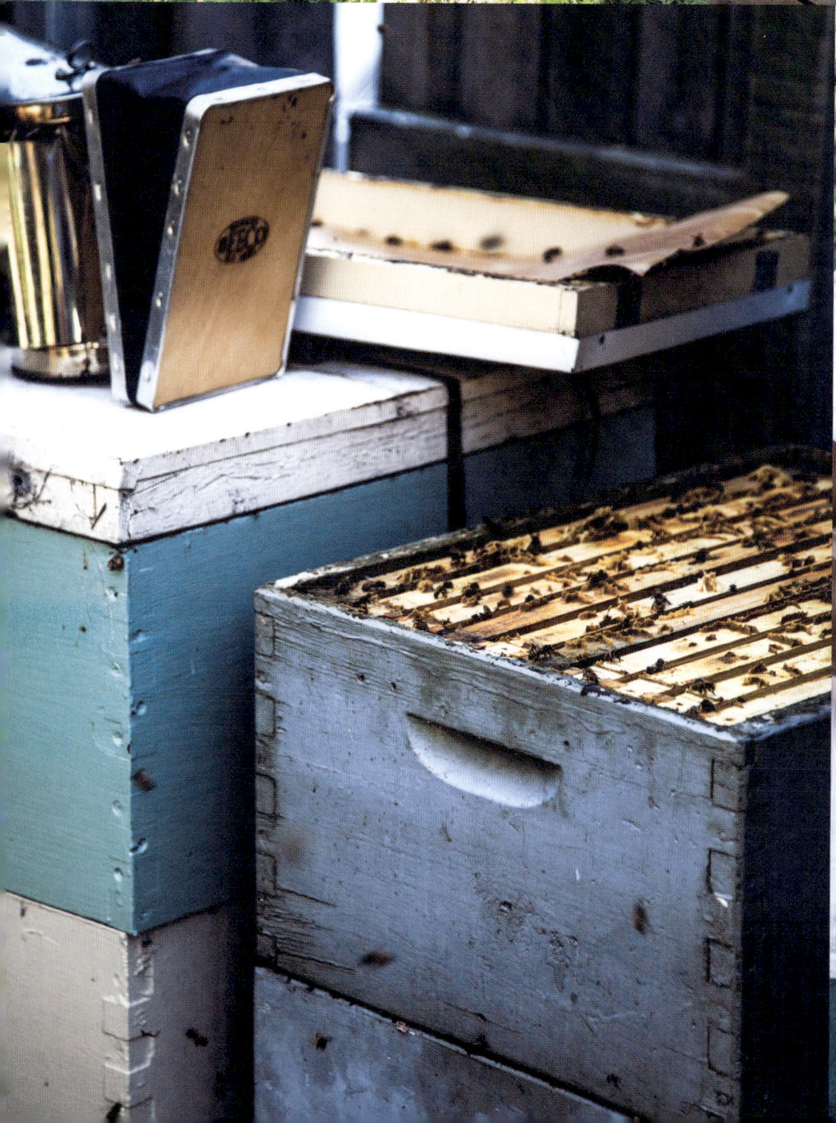

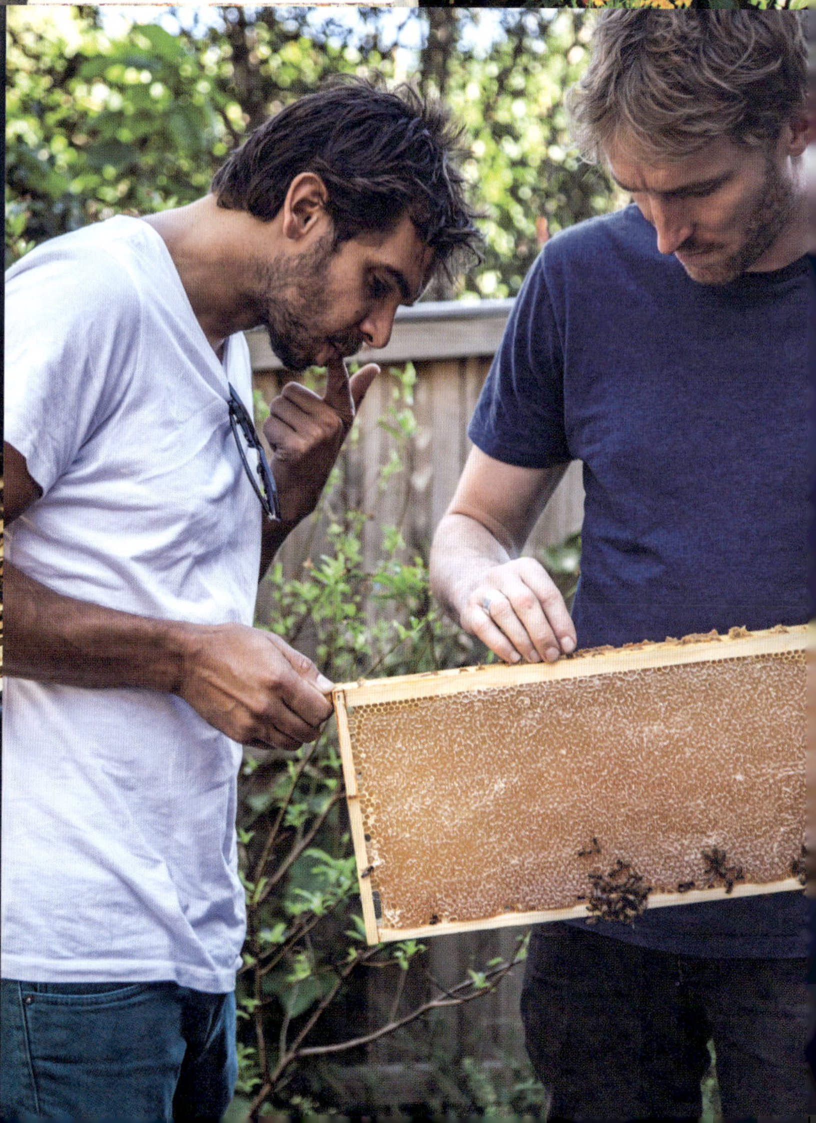

WHERE WILL YOU KEEP THE HIVE?
- Keep the hive in a dry, sunny position, out of the wind. If possible, place the hive away from human traffic areas.
- Don't put the hive between you and a water source; bees use water to control the temperature in the hive and so, particularly in summer, they seek out water.
- Don't face the hive entrance towards an outside light, as the light will attract the bees when it's on.
- Keep the hive elevated from the ground, to protect it from foraging animals like dogs, foxes and chickens.
- It's a good idea to keep your hive behind a hedge, a high fence, or even a garage. This makes the bees fly up and away when leaving the hive. Then when returning, they will enter from above, so aren't flying at human height.

Compared to keeping chickens, having bees is a holiday. They don't require daily attention, and they are almost entirely self-sustaining. In fact, aside from the initial setup period, if a hive is working well, it shouldn't even be touched until time of harvest. Disturbing the bees sets back production and the overall success of the hive. Although cursory checks are important, they need not be carried out frequently. The companies that supply your hive will usually also send someone to safely rob your hive of honey, so you don't upset the bees or aggravate the Queen and find yourself on the wrong end of a stinger.

At least in the beginning, hiring professional hive robbers is probably safest. Via firsthand observation, you can quickly gain important knowledge. For example, bees are cold blooded and their flight and activity increases on warm sunny days as compared to cool, overcast days. Furthermore, the older field bees are the aggressive members of the hive. So, it's usually best to check your hive on warm, sunny days when the field bees will be out working, compared to cold, overcast days when most of the field bees will be home making the hive more aggressive. The very best part of bees, of course, is their honey. Honey is a superfood; jam-packed with nutrients, its floral origins make it a natural fortifier against seasonal allergies, and it is naturally antimicrobial, which means it eliminates bacteria. Not to mention, it's a deliciously syrupy alternative to sugar. We go through 6¬–10 litres of honey every week, which we use to sweeten tea, muesli, pancakes, ice cream and dressings. Annually we collect about 30–40 litres of virgin honey from one healthy hive, which has about 20,000–60,000 bees. This is enough to sustain at least one honey-based dessert on the menu. Potentially the dessert will always taste different too, as the bees are always collecting from different flowers, in keeping with the seasonal flavour philosophy of the Ducks.

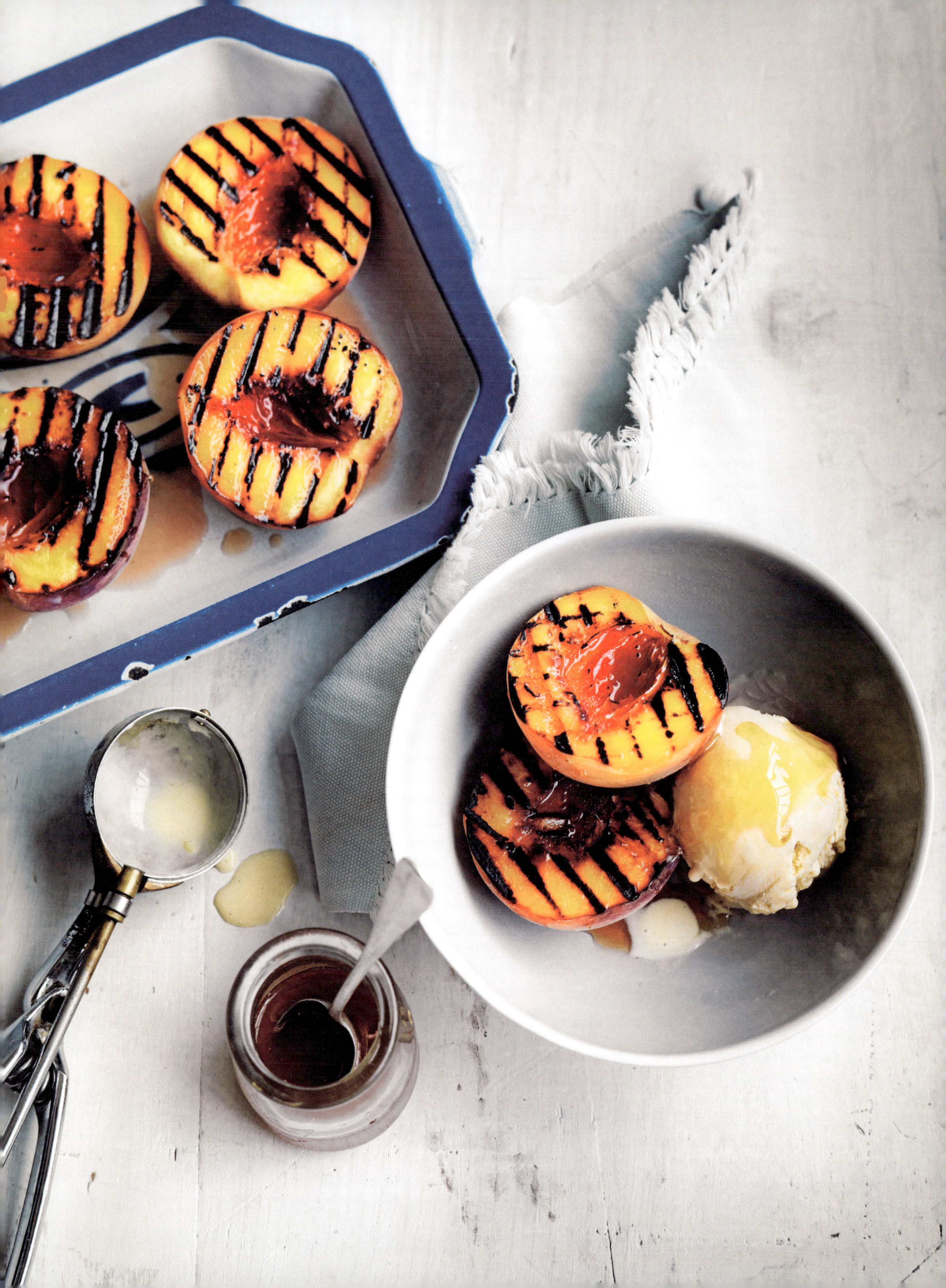

CHAR-GRILLED HONEY PEACHES with VANILLA and ROSEMARY ICE CREAM

If you can't get your hands on ripe peaches try char-grilling pineapple, or pears, figs, bananas or apples. Have a play with the ice cream flavours too – replace the rosemary with lemongrass, star anise, lemon verbena, kaffir lime or liquorice root.

In a large bowl, whisk the egg yolks and sugar together until pale and creamy. Put the milk, cream, vanilla, rosemary and glucose in a saucepan, bring almost to the boil, take off the heat and pour over the yolks while whisking. (Make sure your milk is not too hot or you will curdle the egg mixture.) Return this mixture to the pan, then gently cook while stirring, until it thickens slightly to a consistency that coats the back of a wooden spoon. Strain into a bowl, chill the mixture then churn in an ice cream machine.

To make the peaches, put the char-grill on high heat. Grill the peaches, flat side down, for 2 minutes on the hot grill, turn over, drizzle with the honey, nutmeg and salt, and cook for another minute. Put the peaches in a large bowl, and serve with lots of vanilla and rosemary ice cream.

SERVES 4

4 ripe peaches, halved and stones removed
2 tablespoons honey
pinch of freshly grated nutmeg
pinch of salt

VANILLA AND ROSEMARY ICE CREAM
8 egg yolks
180 g caster sugar
750 ml milk
380 ml cream
1 vanilla pod, split lengthways, seeds scraped
4 sprigs rosemary
30 ml liquid glucose

THE GARDEN

FIGS, BLUE CHEESE and HONEYCOMB

4 fresh figs
200 g good-quality Australian blue cheese or Stilton (UK) or Fourme d'Ambert (France)
50 g honeycomb (page 152)
50 g walnuts, toasted
crackers

A cheese plate is a great way to end a meal, and one of our new favourites has to be Sapphire Blue. It's a hand-made, semi-hard blue cheese made from sheep's milk in Tasmania. Soft yet crumbly, with a slightly spicy-sweet flavour, it goes perfectly with fresh figs and real honeycomb.

Break apart the figs and serve with a generous amount of blue cheese, a good chunk of honeycomb, toasted nuts and crackers.

SERVES 4-6

BANANAS, MILK and HONEY

3 bananas, peeled
400 ml milk
1 tablespoon honey
zest and juice of ½ lime
8 mint leaves
50 g ice

A really refreshing and super easy drink for the summer. Use ripe bananas for maximum sweetness.

Put all the ingredients in a blender, whizz until it's chilled and frothy, and serve in tall glasses.

MAKES 4 GLASSES

CHRISO'S CHAI TEA *and* GARDEN HONEY

This is a lovely little pick-me-up, especially during winter. If you prefer a chai latte, simply reduce this tea to a syrup and add warmed milk.

Put all the ingredients except the tea leaves and honey into a saucepan. Bring to the boil, then lower the heat and simmer, uncovered, for 5 minutes. Leave it to steep for 10 minutes.

Add the tea leaves to the pan and bring to the boil again, then turn off and steep for another 5 minutes.

Strain the mixture and add honey – this is your chai blend.

You can keep your chai blend in the fridge for up to 4 weeks.

MAKES ENOUGH FOR 12 CUPS

5 green cardamom pods
10 whole cloves
1 teaspoon fennel seeds, roasted
2 star anise
1 cinnamon stick
20 g fresh ginger, thinly sliced
2 bay leaves
1 pinch of whole black peppercorns
2 small pieces dried orange peel
1 litre water
3 tablespoons Ceylon tea leaves
6 tablespoons honey

FOR CHAI LATTE
hot milk, to serve

LAVENDER HONEYCOMB

325 g sugar
50 g honey
50 ml liquid glucose
30 ml water
15 g bicarbonate of soda
4 lavender buds, chopped

This is fun to make. There's a real mad scientist feel when the bicarbonate of soda goes into the sugar mix, causing a 'volcanic' reaction. Be careful though, as the bubbling honeycomb can burn – at around 120°C, it's extremely hot. You also have to watch closely – don't wait until the caramel is too dark before adding the bicarbonate of soda as the sugar will continue to cook after removing it from the heat and your honeycomb will have a burnt flavour.

Allow plenty of room to work and spread baking paper on a large baking tray ready for the hot honeycomb mixture.

Put the sugar, honey, glucose and water into a large saucepan. Place over high heat and stir occasionally until the sugar melts. When the sugar mixture starts to caramelise and becomes a pale golden colour, add the bicarbonate of soda and lavender and stir quickly until there are no more lumps (10 seconds), then pour onto the baking paper on the bench. The mixture will triple in volume and will be extremely hot. Don't touch it – it will burn.

Leave the honeycomb to sit for about 20 minutes until it cools down. When it has cooled, break into it chunks and store in an airtight container.

To clean the pan, fill it with hot water and let it sit for 10 minutes. The remaining honeycomb will melt away.

MAKES 500 G

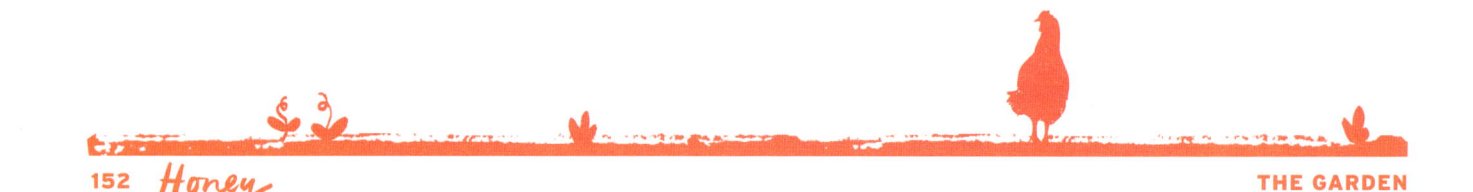

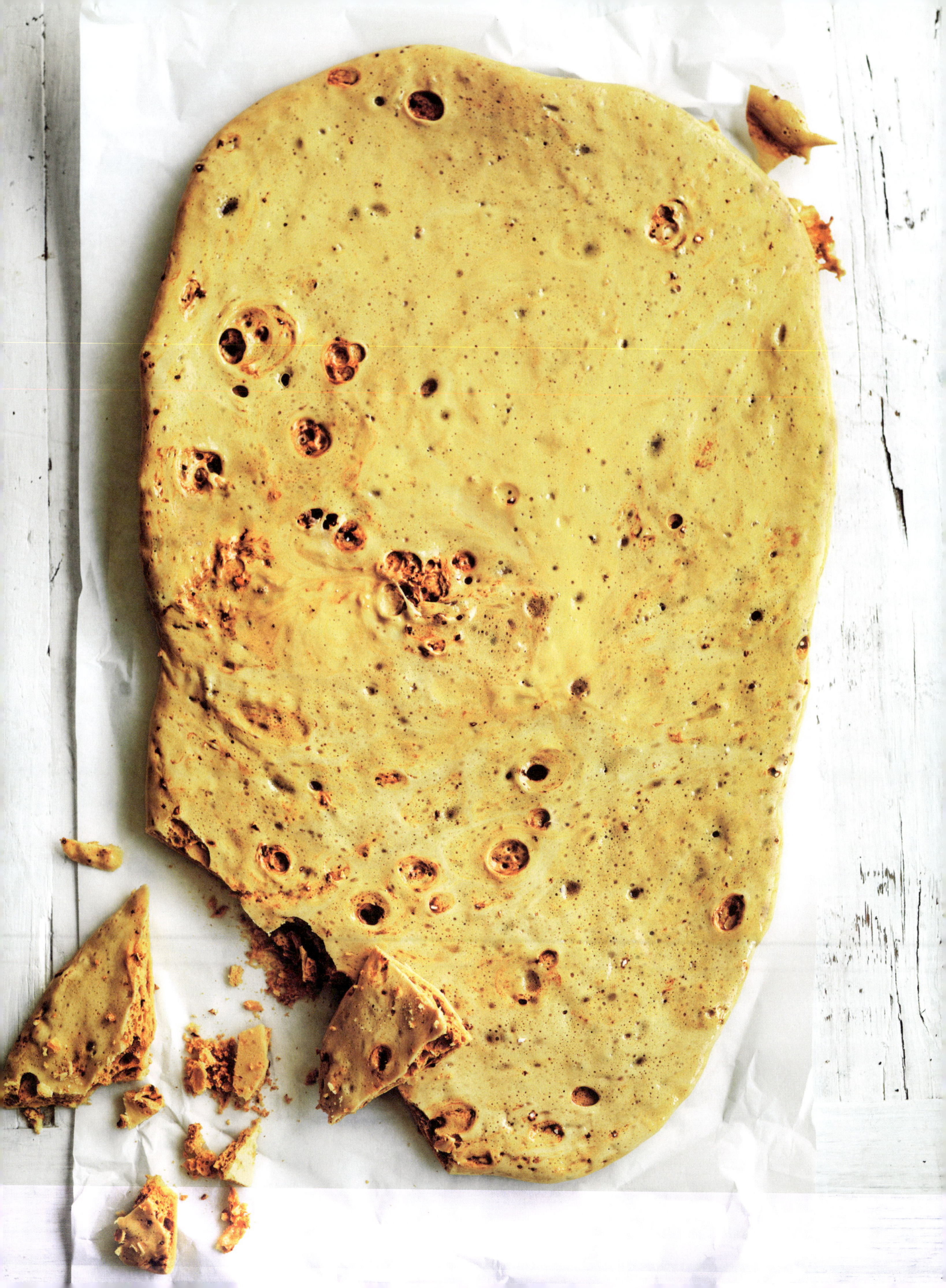

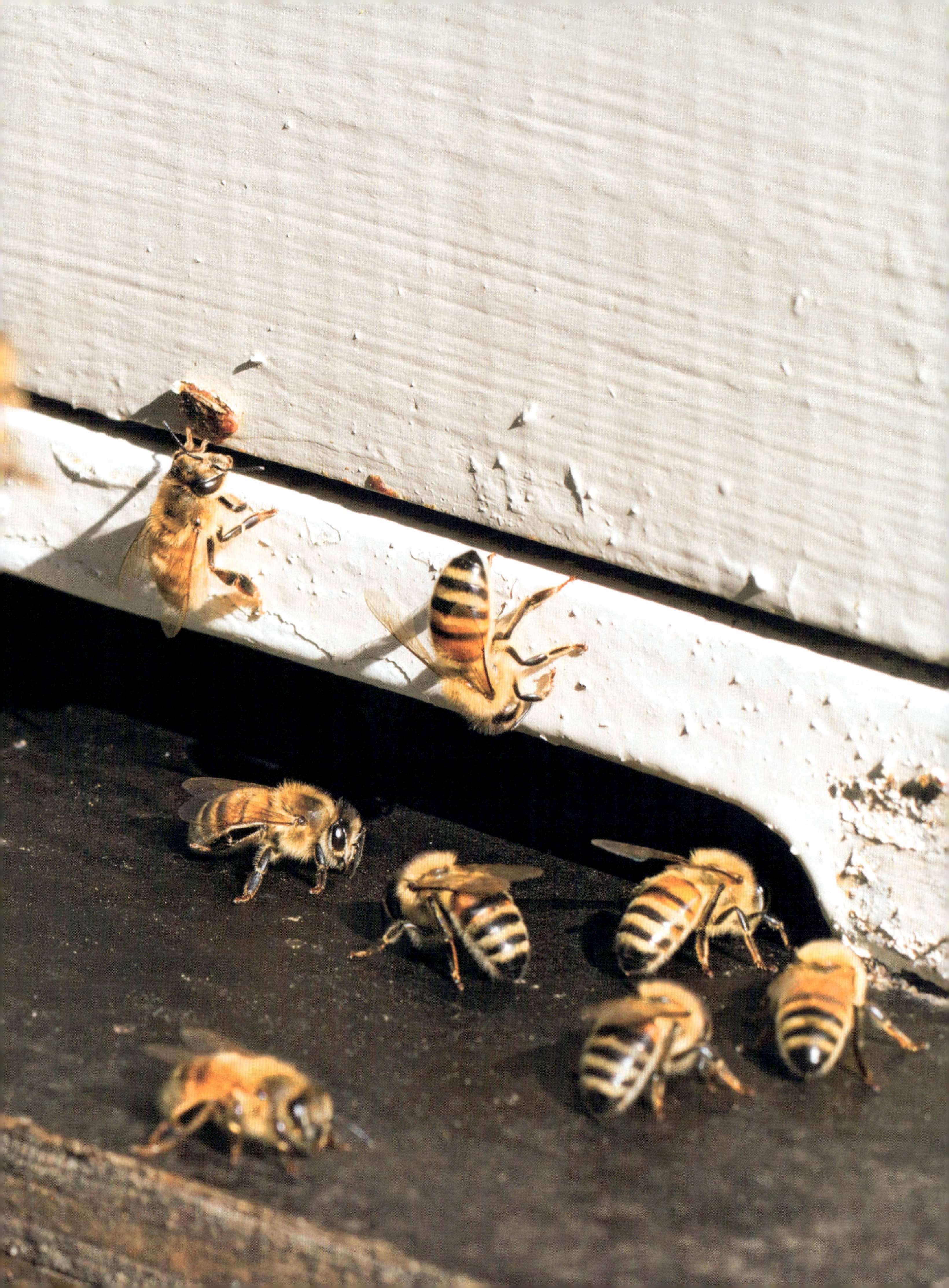

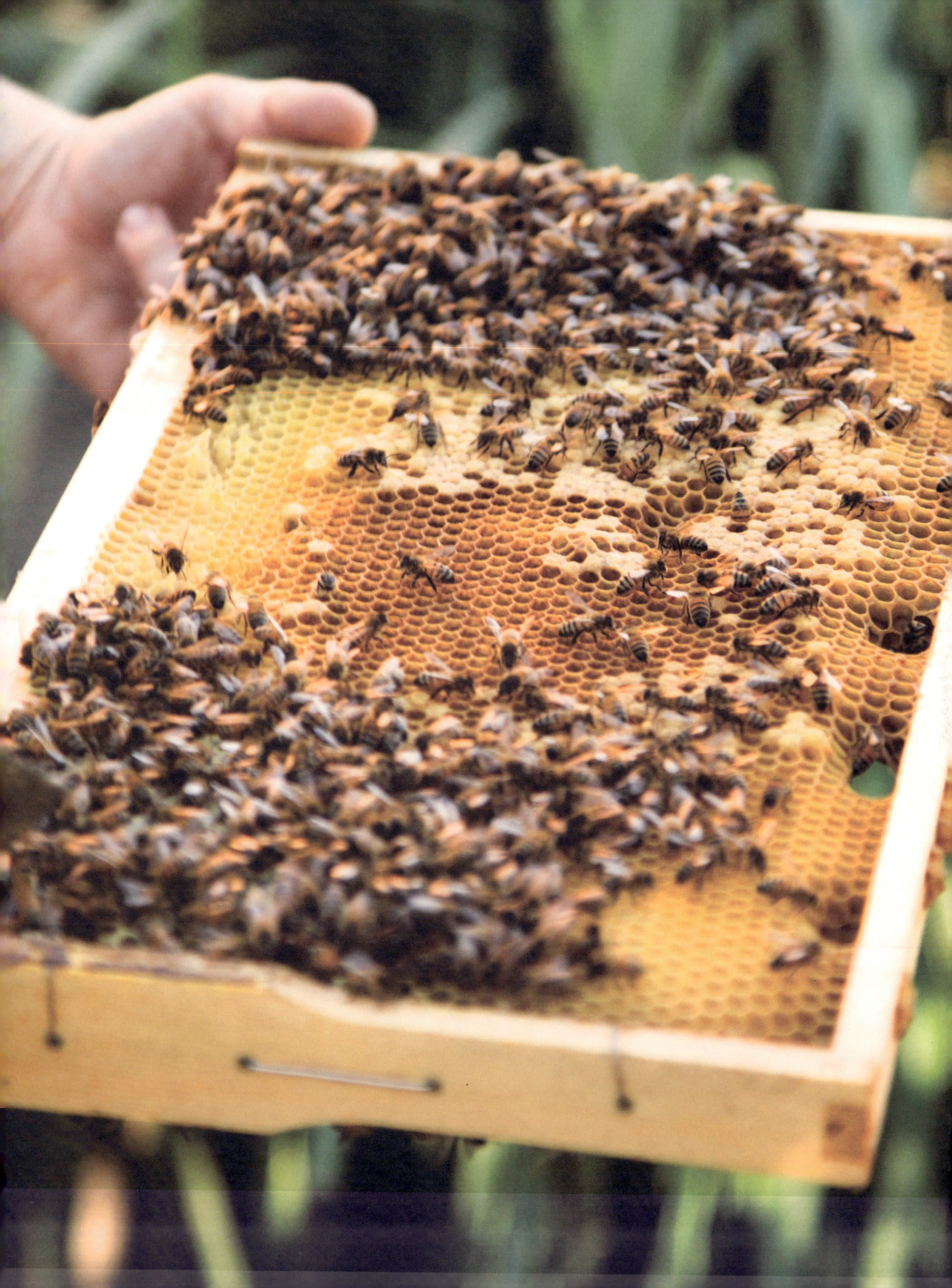

Savoury PRESERVES

These preserves are delicious with charcuterie, cheeses and the chilli jam works well with seafood.

Pickled Baby radishes

50 ml rice wine vinegar
1 teaspoon caster sugar
1 teaspoon salt
200 g baby radishes, washed and halved

Warm the vinegar, sugar, and salt and set aside.

Pour the dressing over the radishes and leave in a sealed jar in the refrigerator for 24 hours.

FILLS A 300 ML JAR

Baby carrots with star anise

400 ml rice wine vinegar
50 g caster sugar
1 bay leaf
1 star anise
300 g of baby carrots

Warm the vinegar, sugar and spices in a saucepan. Leave to cool.

Clean and trim the carrots, place in a container, cover with the cooled brine and leave in the refrigerator for 24 hours to pickle.

FILLS A 750 ML JAR

Pickled Red Onion

1 tablespoon peppercorns
1 bay leaf
1 lemon, halved
1 tablespoon sugar
3 tablespoons apple cider vinegar
½ cup water
1 red onion, sliced 5 mm thick
1 medium-sized bowl of ice

To make the pickling solution, place all the ingredients, except the water, onion and ice, in a small bowl and mix well. The sugar should dissolve into the vinegar in a few minutes. Set aside.

Pour the water into a medium-sized saucepan and bring to the boil. Make sure you have the ice ready close by. Drop the sliced onion into the boiling water for 25 seconds, strain and place the onion in the ice immediately.

When the onion has cooled, strain and place in the pickling solution.

Serve the onion with meats and cheeses. It will last a few days in the fridge but is always better fresh before it starts to loose its crunch.

FILLS A 250-300 ML JAR

Pickled celery and mustard seeds

400 ml rice wine vinegar
70 g caster sugar
1 teaspoon red mustard seeds
1 teaspoon coriander seeds, roasted
1 star anise
5 celery stalks, peeled

Warm the vinegar, sugar and spices in a saucepan. Leave to cool.

Cut the celery into batons, place in a container, cover with the cooled brine and leave in the refrigerator for 24 hours to pickle.

FILLS A 750 ML JAR

Chilli Jam

See overleaf for recipe >

CHILLI JAM

100 ml vegetable oil
25 long red chillies, seeded
2 garlic cloves, chopped
2 large knobs of ginger, chopped (skin on is fine)
1 bunch of lemongrass (about 6 stalks), outer leaves removed, stalks finely chopped
roots only from 2 bunches of coriander, well washed and chopped
250 g French shallots, chopped
250 g palm sugar, grated
150 ml fish sauce
100 ml sweet soy sauce (kecap manis)

This is seriously a must-have in the kitchen. We use it on just about everything ... roast chicken ... lamb ... on sandwiches ... in salad dressings ...

Place a large saucepan over high heat, add the oil and all the other ingredients and fry, stirring occasionally for 15–20 minutes, or until the chillies become translucent. If it becomes too dry, add a little warm water.

When the mixture is bright red in colour, pour into a food processor and blend to make a chunky paste. Pour the jam straight into clean jars while still very hot.

Put a lid on each jar, turn upside down for 15 seconds then place upright again.

Place the jars in the refrigerator. If you have done it correctly, you should have an air-locked jar, which will make a pop sound when you unscrew the lid.

This will last about 6 months if you keep it stored in the fridge.

MAKES ABOUT 2 CUPS

OVEN-DRIED TOMATOES

This is a very satisfying way to preserve a bumper crop of tomatoes at the end of summer or a big buy at a local farmers' market. When they're dried, you can pack them in a jar with olive oil and herbs, or whizz them in the blender for a tasty pasta sauce.

Preheat the oven to 200°C. Line a baking tray with baking paper.

Place the tomatoes on a baking tray, skin-side down, with a thin slice of garlic on each half. Sprinkle with rosemary, thyme, salt and pepper and drizzle with the oil.

Transfer the tray to the oven and roast for 18 minutes, then turn down to 60°C and leave overnight.

Remove the dried tomatoes from the oven.

MAKES 5-6 PORTIONS

5 ripe tomatoes, halved horizontally
2 garlic cloves, thinly sliced
6 sprigs rosemary, finely chopped
6 sprigs thyme, finely chopped
teaspoon each tomato salt and cracked pepper
about 2 tablespoons good olive oil

PICKLED CUCUMBERS

People tend to love or hate pickles. If you love them, here's how to make your own. If you're a hater, try making them and you'll see that it's not hard. They make a refreshing side dish for smoked meats, rillettes and liver parfaits. They're also good tossed into a salad for some extra crunch.

Warm the vinegar, sugar, salt and seeds and set aside. Cut the cucumber into large chunks and put into a bowl. Pour the dressing over the cucumber and serve.

FILLS A 250 ML JAR

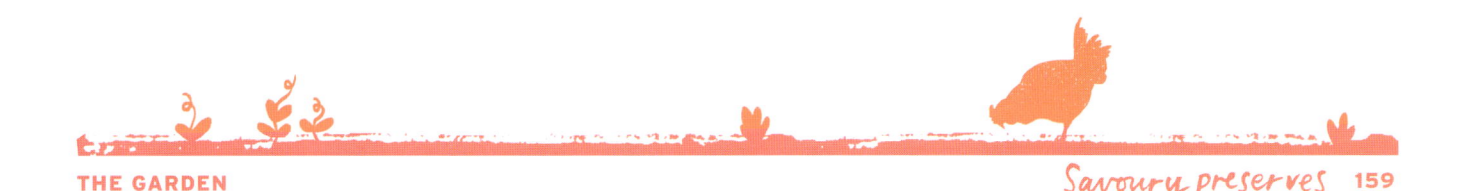

50 ml rice wine vinegar
1 teaspoon caster sugar
1 teaspoon salt
1 teaspoon poppy seeds
1 teaspoon mustard seeds
1 telegraph cucumber

Sweet PRESERVES

Make jam. It's easy, especially when fruit is in season and cheap at your local fruit shop – the flavour combinations are almost endless. Spread your jam on toast, a generous slab of chewy sourdough or soft brioche.

One of the keys to making jam is to get the right consistency for it to set naturally. The pectin in fruit is what helps it set, but different fruits have different levels of pectin. If the jam is too runny, you will need to use a setting agent such as xanthum, agar agar, pectin or good old-fashioned jam-setter. Citrus fruits, some berries and apples all have high levels of pectin. You can add natural ingredients for setting, such as lemon juice and apple cores, which both have large amounts of pectin.

As a general rule, if you are using soft fruit like berries or apricots, start cooking the jam, then remove the fruit after 10 minutes simmering, add some lemon juice or apple cores and cook the jam to reduce the liquid and thicken it. This doesn't apply to oranges, pineapples, green mangoes or any other hard fruit.

If you prefer a jam that is not too sweet, work on a ratio of 60 per cent fruit to 40 per cent sugar. It may seem like a lot of sugar but it's the sugar that preserves the jam and gives it a longer shelf-life.

BOTTLING YOUR JAM
Use recycled glass jars (not plastic) with tight-fitting lids. If you have a dishwasher, put jars and lids only in the machine and run it on the hottest cycle. This should kill most of the bacteria lurking in the jars. If you don't have a dishwasher, use hot soapy water, rinse well with hot water and leave jars upside to drain.

Apple-berry jam

500 g frozen blueberries
500 g frozen strawberries
500 g frozen black currants
8 granny smith apples, washed, peeled and diced (keep the cores and the peel)
1.2 kg caster sugar
1 vanilla pod, halved lengthways, seeds scraped

Place all the ingredients in a large saucepan over medium–high heat, stir until the sugar is dissolved and bring to the boil. Reduce heat and let simmer for 10 minutes. A lot of juice will come out of the fruit. Use a ladle to remove the fruit from the pan and put it into a strainer over a bowl. If you don't take the fruit out at this stage it will break down during the cooking and you won't have those lovely chunks of fruit in your jam.

Place the apple cores and peel into the fruit syrup in the pan, bring to a simmer and cook until it reduces to a thicker consistency. Check if it is ready by drizzling some on a plate and putting it in the refrigerator. If the jam becomes sticky when cold, it's ready.

Remove the cores and peel, then pour the berries and cooked apples back into the syrup and simmer for 5 minutes.

While the jam is hot (preferably above 90°C), ladle it into jars, wipe the rims clean and put the lids on. Turn the jars upside down for 15 seconds, then turn back. This will kill any bacteria in the neck of the jars. As the jam cools, it will create suction, drawing the lid back into the jar (that's why it pops when you open it). Filling the jars is better done with two people – one to fill, one to screw on the lids and tip the jars.

MAKES 2KG

Orange marmalade

3 kg oranges, thinly sliced, keeping the juice and skins
2 kg caster sugar
2 vanilla pods, split lengthways, seeds scraped
big knob of ginger
1 star anise
1 cinnamon stick
3 whole cloves
2 litres water

In a large saucepan, combine all the ingredients and place on high heat until it reaches the boil. Reduce the heat to low and simmer until the orange becomes soft and most of the water has evaporated, leaving a clear syrupy consistency.

Pour the jam into jars while the marmalade is still hot, seal well and keep in the fridge or pantry. (See Bottling your jam, previous page.)

MAKES 5 KG

Grapefruit marmalade

3 kg grapefruit, thinly sliced, keeping the juice and skins
2 kg caster sugar
2 vanilla pods, split lengthways, seeds scraped
1 star anise
1 cinnamon stick
3 whole cloves
2 litres water

In a large saucepan, combine all of the ingredients on high heat until it reaches the boil. Reduce the heat to a mild simmer, and cook until the grapefruit becomes soft and most of the water has evaporated, leaving a clear syrupy consistency.

Pour into jars while the marmalade is still hot, seal well and keep in the fridge or pantry. (See Bottling your jam, previous page.)

MAKES 5 KG

LEMON CURD

3 egg yolks
5 eggs
210 g caster sugar
juice of 4 lemons
zest of 1 lemon
juice and zest of 1 lime
1 vanilla pod, halved lengthways, seeds scraped
100 g butter

This is perfect as the filling for a lemon meringue tart, or as a spread at breakfast time. It's creamy and rich but the lime just cuts the sweetness.

First of all clean some small jars with lids (wash them in the dishwasher on the hottest setting, then leave to dry).

Lightly beat together the egg yolks, eggs and sugar in a large, heat-proof bowl. Add the juices, zests and vanilla seeds and butter and lightly beat until just combined.

Place a saucepan on the stove, add some water and bring to simmering point. Place the bowl with the egg mixture on top (to make a double-boiler). The base of the bowl must not touch the water.

Stir the egg mixture constantly over medium heat for about 10 minutes until the mixture becomes thick. Be careful not to overheat or the mixture might curdle. If you are using a sugar thermometer, keep the mixture at around 75–80°C.

When the lemon curd is thick and coats the back of a wooden spoon, take the bowl off the heat. Pour the curd into clean, dry jars and cover. Leave to cool, then put in the refrigerator. The curd will firm up more when it is chilled.

The curd should keep for about 2 weeks if sealed and kept in the fridge.

MAKES ABOUT 2 CUPS

Grant loves his chooks

keeping CHOOKS

Yes, it does seem insensitive to have advice on keeping pet chooks in the back garden alongside a roast chicken recipe. But getting eggs from your own chooks is a healthy example of local and sustainable food. And if you're talking food miles, you can't get much closer than back garden to bowl.

For us, the decision to raise chooks came naturally. We love eggs. Poached, scrambled, coddled, baked – we go through 2500 eggs per week. Obviously, the size of the garden at the Ducks was never going to be able to cater for the sheer number of eggs needed commercially each week. It was more a decision in keeping with the ethos of the café. The intention was to use the eggs for staff meals, and the chooks to assist with the organic waste management. In fact, the chooks consume hundreds of kilograms of scraps per year. The majority of the natural waste produced by the restaurant is bagged and taken to community gardens in Bondi to be used as fertiliser, but a significant amount is flung into the chook pen throughout the day. The chickens have gotten plump, spending their days feeding off the fat of the Ducks.

Chooks are by no means impulse-buy animals, particularly if you live in an urban area. There are myriad considerations before you can even begin to plan that first omelette. Local council laws for keeping domestic chickens have to be taken into account during the design and build of the chicken coop. These laws regulate rearing, feeding and sheltering chickens and they tend to vary from council to council. For example, our council restricts the number of backyard chickens allowed to 6–10 per residence, stating that there are to be no roosters, and that the coop has to be a minimum of 4.5 metres from any dwelling. The coop needs to be warm, dry, free of vermin, and safe for the chooks. Our pen at the Ducks is renovated constantly as ideas for additional compartments and roofing have left it looking like a Chook Mahal.

The existence of potential predators in the area, such as foxes, dogs or snakes, may also call for the modification of your coop. When we were building the pen at the Ducks, we dug mesh wire about 60 centimetres into the ground below the fence line, so that burrowing predators couldn't prey on the brood. It sounds improbable but urban foxes are a real threat. They build dens in shadowy corners under buildings and bridges and skulk around backyards at night. Usually, if you have a flock of chickens, a rooster is the best defence against predators. Particularly if the rooster is mean or arrogant, which they tend to be, they flap and squawk, chasing away attackers. But in the suburban patchwork of Bronte, there was no way we could have a rooster. Can you imagine the collective fury of Bronte with every 5 am crow? Our hands were tied. However, roosters aren't necessary for egg production and they also make the hens flirty and broody, so that they sit on the eggs trying to hatch chicks, reducing the number of eggs laid.

Chooks lay the majority of their eggs in their first three years, after that there is a natural decline. By buying chickens progressively, we plan to stagger the ages of the chooks to keep up a steady supply of eggs.

By nature, chooks are not particularly needy, however, they are not a wild animal, and so can't be expected to survive without attention. Feed them your green scraps, but supplement their diet with commercial chicken feed, for vitamins and minerals. Chooks need fresh water daily, and their coop needs to be cleaned and the straw on the ground changed regularly. Obviously, if you go on holiday, a friend or neighbour must be enlisted to feed and water them.

Choosing the right breed of chook is dependent on what trait you value most. Generally, chicken breeds are divided into two groups – birds for eggs and birds for meat – but there are other considerations. For example, different breeds have different temperaments. Do you want show-standard birds, or birds that require less maintenance? We were advised to get female pullets aged between 14 and 16 weeks. But then what? Heritage breeds? Hybrids? The list of chicken breeds reads like an encyclopaedia of cartoon characters: Leghorn, Golden Comet, Cherry Egger, Rhode Island Red, Plymouth Rock, Marsh Daisy, Cinnamon Queen, Jersey Giant, Red Cap. Our emphasis was on having nutritious, tasty eggs. And lots of them. For egg-production, crossbred chooks are ideal. They have been selectively bred to remove the trait to become broody. Another consideration was the climate; we needed to have a winter-hardy breed, with dense feathers to keep insulated and warm, but also a breed that would be able to survive a hot, dry summer. We settled on 6 ISA Browns. Hyperactive by nature, ISA Browns are egg-laying machines, sometimes laying two eggs a day. The ideal temperature for egg production for ISA Browns is 21–26°C, and so far they have managed beautifully through the changing Sydney seasons.

The chickens have been a lively addition to the atmosphere of the restaurant. Customers head out the back and wander through the garden to admire the chooks. Kids push crumbs from their muffin through the wire mesh and everyone has a tip to offer us:

- put lime on the floor of the coop to neutralise odour
- place golf balls in the nest boxes to encourage the chickens to lay
- feed the chooks molasses to make their coats shiny
- build a straw yard for the chooks: an enclosed area covered in straw, sawdust, or woodchips, adjacent to the coop, which can be harvested twice a year as ripe compost for your garden
- if you don't collect the eggs regularly, chooks develop a habit of pecking at and eating the eggs and it's a very hard habit to break
- artificial light in the coop, from an LED or halogen bulb, will encourage chooks to lay for longer throughout the winter
- fresh eggs will sink in a glass of water, whereas old eggs will float.

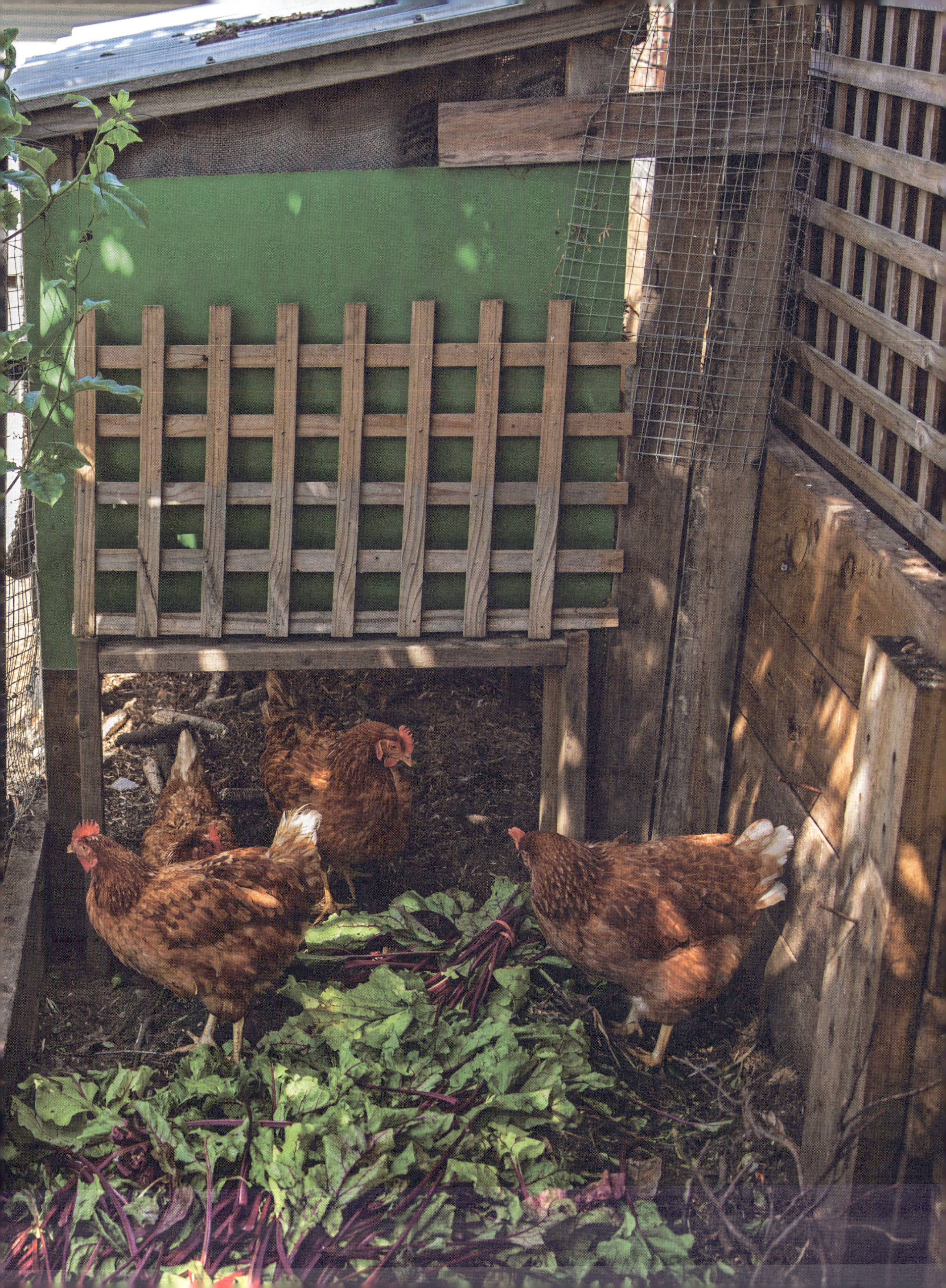

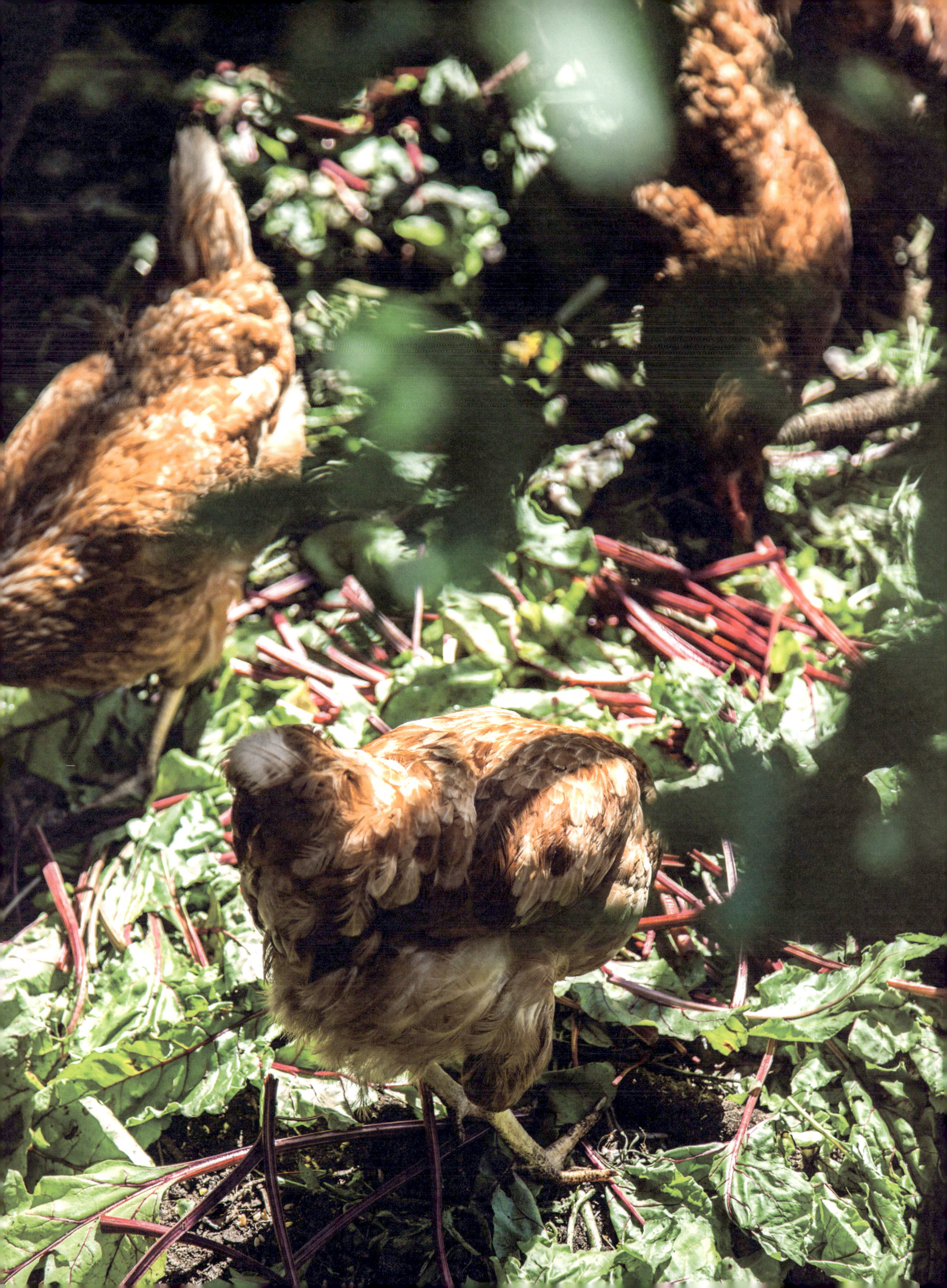

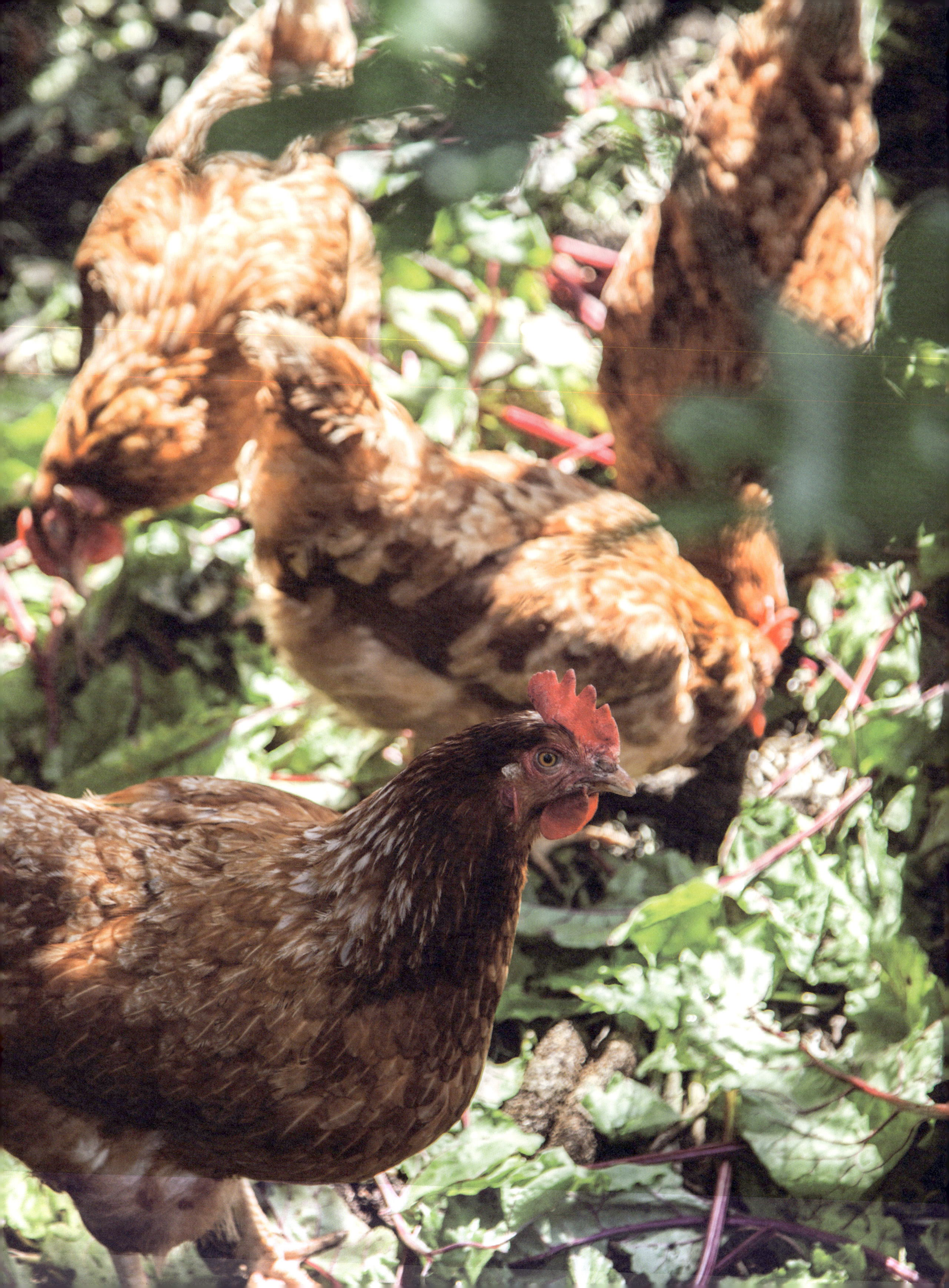

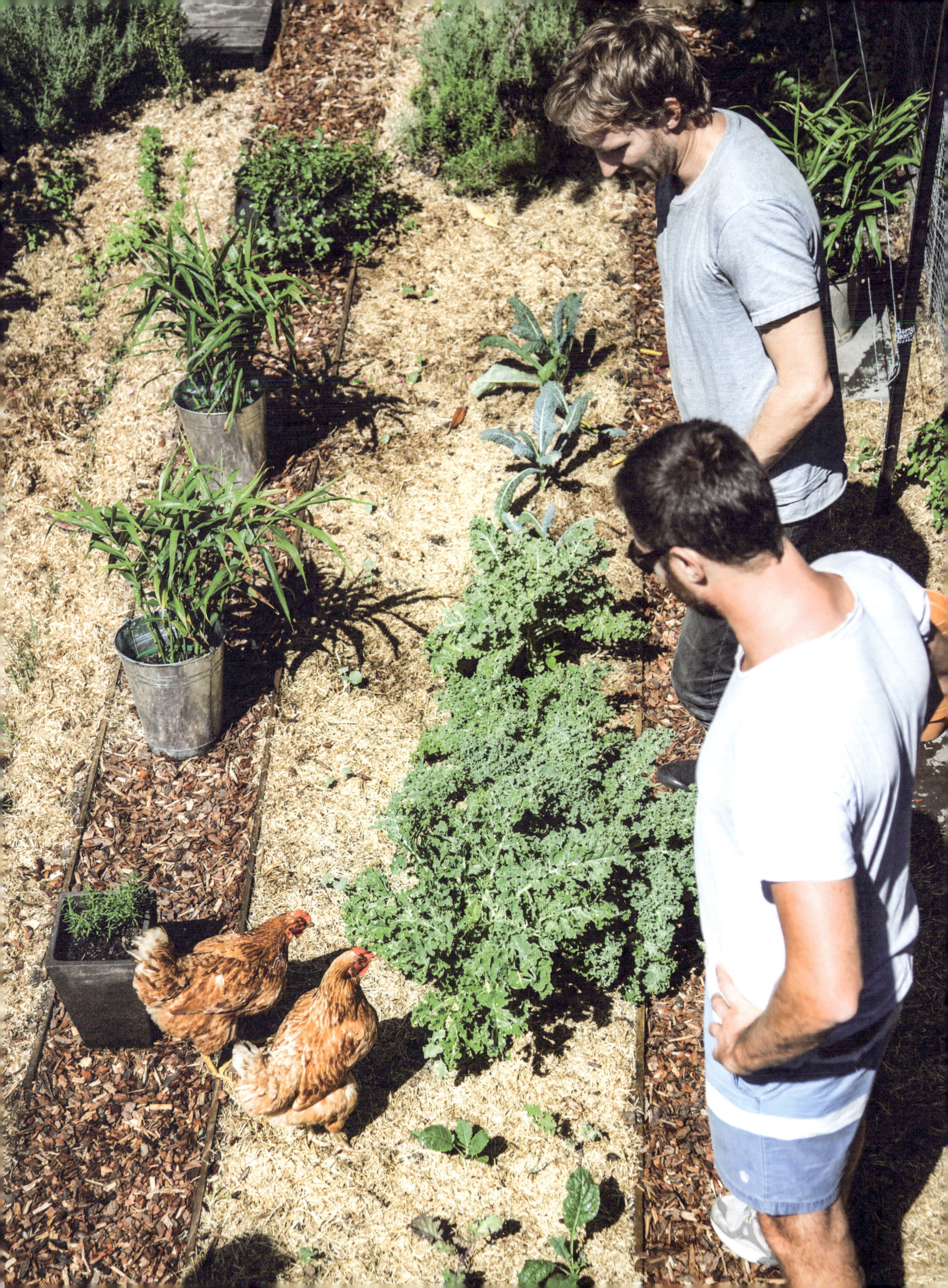

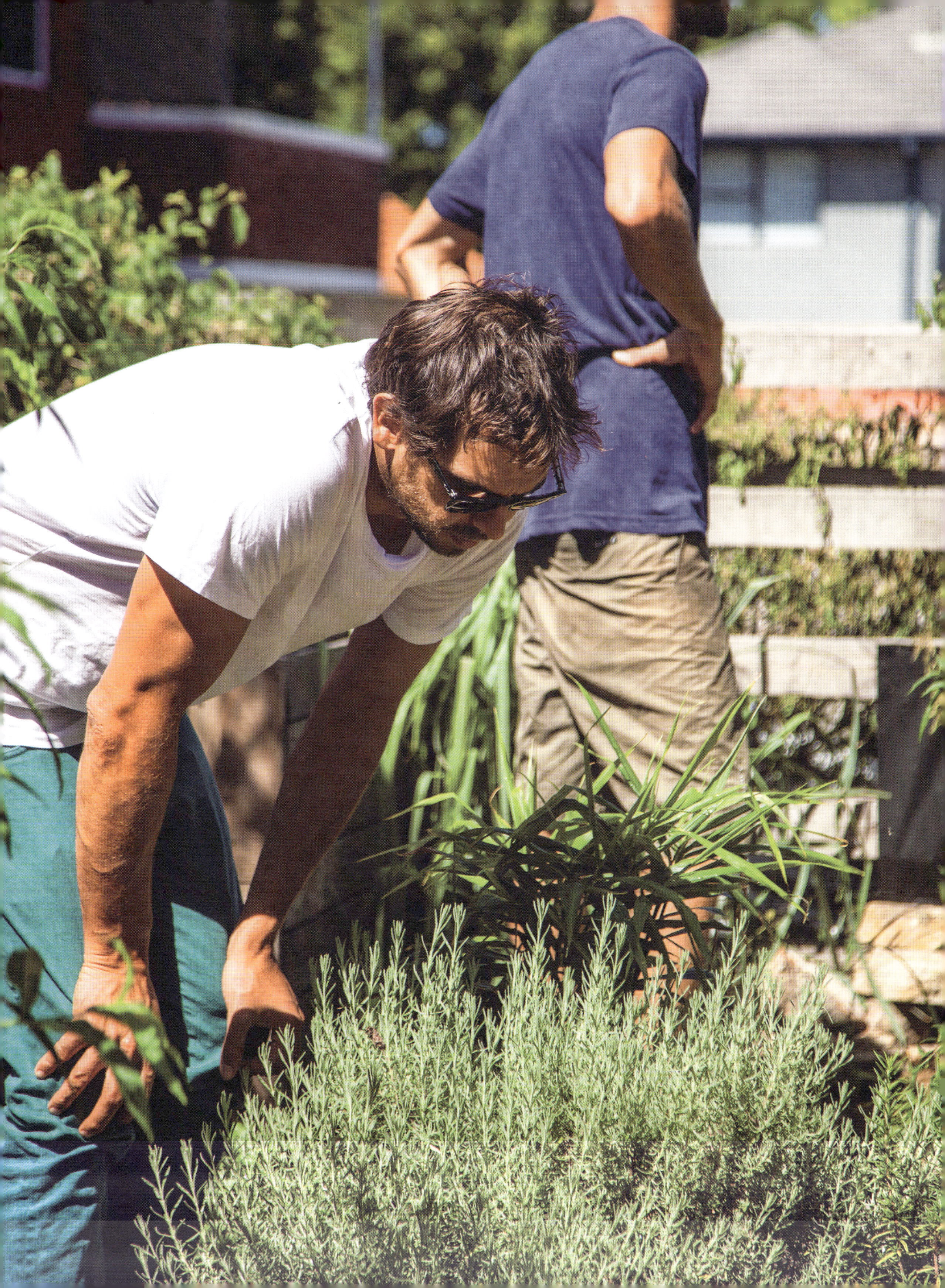

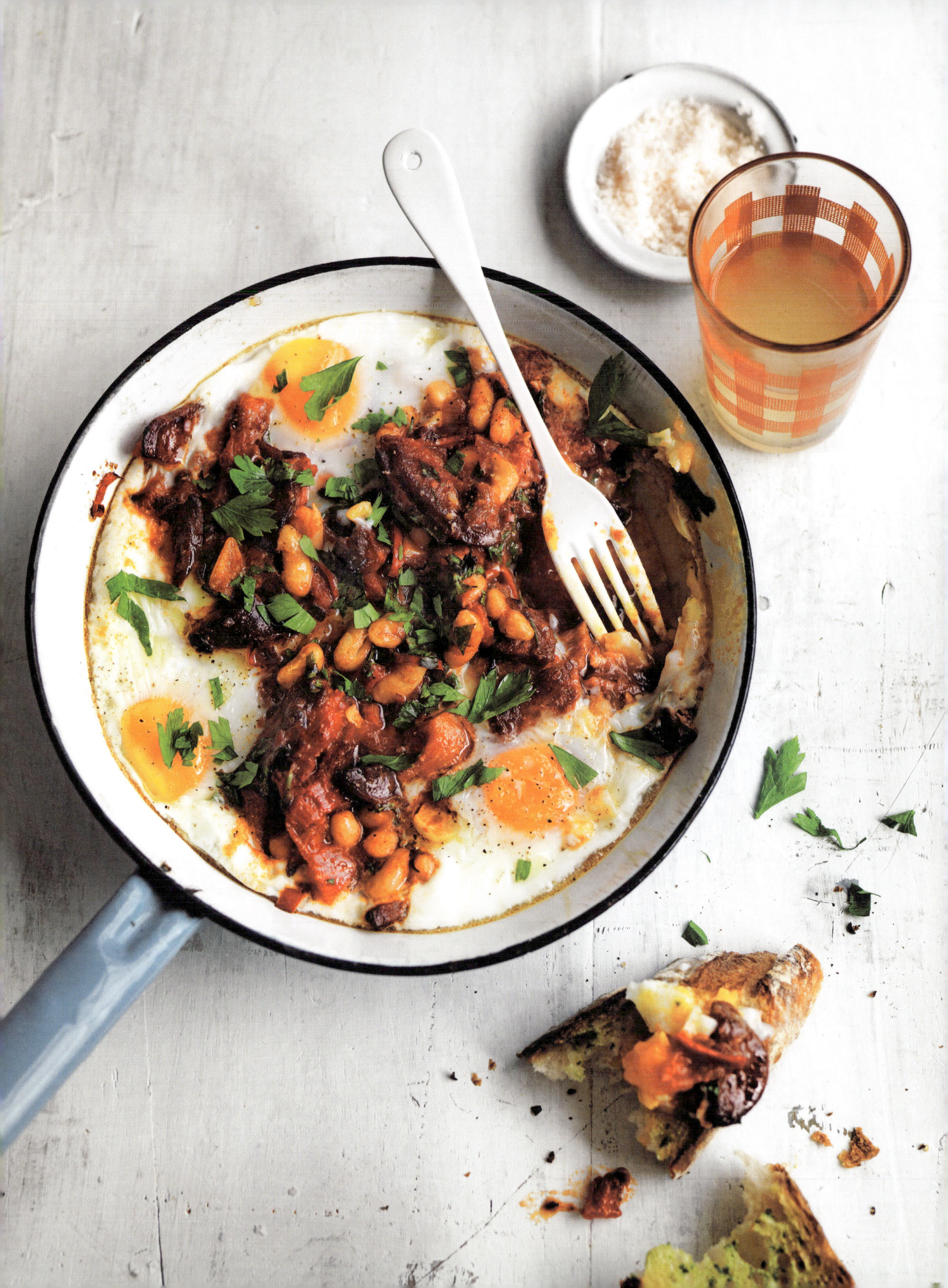

DELICIOUS SUNDAY BREAKFAST of BAKED EGGS with CHORIZO and CANNELLINI BEANS

This is an excellent dish for a Sunday morning breakfast. It doesn't take long to make on the spot, or you can get the chorizo and beans ready ahead of time, spoon it into dishes, then just add the eggs and bake when you need them. Easy.

Heat the oil in a large frying pan, add the onion, garlic and chorizo and fry until the onion becomes translucent. Add the capsicum, chilli, beans, tomatoes and paprika, stir and simmer for a further 10 minutes. The mixture should become thick but still be saucy. Season to taste, add the parsley and take off the heat.

Preheat the oven to 200°C.

Place a large spoon of the bean mix in the centre of 6 individual terracotta bowls or ramekins, then crack an egg either side of the beans. Season, place in the oven and bake for 6–8 minutes, depending on how well cooked you like your eggs.

Serve with crusty sourdough bread a herb salad, and a red onion, basil and cherry tomato salad with balsamic dressing.

SERVES 6

a few tablespoons vegetable oil
1 red onion, chopped
3 garlic cloves, finely chopped
250 g spicy chorizo sausage, thinly sliced
1 red capsicum, roughly chopped
1 long red chilli, finely chopped
1 x 400 g can cannellini beans, well rinsed and drained
1 x 400 g can diced tomatoes
1 tablespoon paprika
salt and pepper
1 handful of flat-leaf parsley, chopped
12 eggs
sourdough bread, to serve
herb salad and salad of red onion/basil/cherry tomatoes, to serve

CHAWANMUSHI
(Japanese savoury custard)

4 eggs
300 ml water
25 ml dashi
75 ml cream

This savoury custard, or chawanmushi, has a delicate texture and subtle flavour. In Japan it is traditionally eaten hot in winter and chilled in summer, either plain or with mushrooms, seafood, herbs or other ingredients. Dashi is a soup stock made with kelp and bonito fish flakes – have a look in the Asian food stores but even supermarkets sometimes have it these days.

Put all the ingredients into a bowl and whisk gently to combine.

Strain the custard into 6 x 150-ml moulds or small teacups, and then cover them with cling wrap.

Put a bamboo steamer over boiling water, carefully place the moulds in the steamer, then turn to simmer, so that it is on a very low heat. Steam for around 15–20 minutes until the custard is set (it will still be a bit wobbly though).

You can leave the custard plain (the dashi gives it a great savoury taste) or you can add lots of other flavours. Before pouring in the custard, put in a spoonful of roasted leeks, sautéed mushrooms, fresh herbs or – our absolute favourite – crabmeat.

SERVES 6

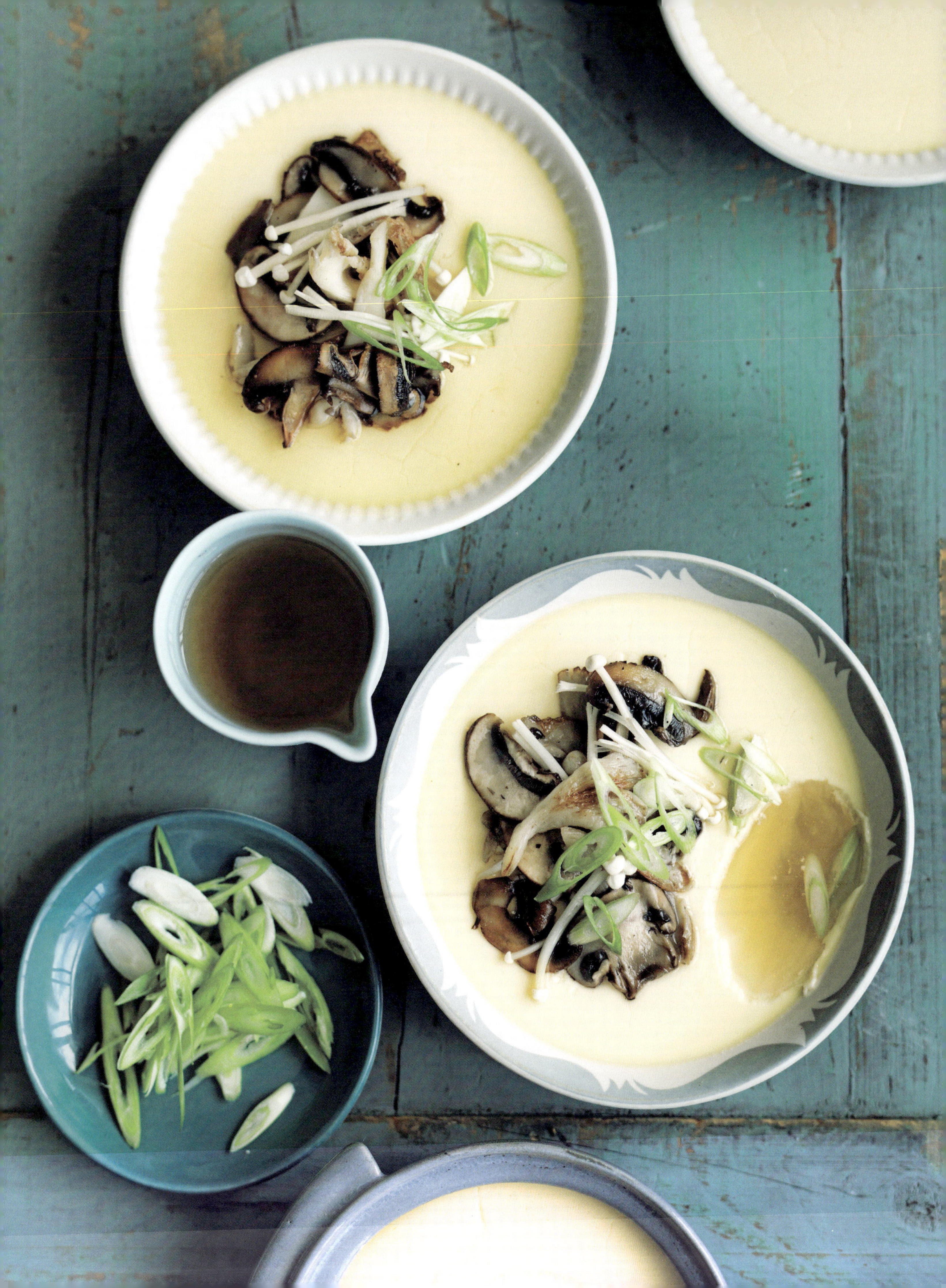

THE DUCKS' PERFECT SCRAMBLED EGGS

1 tablespoon vegetable oil
2 eggs per person, lightly beaten
sea salt and cracked pepper

This is how we make our scrambled eggs – and we make lots! It's very easy and literally takes 1 minute. Make sure your pan is hot, and don't add salt before cooking the eggs, or they will go a dull orange colour and won't fluff up.

Put a non-stick frying pan over very high heat and add the oil.

When the oil is hot, pour in the eggs, and season with pepper when the eggs hit the pan. Don't start playing with the eggs. As the bottom surface of the eggs starts to cook and become firm, push the mixture into a pile with a spatula so the uncooked egg comes into contact with the hot frying pan.

Repeat until the eggs are cooked to your liking.

Season with salt and serve.

SERVES 1

SEA SALT MERINGUES

Sea salt is a bit unexpected with meringues, but try it – it's a winner. These little meringues are a useful treat to have on hand for a quick dessert. Add fresh berries, mascarpone, passionfruit, grilled pineapple, mint, sour cherries and cream – whatever you like really.

220 g egg whites (you need about 8 egg whites)
220 g caster sugar
1 teaspoon fine sea salt

Preheat the oven to 100°C. Line a baking tray with baking paper.

Put the egg whites in an electric mixer, turn to high and slowly incorporate the sugar. Leave the whites to mix for 8 minutes until smooth and glossy. Add the salt and stop mixing.

Spoon the meringue into small mounds onto the prepared tray and bake for 1 hour.

Remove from the oven and leave on a wire rack to cool.

MAKES ABOUT 16 MERINGUES

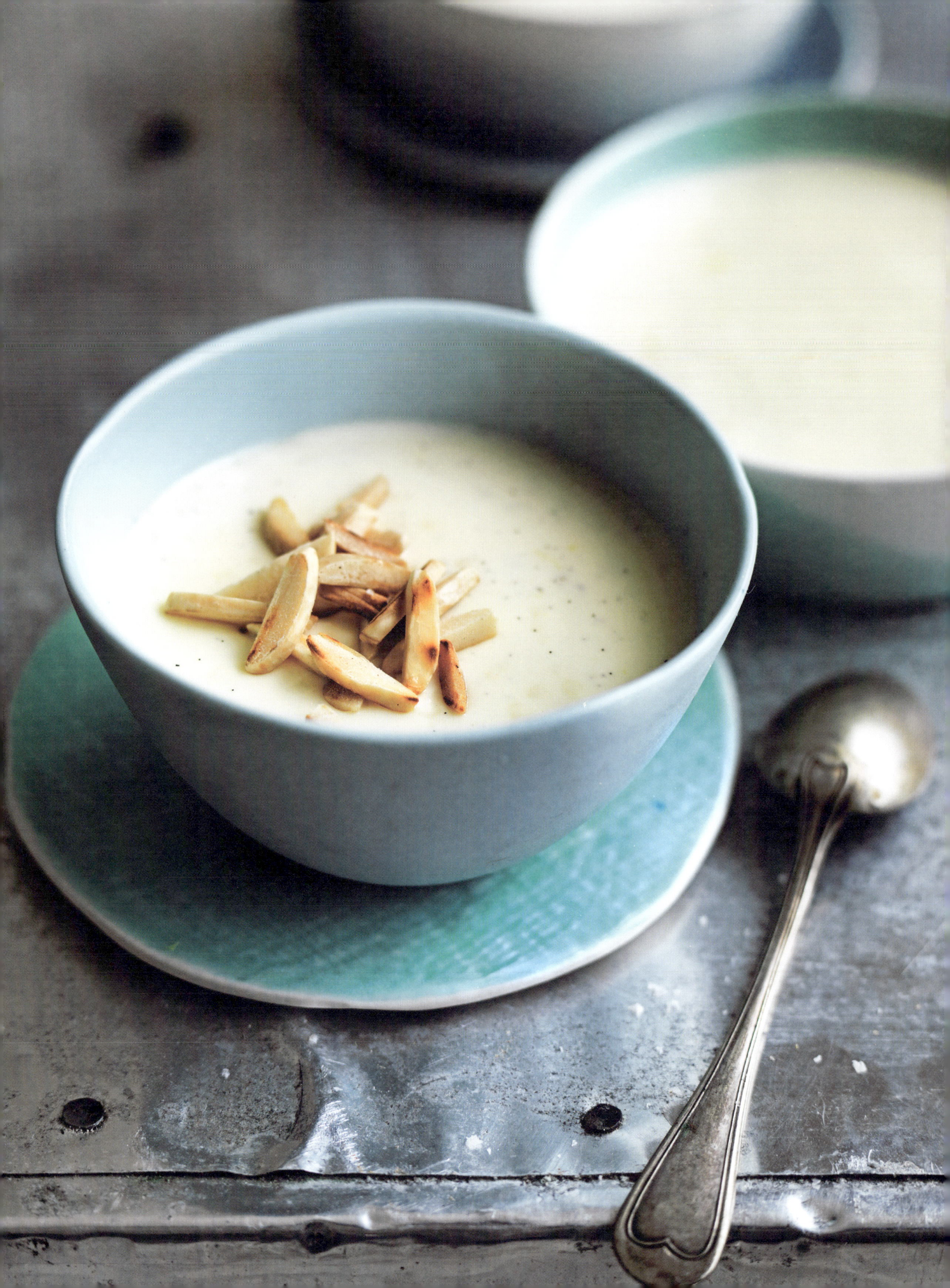

VANILLA PANNA COTTA

This panna cotta recipe is foolproof and you can flavour it with anything you like – try infusing the cream with bay leaves, mint, blue cheese, grated blood orange, lemon myrtle or wattle seeds.

Place the gelatine sheets in cold water to soak for 4–5 minutes, then gently squeeze out the excess water.

Put the cream, sugar and vanilla pod in a saucepan over medium heat and bring to the boil.

Remove the pan from the heat, then whisk in the lemon zest, milk and gelatine. Put the pan over a bowl of ice to chill the cream mixture, and stir it so the vanilla seeds are evenly distributed. Remove the vanilla pod.

Pour the panna cotta into moulds and set for 8 hours.

Serve, scattered with the toasted almond slivers.

SERVES 6

2 gelatine sheets
250 ml cream
60 g caster sugar
1 vanilla pod, split lengthways
zest of 1 lemon
250 ml milk
toasted almond slivers, to serve

ORANGE and YOGHURT PANCAKES

8 eggs, separated
150 g caster sugar
zest and juice of 6 oranges
500 g natural yoghurt
400 g plain flour, sifted
butter
fresh orange segments and natural yoghurt, to serve

Many people who have visited us at the Ducks will know that the weekend means orange and yoghurt pancakes! They are moist, yet light and packed with citrus flavour – just be careful not to overwork your batter as you'll get a denser pancake as a result. The secret to these is to fold in the beaten egg whites very gently – if you're heavy-handed you won't end up with light pancakes.

Beat the egg whites in a clean, dry bowl until they form stiff peaks, then set aside.

Place the egg yolks, sugar and orange zest in a large mixing bowl and whisk by hand until smooth and lighter in colour. Add the yoghurt and orange juice. The mixture should be very wet at this stage. Stir in the flour, a quarter at a time, until the mixture is smooth and firm.

Fold in the egg whites very gently, to keep the batter light and aerated.

Heat 1 tablespoon of butter in a heavy-based, non-stick frying pan over medium heat, then add three spoonfuls of batter. When you see bubbles forming and popping on top of the pancakes, turn them over and cook until golden brown.

Serve with fresh orange segments and natural yoghurt.

SERVES 6

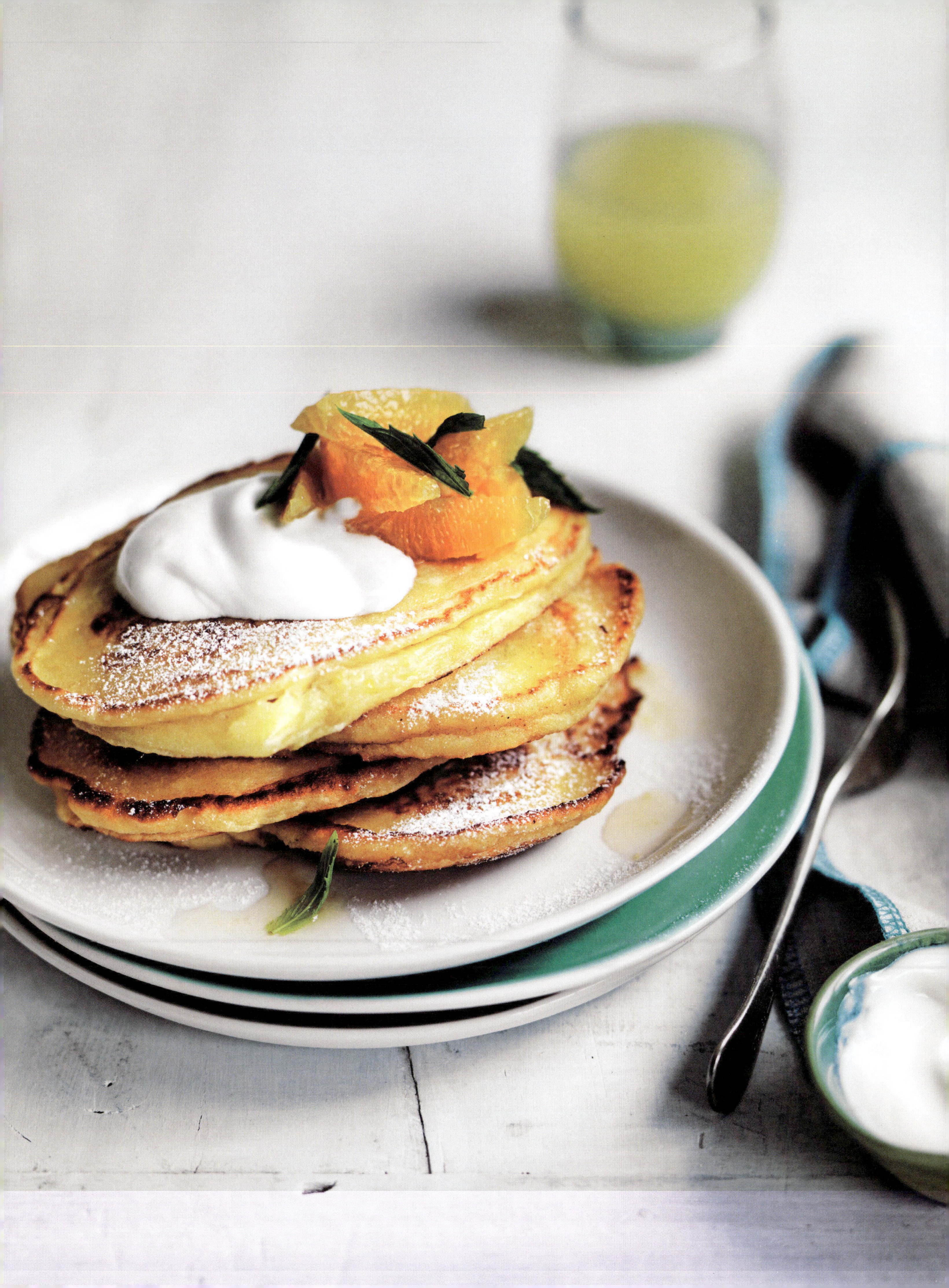

CHOCOLATE and BEETROOT BROWNIE

10 eggs
330 g sugar
1.5 kg dark chocolate, 60 per cent cacao, broken into pieces
500 g butter, chopped
365 g plain flour, sifted
200 g beetroot, diced
3 tablespoons grapeseed oil

These brownies are rich, dark and extra chocolatey – make sure to have a glass of cold milk ready for when they come out of the oven. This makes a big batch, but you could halve it if you wanted to.

Preheat the oven to 150°C. Line a 40 cm x 30 cm baking pan or brownie tray with baking paper.

Put the eggs and 250 g sugar in a large mixing bowl and beat until light and fluffy.

Pour boiling water into a medium-sized saucepan and place a large heatproof bowl on top (to make a double boiler). Place the pan over medium heat, add the chocolate and butter to the bowl and stir occasionally until it melts and becomes a smooth consistency. Remove the bowl from the heat.

Place a large frying pan over medium heat, add the oil and beetroot and cook for 5–10 minutes, until the beetroot starts to soften. Add the remaining sugar and toss until a dark caramel forms.

Fold the beetroot into the melted chocolate, then fold the chocolate mixture into the beaten eggs and mix well.

Add the flour gradually, stirring after each addition. The batter should be thick and chocolatey.

Pour the mixture into the prepared pan, leaving 3–4 cm at the top and bake for approximately 1 hour. After 45 minutes, insert a small knife in the centre of the brownie – if the knife comes out clean, the brownie is ready.

MAKES 20 LARGE WINTER-SIZED PIECES OF BROWNIE

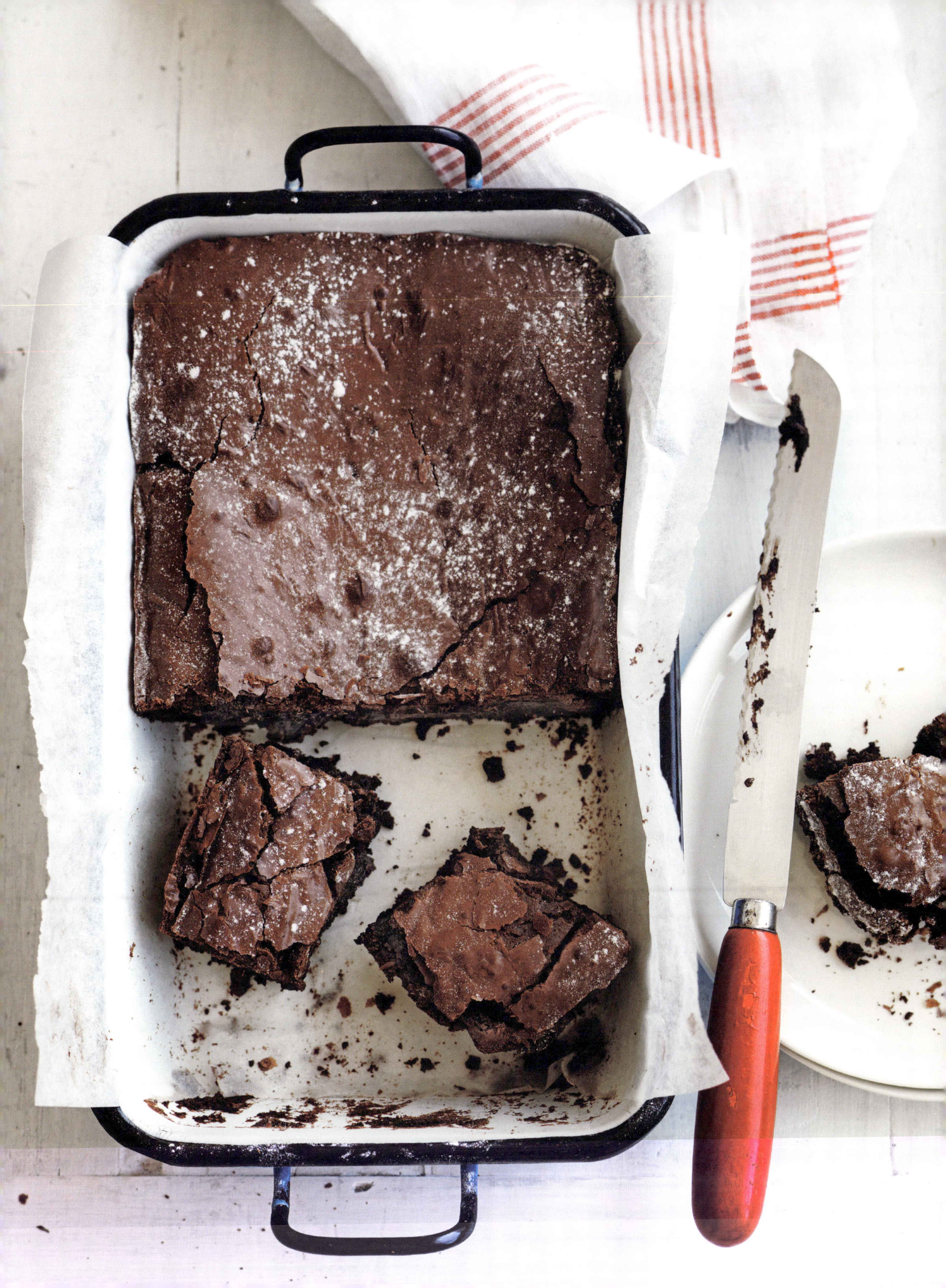

FENNEL ICE CREAM

8 large egg yolks
180 g caster sugar
475 ml milk
475 ml cream
2 tablespoons fennel seeds, roasted
200 g fennel bulb, chopped
60 ml liquid glucose
20 ml pastis (such as Pernod)

We try to use every part of all ingredients that come through our kitchen so, we thought, instead of discarding the fennel trimmings, why not make them into ice cream? This ice cream is quite easy to make, especially considering how good it tastes – the liquorice flavour is a bit unexpected and the pastis adds an extra kick. Try it with chocolate brownies – it's a great combination.

In a large bowl, whisk the egg yolks and sugar together until pale and creamy.

Put the milk, cream, seeds, fennel and glucose in a saucepan, bring almost to the boil, remove from the heat and leave to infuse for 1 hour.

Bring the mixture back up to the boil, strain into a large jug, then pour onto the egg yolks and whisk. Return this mixture to the pan, then gently cook while stirring, until it thickens slightly to a consistency that coats the back of a wooden spoon.

Strain into a bowl, chill the mixture, then churn in an ice-cream machine.

MAKES ABOUT 1 LITRE

LEMON, BASIL *and* MINT PRALINE

We try to use this pretty sparingly as it does contain quite a bit of sugar, but it is a great way to add sweetness and texture to desserts and sour fruits.

Sprinkle the zest, leaves and nuts onto a sheet of baking paper.

In a non-stick saucepan, gently heat the sugar until it turns a light caramel. Carefully but quickly remove the pan from the heat and pour over the nuts and leaves. Leave for 10–15 minutes to set.

When completely firm, smash up the toffee using a mortar and pestle. Store in airtight container in your pantry.

MAKES ABOUT 400 G

grated zest of ½ lemon
5 basil leaves
3 mint leaves
100 g peeled hazelnuts
300 g sugar

THE GARDEN

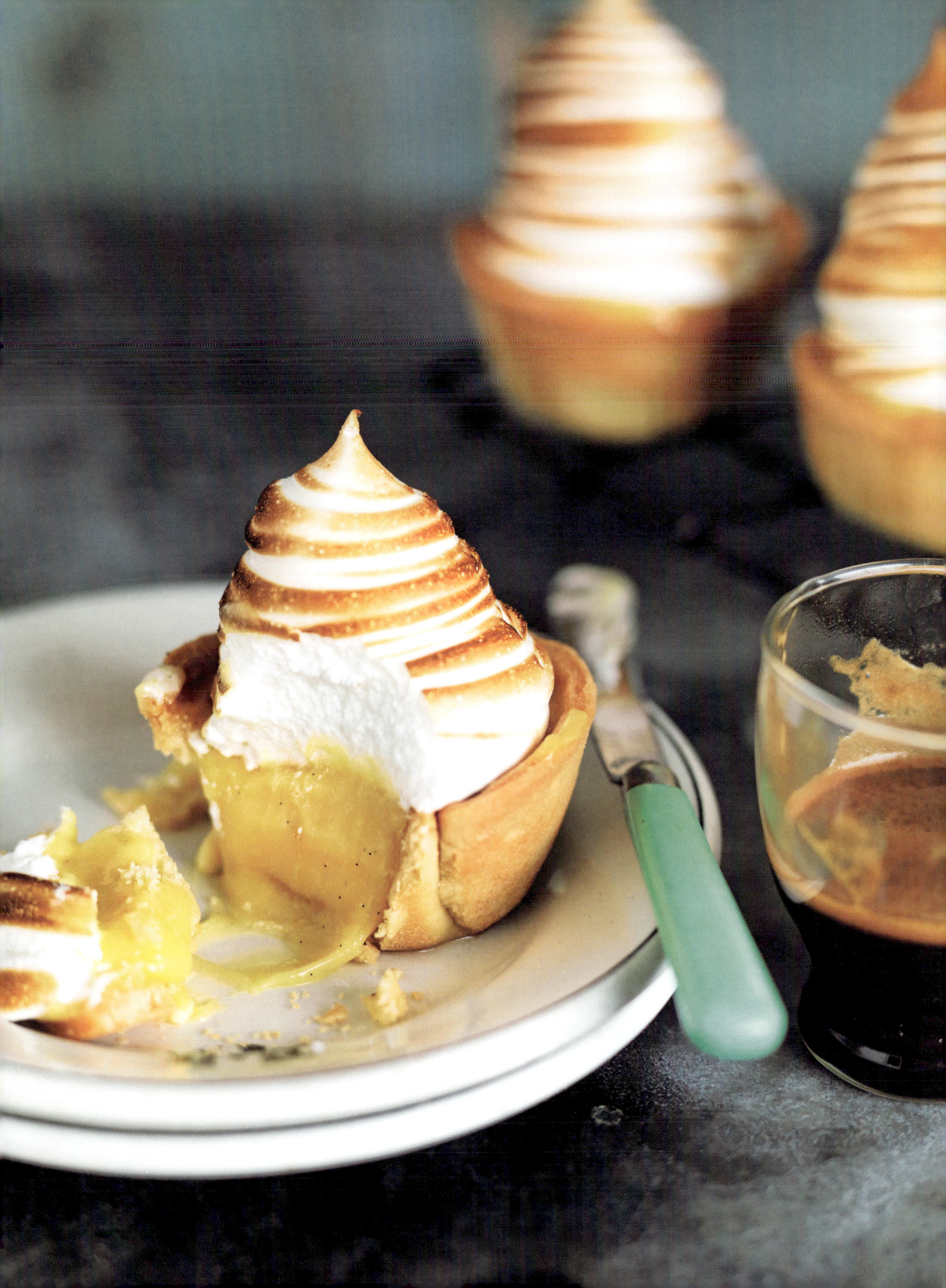

LEMON MERINGUE TARTLETS

This is one of the staple front-cabinet 'sweet things' at the Ducks – extremely yummy with a piccolo or ristretto. The meringue recipe can be used to make a pavlova base or baked meringues for desserts. Keep the same ratio (one part egg white to two parts caster sugar) but increase the quantity.

To make the meringue, put the egg whites into a medium-sized, clean, dry bowl and whisk on high speed until the whites start to rise and become fluffy. Very slowly add the caster sugar, still whisking, until the mixture becomes silky, smooth and shiny. When the meringue is thick and stable and will stand up in peaks, it's ready.

To assemble, fill the baked pastry tart shells with lemon curd.

Scoop the meringue on top of the tarts. Using the flat part of a spatula, lift the meringue into peaks. The uneven surface will make for nice little burnt bits on the tips of the spikes.

When you're happy with the look of the tarts, use a blowtorch to brown the top a little, or put the tarts under the grill on high heat for a few minutes until lightly browned.

If you want to make one large meringue tart, preheat the oven to 200°C, put the tart in for 5 minutes to set the meringue, then use the blowtorch to get those crispy little spikes on top.

SERVES 6

½ quantity sweet shortcrust pastry, baked into 6 small tart shells (page 188) or 350 g of bought tart shells
1 quantity lemon curd (page 162)

MERINGUE
2 large egg whites, at room temperature
120 g caster sugar

SWEET SHORTCRUST PASTRY

500 g plain flour
200 g icing sugar
200 g butter, grated
2 eggs
pinch of salt

This recipe is ideal for sweet tart shells to use when making lemon meringue or chocolate tarts. You can make the pastry by hand or using a food processor. Either way, you'll need a nice clean bench for rolling the pastry.

Sift the flour and icing sugar together.

If using a food processor, fit the paddle attachment, add all the ingredients and mix until the dough comes together.

If making by hand, pile the flour and sugar on the bench and form a well in the middle. Put the butter and the eggs in the well. Using your fingers, bring the ingredients together, gradually pulling in the dry mixture from the walls of the well. Fold and mix, as you would if making bread by hand, until you have a silky, smooth dough.

Cut the dough in half, press flat and wrap in cling film. Chill in the refrigerator for at least 2 hours before rolling out.

ROLLING OUT

Remove the dough from the refrigerator. Dust the bench and rolling pin well with flour.

Roll the pin over the dough, then turn and roll the other side. Continue until the dough is 3–4 mm thick.

Lightly grease individual tart pans and dust with flour. Cut rounds of pastry, using one of the tart pans as a template, leaving about an extra 2 cm.

Lay a circle of pastry over each tart pan, then gently press it into position and trim the edges, leaving a little overhang as the pastry may shrink when baked.

BLIND BAKING

Blind baking means to bake a pastry shell without a filling and without colouring the pastry.

Preheat the oven to 170°C.

When the pastry is in the tart pan, line the shell with baking paper and fill the base evenly with dry rice or dried beans. This will keep the pastry in shape and stop it rising when baking.

Place the pastry shells in the oven and bake for about 15 minutes, or until the top edges are golden and the shells are crisp and cooked through. If they're not cooked, your filling will leak through the pastry.

MAKES 900 G PASTRY (CAN BE WRAPPED AND FROZEN)

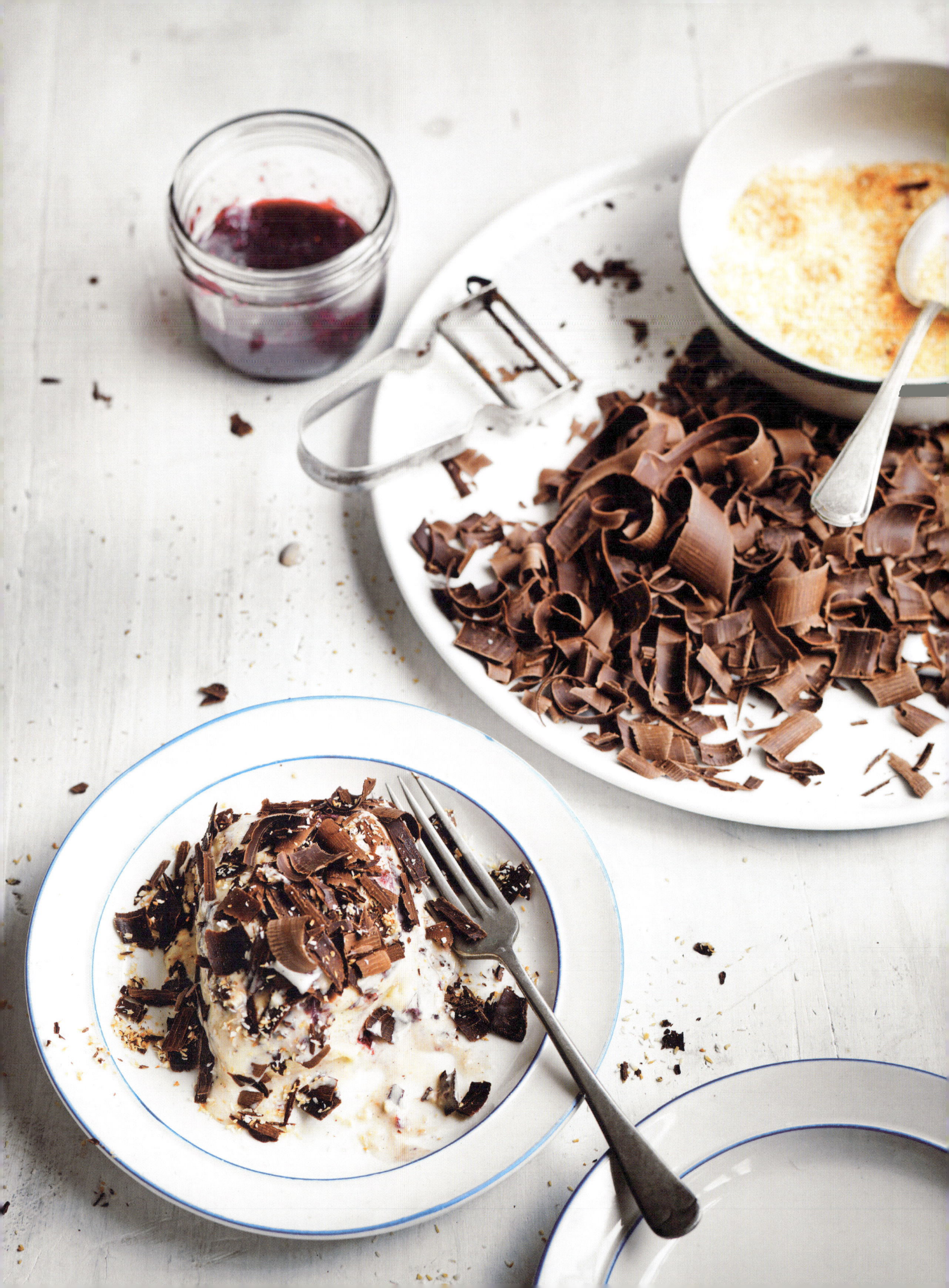

LAMINGTON ICE CREAM

Wherever the lamington came from – NZ or Oz – one thing's for sure, it is a no-brainer! Toasted coconut with shaved chocolate and berries is a great combination. Add whatever berries are in season and you're winning!

To make the jam, dissolve the sugar with the berries over a medium heat. When the sugar has fully dissolved, strain the liquid, retaining the berries. Put the liquid back over a medium heat and reduce to a third of its volume. Add the reserved berries and set aside.

In a large bowl, whisk the egg yolks and sugar together until pale and creamy.

Put the milk, cream, vanilla and glucose in a saucepan, bring almost to the boil, take off the heat and pour over the yolk mixture while whisking. (Make sure your milk is not too hot or you will curdle the eggyolks.) Return this mixture to the pan, then gently cook while stirring, until it thickens slightly to a consistency that coats the back of a wooden spoon. Strain into a bowl, chill the mix, then churn in an ice-cream machine.

Fold in the berry jam making sure to keep nice lumps of fruit in the mixture. Using an ice-cream scoop, or a melon baller if you want small scoops, ball the ice cream, lay them on a tray and set in the freezer to re-freeze. Just before serving, mix the chocolate, nuts and coconut together and roll the ice cream in the mixture. Serve straight away.

MAKES ABOUT 1.2 LITRES OF ICE CREAM

8 large egg yolks
160 g caster sugar
750 ml milk
380 ml coconut cream
1 vanilla pod, split lengthways, seeds scraped
30 ml liquid glucose
100 g dark chocolate, grated
50 g crushed almonds, toasted
100 g shredded coconut, toasted

BERRY JAM
200 g sugar
500 g mixed frozen berries

SPICED PARSNIP CAKE

200 ml canola oil
2 eggs
200 g soft brown sugar
zest of 1 orange
250 g plain flour
1 teaspoon sea salt
1 teaspoon baking powder
1 teaspoon ground cinnamon
½ teaspoon ground cumin
200 g dark chocolate, chopped
280 g parsnips, peeled and grated
100 g walnuts, roughly chopped
150 g nibbed almonds, toasted

Vegetables shouldn't just be used to accompany the main course – they're fantastic in sweets too. Candied beetroot with chocolate brownies, fennel ice cream and parsnip cake are all great treats. This is really a play on carrot cake, just a little spicier. Serve with a dollop of mascarpone and a pot of tea.

Preheat the oven to 180°C. Lightly grease a 24 cm x 12 cm cake pan and line the base and sides with baking paper.

In a large bowl, whisk the oil, eggs, sugar and zest until pale.

Sift the flour, salt, baking powder and spices into the egg mixture, mix to blend together. Stir in the chocolate, parsnip and nuts. Pour into the prepared pan and bake for 1 hour and 10 minutes.

Remove from the oven and cool on a wire rack.

SERVES 8

STICKY DATE PUDDINGS with BUTTERSCOTCH SAUCE

This recipe is pretty special. I've used it since I was an apprentice – it's foolproof, it works a treat and it's very moreish. Serve it with ice cream or cream. Make that double cream.

Cream the butter, sugar and vanilla seeds using an electric mixer until pale. Add the eggs, one at a time, beating after each addition. Then add the flour, a quarter at a time, still beating.

Bring the water to the boil in a large saucepan, add the dates and bicarbonate of soda. The mixture will rise and froth as the bicarbonate of soda is activated. Pour the dates and liquid into the creamed butter and eggs and stir until combined.

Preheat the oven to 190°C. Grease 8 coffee cups with butter.

Pour the batter into the prepared cups, until about 2–3 cm from the top.

Place the cups in a baking pan. Fill the pan with water until it comes halfway up the side of the cups. Cover the pan with foil. Place in the oven and bake for 35 minutes.

To test if a pudding is cooked, insert a skewer in the centre. If the skewer comes out clean, then it's ready.

To make the butterscotch sauce, pour the caster sugar into a very clean saucepan over medium heat. Don't stir it. When the sugar has melted and become a dark caramel colour, add the butter and cream while stirring. The butterscotch will boil intensely until the temperature drops. Remove the pan from the heat immediately.

If there are any crystallised sugar clumps, pass the sauce through a fine strainer. If not, pour the sauce into a container. Don't refrigerate the sauce.

When the puddings are cooked, dollop a tablespoon of butterscotch on top and it will melt down the sides. Serve with double cream or ice cream.

SERVES 8

110 g butter, at room temperature
320 g sugar
1 vanilla pod, halved lengthways and seeds scraped
4 eggs
320 g plain flour, sifted
320 g dates, roughly chopped
600 ml water
2 teaspoons bicarbonate of soda
double cream or ice cream, to serve

BUTTERSCOTCH SAUCE
200 g caster sugar
90 g butter
90 ml cream

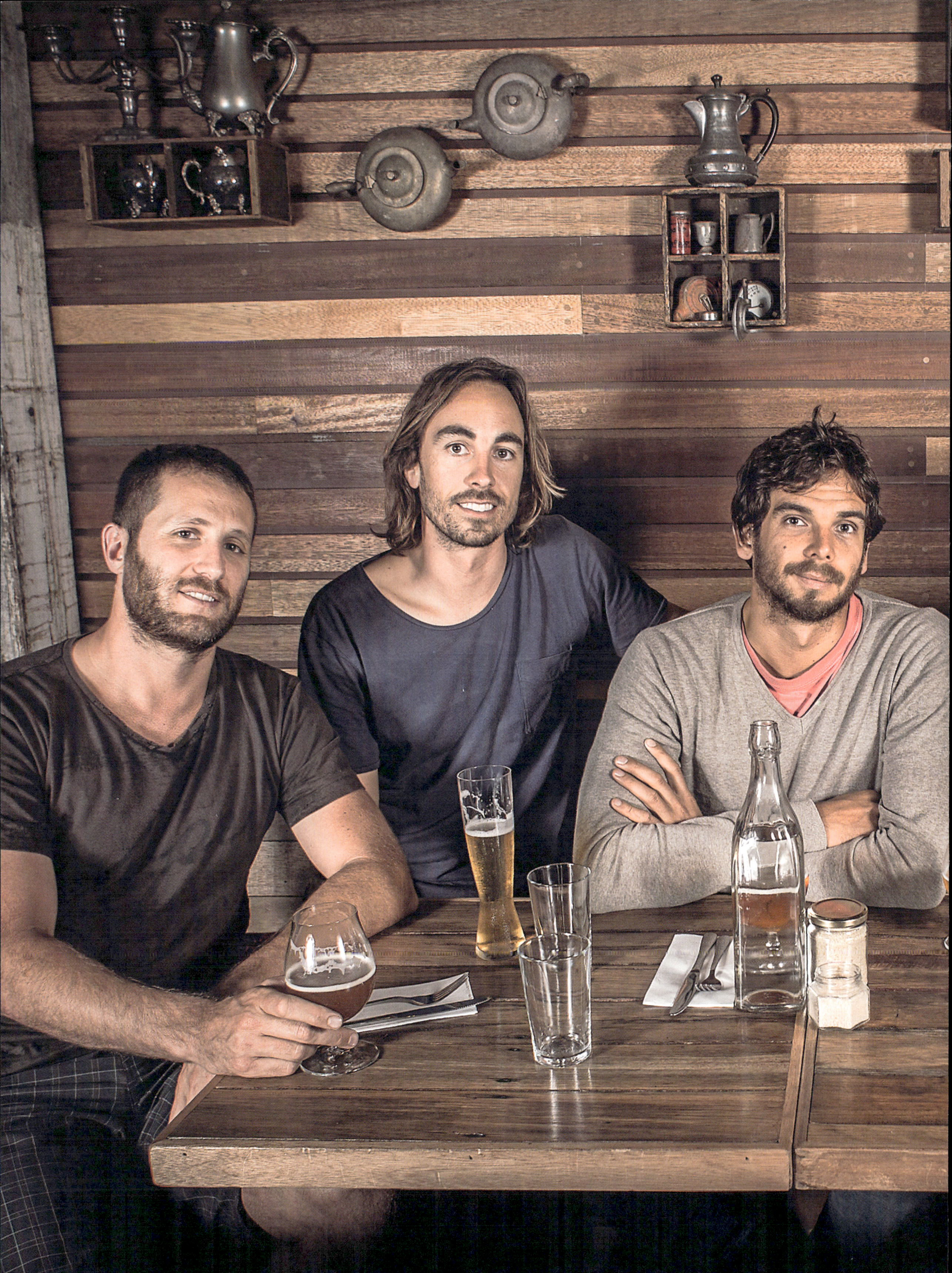

Big thanks! →

Mark

I would like to thank my dad and Cazza, for lending me the money to get this started; Georgie, for all the planning and support; Dion from Single Origin Roasters; Brian from Pumpkin Head; the guys at Goldstein; Brad from Frothers; the amazing Iggy's family; Pete, Francesco, Frenchie, Gus, Shazza and Danni; everyone I have worked with who has helped me become the chef I am today; my uncle Nils, for putting me in the kitchen at such a young age and for his tough-love teaching methods. A very special thankyou to Grant, my incredible brother. Grant has stood by me from the start, made the Ducks the most fun and exciting place to work, and has helped the business become what it is today. And lastly, to Hannah, for helping to write such a lovely book, and for being the most amazing partner anyone could wish for.

Darren

Huge thanks to Mum, Abbie and Jamie, Magdalena, Geremy Glew, Mark Tzen, Jonny NBS Wilson (for the surfs), Danielle O' Keefe. Easy E, Mike Clift, Luke Powell, Hongy, Jowett, Lou Dog and all the old Tetsuya's crew, Amanda Ryan, Morgs and the TOYS crew, Shannon Debreceny, Big Mike, Limbo, Fassy, and Ben Shewry. Thanks to our brilliant suppliers: Joto, Pumpkin Head, Cath and Hapi. Also to J. Sussman, A. Huxstep, Martin Benn, Mark Raffan, Ann Swan, Justine May, Tracy Gualano, Franz Scheurer, Seamus and Rosie, the Iggy's family, the Single Origin crew, Brad at www.frothers.com.au, Caleb Reid and Benny Reid, for all the sick artwork around the place, Pete, Francesco, Danni, Gus, Zlata, Byron, Kiwi Mark, Rosco, Frenchie, Max, Tom, James, Jesse, Mitch, Chris and all of our amazing team. And to Hannah, for writing our story.

We'd both like to thank Tara Wynne, Mary, Ellie and all at Pan Macmillan, Will Meppem and Emma Knowles for the incredible photography and styling, Allison Colpoys for the design, and Margaret Barca, for making us read so much better. And special thanks to Leonie McRae.

INDEX

A

almonds
   quinoa and spelt salad with roasted almonds 90
apple–balsamic dressing 110
apple–berry jam 160
artichoke
   parsnip and Jerusalem artichoke soup 114
asparagus, charred, with coddled eggs and butter sauce 127
avocado
   prawn, corn and avocado salad 13

B

bacon
   barramundi, peas and bacon 22
bananas
   the best banana bread we've ever had – thanks Pauly! 91
   bananas, milk and honey 150
   salted caramel–banana muffins 97
barbecued calamari with tomato and olive salsa 10
barley
   mushrooms and pearl barley with macadamia bread sauce 84
barramundi, peas and bacon 22
beef
   braised beef cheeks, pickled celery and burnt onion puree 73
   braised and charred ox tongue 50
   kick-arse steak sandwich 41
   the perfect steak 63
beetroot
   chocolate and beetroot brownie 182
   roasted vegetable salad 132
bircher muesli with honey for a crowd 94
braised beef cheeks, pickled celery and burnt onion puree 73
braised and charred ox tongue 50

bread
   the best banana bread we've ever had – thanks Pauly! 91
   bread and butter pudding with a few herbs 102
   dark chocolate, date and walnut bread 99
   flat bread 83
   roti 82
   seedy soda bread 83
breakfast
   bircher muesli with honey for a crowd 94
   delicious Sunday breakfast of baked eggs with chorizo and cannellini beans 173
   the Duck's perfect scrambled eggs 176
   orange and yoghurt pancakes 180
   salmon and poached egg on toast for 6 hungry people 12
   spiced black quinoa porridge 95
   toasted muesli, the way we like it 93
Bronte fish cakes 33
Brussels sprouts with roasted chestnuts 142
burnt onion puree 73
butter sauce 127
butterscotch sauce 193

C

cakes
   chocolate and beetroot brownie 182
   lime, polenta and ricotta cake 100
   muffins 96–7
   spiced parsnip cake 192
   white chocolate and vanilla friands 98
calamari
   barbecued calamari with tomato and olive salsa 10
cannellini beans
   delicious Sunday breakfast of baked eggs with chorizo and cannellini beans 173
capsicum
   red capsicum mayo 41
carrots
   baby carrots with star anise 156

cauliflower cheese, our way 128
celery
   pickled celery and mustard seeds 157
   pickled celery salad 73
chai
   chai latte 151
   Chriso's chai tea and garden honey 151
char-grilled honey peaches with vanilla and rosemary ice cream 149
char-grilled lamb kebabs ready for wrapping 74
charred asparagus with coddled eggs and butter sauce 127
chawanmushi (Japanese savoury custard) 174
cheese
   cauliflower cheese, our way 128
   fig, walnut and goat's cheese salad 140
   figs, blue cheese and honeycomb 150
   lime, polenta and ricotta cake 100
   pear and ricotta muffins 97
   tomato and torn mozzarella salad 108
chicken
   chicken and charred leek soup 115
   chicken liver parfait 64
   coconut, lime and lemongrass chicken soup 77
   our green chicken 67
   spiced chicken in a brown paper bag 48
chillies
   chilli duck salad with green mango and mint 42
   chilli jam 158
   chilli and lime oyster topping 19
   chilli oil 125
   chilli paste 9
   mussels and pipis with chilli and coconut 9
   nahm jim 111
   prawn, corn and avocado salad 13
   shellfish, chilli and lemon pasta 16

sweet corn soup with toasted
    coconut and chilli **125**
chocolate
    chocolate and beetroot
        brownie **182**
    chocolate and macadamia
        muffins **97**
    chocolate pots with whatever you
        fancy **105**
    dark chocolate, date and walnut
        bread **99**
    lamington ice cream **191**
    white chocolate and vanilla
        friands **98**
chorizo
    chorizo oyster topping **19**
    delicious Sunday breakfast
        of baked eggs with chorizo and
        cannellini beans **173**
Chriso's chai tea and garden
    honey **151**
coconut
    coconut, lime and lemongrass
        chicken soup **77**
    coconut sambal **9**
    mussels and pipis with chilli
        and coconut **9**
    sweet corn soup with toasted
        coconut and chilli **125**
corn
    prawn, corn and avocado
        salad **13**
    sweet corn soup with toasted
        coconut and chilli **125**
cucumber
    pickled cucumbers **159**
    wasabi and cucumber granita
        oyster topping **19**
cuttlefish and summer herb soba
    noodle salad **35**

D
dark chocolate, date and walnut
    bread **99**
dates
    dark chocolate, date and walnut
        bread **99**
    sticky date puddings with
        butterscotch sauce **193**
dead simple char-grilled sardines **30**
delicious Sunday breakfast of baked
    eggs with chorizo and cannellini
    beans **173**
desserts
    bread and butter pudding with a
        few herbs **102**
    char-grilled honey peaches with
        vanilla and rosemary ice
        cream **149**
    chocolate pots with whatever
        you fancy **105**
    fennel ice cream **184**
    lamington ice cream **191**
    lavender honeycomb **152**
    lemon and basil praline **185**
    lemon meringue tartlets **187**
    orange and yoghurt pancakes
        180
    rice pudding with cinnamon,
        honey and lime **103**
    sea salt meringues **177**
    sticky date puddings with
        butterscotch sauce **193**
    vanilla panna cotta **179**
dressings *see* sauces and dressings
drinks
    bananas, milk and honey **150**
    chai latte **151**
    Chriso's chai tea and garden
        honey **151**
duck
    chilli duck salad with green mango
        and mint **42**
    fragrant duck soup **76**
    honey-roasted brined duck
        breast **51**

E
eggs
    charred asparagus with coddled
        eggs and butter sauce **127**
    delicious Sunday breakfast
        of baked eggs with chorizo and
        cannellini beans **173**
    the Duck's perfect scrambled
        eggs **176**
    Japanese savoury
        custard (chawanmushi) **174**
    mayonnaise **113**
    salmon and poached egg on toast
        for 6 hungry people **12**
    sea salt meringues **177**

F
fennel
    fennel ice cream **184**
    pasta with pancetta and toasted
        fennel seeds **62**
fig
    fig, walnut and goat's cheese
        salad **140**
    figs, blue cheese and honeycomb
        150
fish
    barramundi, peas and bacon **22**
    Bronte fishcakes **33**
    dead simple char-grilled
        sardines **30**
    salmon and poached egg on toast
        for 6 hungry people **12**
    see also seafood
flat bread **83**
fragrant duck soup **76**

G
grapefruit marmalade **161**

H
honey
    bananas, milk and honey
        150
    bircher muesli with honey for
        a crowd **94**
    char-grilled honey peaches with
        vanilla and rosemary ice cream
        149
    Chriso's chai tea and garden
        honey **151**
    figs, blue cheese and honeycomb
        150
    honey, mustard and citrus
        dressing **111**
    honey-roasted brined duck
        breast **51**
    lavender honeycomb **152**
    rice pudding with cinnamon,
        honey and lime **103**

I
ice cream
    fennel ice cream **184**
    lamington ice cream **191**
    vanilla and rosemary
        ice cream **149**

198

J

jams
- apple–berry 160
- chilli 158
- see also marmalade

Japanese savoury custard (chawanmushi) 174

K

kebabs
- char-grilled lamb kebabs ready for wrapping 74

kick-arse steak sandwich 41

L

lamb
- char-grilled lamb kebabs ready for wrapping 74
- Middle Eastern lamb with zucchini and labna 70
- slow-cooked lamb shanks for a cold day 44

lamington ice cream 191
lavender honeycomb 152
leeks
- chicken and charred leek soup 115

lemon and basil praline 185
lemon curd 162
lemon dressing 140
lemon meringue tartlets 187
lime
- chilli and lime oyster topping 19
- coconut, lime and lemongrass chicken soup 77
- lime, polenta and ricotta cake 100
- rice pudding with cinnamon, honey and lime 103

M

macadamia nuts
- chocolate and macadamia muffins 97
- macadamia bread sauce 84

marmalade
- grapefruit marmalade 161
- onion marmalade 41
- orange marmalade 161
- see also jams

mayonnaise
- mayonnaise 113
- red capsicum mayo 41

Middle Eastern lamb with zucchini and labna 70
muesli
- bircher muesli with honey for a crowd 94
- toasted muesli, the way we like it 93

muffins
- basic recipe 96
- chocolate and macadamia 97
- pear and ricotta 97
- rocky road 96
- salted caramel–banana 97

mushrooms and pearl barley with macadamia bread sauce 84
mussels and pipis with chilli and coconut 9

N

nahm jim 111

O

olive
- tomato and olive salsa 10

one-pot rabbit stew 45
onions
- burnt onion puree 73
- onion marmalade 41
- pickled red onion 157
- rice wine and shallot vinegar oyster topping 19

orange marmalade 161
orange and yoghurt pancakes 180
our green chicken 67
oven-dried tomatoes 159
oysters
- toppings 19

P

pancetta
- pasta with pancetta and toasted fennel seeds 62

parsnip
- parsnip and Jerusalem artichoke soup 114
- spiced parsnip cake 192

pasta
- pasta with pancetta and toasted fennel seeds 62
- shellfish, chilli and lemon pasta 16

pastry
- sweet shortcrust pastry 188–9

peaches
- char-grilled honey peaches with vanilla and rosemary ice cream 149

pear and ricotta muffins 97
peas
- barramundi, peas and bacon 22

pesto 130
pickles
- pickled baby carrots with star anise 156
- pickled baby radishes 156
- pickled celery and mustard seeds 157
- pickled cucumbers 159
- pickled celery salad 73
- pickled red onion 157

pipis and mussels with chilli and coconut 9
polenta
- lime, polenta and ricotta cake 100

pork
- sticky pork belly 53
- twice-cooked sticky pork ribs 61

potatoes
- warm salad of kipfler potatoes 126

prawns
- prawn, corn and avocado salad 13
- shellfish, chilli and lemon pasta 16

preserves
- savoury 156–9
- sweet 160–2
- see also jams; marmalade

puddings see desserts

Q

quinoa
- quinoa and spelt salad with roasted almonds 90
- quinoa, smoked eggplant and yoghurt salad 88
- spiced black quinoa porridge 95

R

rabbit
- one-pot rabbit stew 45

red capsicum mayo **41**
rice pudding with cinnamon, honey and lime **103**
rice wine and shallot vinegar oyster topping **19**
ricotta
    lime, polenta and ricotta cake **100**
    pear and ricotta muffins **97**
roasted vegetable salad **132**
rocky road muffins **96**
roti **82**

S
salad dressings **110–11**
salads
    chilli duck salad with green mango and mint **42**
    cuttlefish and summer herb soba noodle salad **35**
    fig, walnut and goat's cheese salad **140**
    pickled celery salad **73**
    prawn, corn and avocado salad **13**
    quinoa and spelt salad with roasted almonds **90**
    roasted vegetable salad **132**
    tomato and torn mozzarella salad **108**
    warm salad of kipfler potatoes **126**
salmon and poached egg on toast for 6 hungry people **12**
salt
    salted caramel–banana muffins **97**
    sea salt meringues **177**
sardines
    dead simple char-grilled sardines **30**
sauces and dressings
    apple–balsamic dressing **110**
    butter sauce **127**
    butterscotch sauce **193**
    honey, mustard and citrus dressing **111**
    lemon dressing **140**
    macadamia bread sauce **84**
    mayonnaise **113**
    nahm jim **111**
    red capsicum mayo **41**
    soy–mirin dressing **111**
savoury custard, Japanese (chawanmushi) **174**

savoury preserves **156–9**
    see also pickles
sea salt meringues **177**
seafood
    barbecued calamari with tomato and olive salsa **10**
    barramundi, peas and bacon **22**
    Bronte fishcakes **33**
    cuttlefish and summer herb soba noodle salad **35**
    dead simple char-grilled sardines **30**
    mussels and pipis with chilli and coconut **9**
    salmon and poached egg on toast for 6 hungry people **12**
    shellfish, chilli and lemon pasta **16**
seedy soda bread **83**
shellfish, chilli and lemon pasta **16**
slow-cooked lamb shanks for a cold day **44**
soup
    chicken and charred leek soup **115**
    coconut, lime and lemongrass chicken soup **77**
    fragrant duck soup **76**
    parsnip and Jerusalem artichoke soup **114**
    sweet corn soup with toasted coconut and chilli **125**
soy–mirin **111**
spiced black quinoa porridge **95**
spiced chicken in a brown paper bag **48**
spiced parsnip cake **192**
steak
    kick-arse steak sandwich **41**
    the perfect steak **63**
sticky date puddings with butterscotch sauce **193**
sticky pork belly **53**
sweet corn soup with toasted coconut and chilli **125**
sweet preserves **160–2**
    see also jams; marmalade
sweet shortcrust pastry **188–9**

T
tea
    Chriso's chai tea and garden honey **151**

the best banana bread we've ever had – thanks Pauly! **91**
the Duck's perfect scrambled eggs **176**
the perfect steak **63**
toasted muesli, the way we like it **93**
tomatoes
    oven-dried tomatoes **159**
    tomato and olive salsa **10**
    tomato and torn mozzarella salad **108**
twice-cooked sticky pork ribs **61**

V
vanilla
    vanilla and rosemary ice cream **149**
    vanilla panna cotta **179**
    white chocolate and vanilla friands **98**

W
walnuts
    dark chocolate, date and walnut bread **99**
    fig, walnut and goat's cheese salad **140**
warm salad of kipfler potatoes **126**
wasabi and cucumber granita oyster topping **19**
white chocolate and vanilla friands **98**
winter Brussels sprouts with roasted chestnuts **142**

Y
yoghurt
    orange and yogurt pancakes **180**

Z
zucchini
    Middle Eastern lamb with zucchini and labna **70**

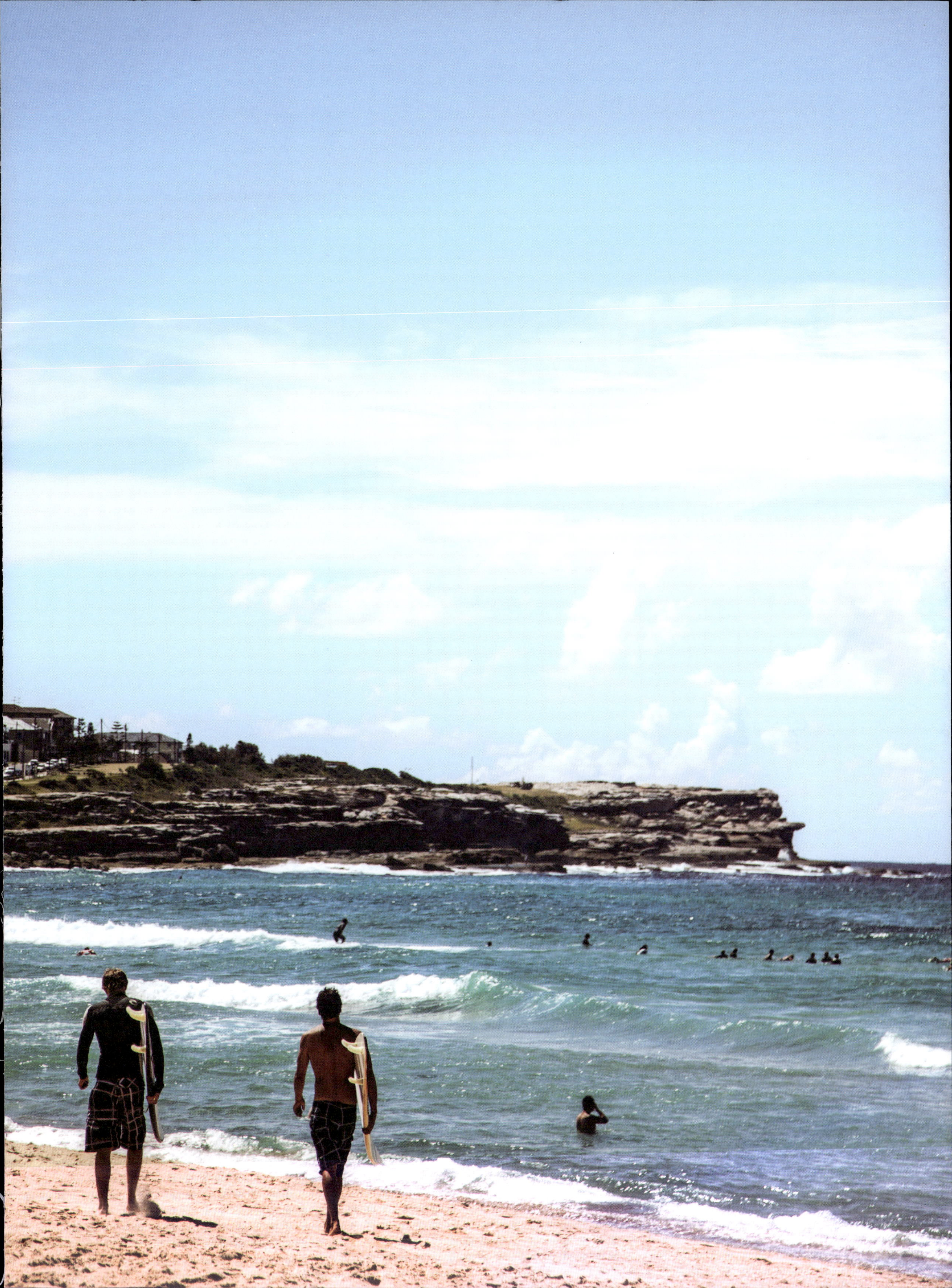

A PLUM BOOK

First published in 2013 by
Pan Macmillan Australia Pty Limited
Level 25, 1 Market Street
Sydney, NSW 2000, Australia

Level 1, 15–19 Claremont Street,
South Yarra, Victoria 3141, Australia

Text copyright © Darren Robertson and Mark LaBrooy 2013
Photography © William Meppem 2013, with the exception of the photographs on pages 144–5, top photograph on page 146, page 154 and page 155 © Justin Guadagnin 2013; page 107 © Shutterstock 2013; and the photographs on pages 4–5, 24–5, 80–1, 86–7 and 194–5 © ocean photographer Brad Malyon and his Frothers Gallery in Bronte 2013

The moral right of the authors has been asserted.

All rights reserved. No part of this book may be reproduced or transmitted by any person or entity (including Google, Amazon or similar organisations), in any form or by any means, electronic or mechanical, including photocopying, recording, scanning or by any information storage and retrieval system, without prior permission in writing from the publisher.

A CIP catalogue record for this book is available from the National Library of Australia.

Photography by William Meppem (with additional images from Justin Guadagnin and Brad Malyon)
Design by Allison Colpoys
Prop and food styling by Emma Knowles
Edited by Margaret Barca
Indexed by Jo Rudd

Colour reproduction by Splitting Image Colour Studio
Printed and bound in China by 1010 Printing International Limited

10 9 8 7 6 5 4 3 2